PERGAMON INTERNATIONAL LIBRARY
of Science, Technology, Engineering and Social Studies

*The 1000-volume original paperback library in aid of education,
industrial training and the enjoyment of leisure*

Publisher: Robert Maxwell, M.C.

TEACHING SCIENCE AND HEALTH FROM A FEMINIST PERSPECTIVE

THE PERGAMON TEXTBOOK
INSPECTION COPY SERVICE

An inspection copy of any book published in the Pergamon International Library
will gladly be sent to academic staff without obligation for their consideration for
course adoption or recommendation. Copies may be retained for a period of 60 days
from receipt and returned if not suitable. When a particular title is adopted or
recommended for adoption for class use and the recommendation results in a sale
of 12 or more copies the inspection copy may be retained with our compliments.
The Publishers will be pleased to receive suggestions for revised editions and new
titles to be published in this important international Library.

THE ATHENE SERIES
An International Collection of Feminist Books
General Editors: Gloria Bowles and Renate Duelli-Klein
Consulting Editor: Dale Spender

The ATHENE SERIES assumes that all those who are concerned with formulating explanations of the way the world works need to know and appreciate the significance of basic feminist principles.

The growth of feminist research has challenged almost all aspects of social organization in our culture. The ATHENE SERIES focuses on the construction of knowledge and the exclusion of women from the process — both as theorists and subjects of study—and offers innovative studies that challenge established theories and research.

ON ATHENE — When Metis, goddess of wisdom who presided over all knowledge was pregnant with ATHENE, she was swallowed up by Zeus who then gave birth to ATHENE from his head. The original ATHENE is thus the parthenogenetic daughter of a strong mother and as the feminist myth goes, at the "third birth" of ATHENE she stops being Zeus' obedient mouthpiece and returns to her real source: the science and wisdom of womankind

---

Volumes in the Series

MEN'S STUDIES MODIFIED
edited by Dale Spender

MACHINA EX DEA
edited by Joan Rothschild

WOMEN'S NATURE
edited by Marian Lowe and Ruth Hubbard

SCIENCE AND GENDER
Ruth Bleier

WOMAN IN THE MUSLIM UNCONSCIOUS
Fatna A. Sabbah

MEN'S IDEAS/WOMEN'S REALITIES
edited by Louise Michele Newman

BLACK FEMINIST CRITICISM
Barbara Christian

THE SISTER BOND
edited by Toni A.H. McNaron

EDUCATING FOR PEACE
Birgit Brock-Utne

STOPPING RAPE
Pauline B. Bart and Patricia H. O'Brien

FEMINIST APPROACHES TO SCIENCE
edited by Ruth Bleier

NOTICE TO READERS

May we suggest that your library places a standing/continuation order to receive all future volumes in the Athene Series immediately on publication?
Your order can be cancelled at any time.

Also of Interest

WOMEN'S STUDIES INTERNATIONAL FORUM*
Editor: Dale Spender
*Free sample copy available on request

TEACHING SCIENCE AND HEALTH FROM A FEMINIST PERSPECTIVE

A Practical Guide

Sue V. Rosser
Mary Baldwin College

Pergamon Press
New York Oxford Toronto Sydney Frankfurt

Pergamon Press Offices:

U.S.A.   Pergamon Press Inc., Maxwell House, Fairview Park,
                 Elmsford, New York 10523, U.S.A.

U.K.   Pergamon Press Ltd., Headington Hill Hall,
                 Oxford OX3 0BW, England

CANADA   Pergamon Press Canada Ltd., Suite 104, 150 Consumers Road,
                 Willowdale, Ontario M2J 1P9, Canada

AUSTRALIA   Pergamon Press (Aust.) Pty. Ltd., P.O. Box 544,
                 Potts Point, NSW 2011, Australia

FEDERAL REPUBLIC Pergamon Press GmbH, Hammerweg 6,
OF GERMANY   D-6242 Kronberg-Taunus, Federal Republic of Germany

BRAZIL   Pergamon Editora Ltda., Rua Eça de Queiros, 346,
                 CEP 04011, São Paulo, Brazil

JAPAN   Pergamon Press Ltd., 8th Floor, Matsuoka Central Building,
                 1-7-1 Nishishinjuku, Shinjuku, Tokyo 160, Japan

PEOPLE'S REPUBLIC Pergamon Press, Qianmen Hotel, Beijing,
OF CHINA   People's Republic of China

Copyright © 1986 Pergamon Press Inc.

Library of Congress Cataloging in Publication Data

Rosser, Sue Vilhauer.
    Teaching science and health from a feminist
perspective.

    (Athene series)
    Includes index.
    1. Science--Study and teaching. 2. Health
education. 3. Women--Study and teaching.
4. Curriculum planning. 5. Feminism. I. Title.
II. Series.
Q181.R684   1986   507'.1   85-17012
ISBN 0-08-033135-1
ISBN 0-08-033997-2 (pbk.)

Printed in Great Britain by A. Wheaton & Co. Ltd., Exeter

For Charlotte

Contents

Acknowledgments

To all of the people who gave me help and encouragement throughout this project, I am truly grateful. Several individuals were particularly supportive; without their aid and contributions, the book would never have been possible.

Charlotte Hogsett provided inspiration for me to write the book, and she continued her daily support at every step during the process. Her suggestions, revisions, and ideas were invaluable. The role of Ruth Bleier as my mentor in science and feminism in general, and for this project in particular, is very significant. Her critical reading of the final manuscript provided additional insights for some of the chapters. I appreciated the initial conversations with Mariamne Whatley about the project which delineated important parameters for the focus and scope of the book.

Without the sabbatical leave during the spring of 1985 from Mary Baldwin College, I would not have had the concentrated period of time necessary to complete this work. I owe a special debt to my colleagues in the Biology Department, Bonnie Hohn, John Mehner, and Lundy Pentz who assumed my departmental duties and thus allowed me to have the sabbatical. I am also grateful to Betty Hairfield who served as Coordinator of the Division of Natural and Theoretical Sciences in my absence.

The people with whom I worked at Pergamon Press facilitated every detail involved with the process of publication. From the beginning, Phyllis Hall was encouraging and constructive in her support for the project. She and her staff were always efficient, yet also warm and human in conducting business. I would particularly like to thank Sarah Biondello for her extensive work in organizing and editing the appendix of syllabi. I also appreciate the work of Angela Piliouras in supervising the copyediting of the manuscript.

Finally I would like to express my thanks to my daughters, Meagan and Caitie, for their patience with the interruptions in our daily lives which this project caused. Without their love and aid, and that of my friends and colleagues at Mary Baldwin College, the University of Wisconsin — Madison, and Pergamon Press, I would never have undertaken or completed the book.

1
INTRODUCTION

Chapter 1
Feminist Perspectives on Science: Is Reconceptualization Possible?

Currently, we who are feminists in science find ourselves in an ironic position. Finally, the rest of the world, including scientists who are not feminists and feminists who are not scientists, are interested in our perspective. They have become aware of the feminist courses in biology, health, and science education and the feminist critiques of traditional science which we have developed over the last decade. For the first time, many of them are eager to incorporate feminist courses and critiques into their curricula and research. This provides positive feedback and new inspiration for those of us who are feminist scientists. Yet, simultaneous with this awakened interest in the possibilities for women in science and for the theory of a feminist science, discouragement on the part of feminist scientists has surfaced. On two separate occasions within the last six months, during public lectures at women's studies events, I have heard two different scientists, each associated for more than a decade with the feminist critique of science, each say that she has stopped her work on a feminist science and returned to working full-time on her traditional scientific research. We obviously need competent women scientists who have the benefit of the feminist perspective to work on traditional scientific research. However, I was very upset at their disillusionment and shocked by the assumptions on which they based their decisions to cease active pursuit of the theory of a feminist science. Their actions indicate that they see little hope of developing such a theory; it seems to them that feminists in science will never move beyond demonstrating the unscientific biases behind current biologically deterministic theories such as sociobiology, where genes are said to determine behavior, and endocrinology, where hormonal levels are assumed to differentially affect thought and behavior in males and females. In short, they feel, apparently, that we can never provide more than a

3

critique of science—that a feminist reconceptualization of science will never be possible.

The impetus for this book arises from a desire to unite the new-found enthusiasm of scientists and feminists with work produced over the last ten years by feminist scientists, in the hope that this union will provide the support each group needs. The descriptions of a variety of sample courses in biology, health, women's studies, and science education based on many semesters of classroom usage should furnish scientists and nonscience women's studies faculty with information regarding the pedagogical methods and content of those courses when taught from a feminist perspective. The syllabi, pragmatic comments, and bibliographic references should allow them to build on our experiences in their teaching and research. At the same time, describing the large number of science courses already developed may make the discouraged feminist scientists aware that we have undoubtedly taken the first steps towards the reconceptualization of traditional science into a feminist science. It is important not to become discouraged because we cannot yet see the exact form that the reconceptualization will take. In fact, it would be very surprising if we could conceptualize a feminist science from within our current sexist society. Fee has stated that a sexist society should be expected to develop a sexist science. Conceptualizing a feminist science from within our society is "like asking a medieval peasant to imagine the theory of genetics or the production of a space capsule" (Fee 1982, 231). However, it seems possible that development towards the feminist form may be embedded in the very work we have done and are continuing to pursue. The interest and addition of more scientists teaching and carrying out research from a feminist perspective increases the speed at which reconceptualization is likely to occur. It was not until a significant percentage of feminists had been working in disciplines in the humanities and social sciences for an extended period of time that basic theoretical transformations occurred in those disciplines.

Like all of the other disciplines in academe, science seeks to discover and explore the truth. The particular aspects of the truth that science attempts to describe are the laws of the physical and natural world. Chemists and physicists search for the universal laws that govern the physical world in all places and at all times. Biologists examine the realities and interrelationships among the living beings that inhabit the physical world.

In science, it is rarely admitted that data have been gathered and interpreted from a particular perspective. Science describes reality and is presumed "objective"; therefore, the term *perspective* does not apply to it. The decisions, either conscious or unconscious, regarding what questions are asked, who is allowed to do the asking, what information is collected, and who interprets that information create a particular vantage point from which the knowledge or truth is perceived. In many disciplines some of the perspectives from which the knowledge is approached are recognized and admitted: a Marxist approach to sociology, a psychoanalytic approach to literature.

Historians of science, particularly Thomas Kuhn (1970) and his followers, have pointed out that scientific theories are not objective and value-free but are paradigms that reflect the historical and social context in which they are conceived. Many biologists do not see the connection between the Victorian, capitalistic, industrial British society in which Darwin lived and his description of the natural world as competitive and hierarchical, with a struggle for survival of the fittest (Hubbard 1979).

Scientific truths have traditionally been considered to be valid and repeatable by anyone in any place or time. Many scientists still contend that our hypotheses test the truth and that our experiments are designed, run, and interpreted without bias. With several thousand years of distance, most scientists admit that Aristotle's experiments, in which he counted fewer teeth in the mouths of women than men, were biased by views that women are inferior to men (Arditti 1980). When shown Kuhn's example of an observer who "sees" a black ace of spades when in fact shown a red ace of spades, scientists are willing to concede that facts which in reality contradict the paradigm may actually be "seen" by the observer as supporting the system of beliefs (Hubbard and Lowe 1979). However, few scientists are as candid about our recognition of the current social and historical contexts that influence the basic theories from which our hypotheses emanate.

Thus, in science, the traditional belief in objectivity makes it difficult for scientists to admit the validity of considering the perspectives by which our data and theories are influenced. Recognizing the influence of the androcentric perspective (a recognition that has been difficult in the disciplines of the humanities and social sciences, where the concept of a perspective in approaching knowledge is more acceptable) is doubly difficult for the scientists. Fee (1981; 1982), Haraway (1978), Hein (1981), and Keller (1982) have described the specific ways in which the very objectivity said to be characteristic of scientific knowledge and the whole dichotomy between subject and object are, in fact, male ways of relating to the world, which specifically exclude women.

Keller (1982) documents the different levels from which women are excluded from science:

1. Unfair employment practices prevent women from reaching the theoretical and decision-making level of science.
2. Androcentric bias in the choice and definition of problems studied so that subjects concerning women, such as menstrual cramps, childbirth, and menopause, receive less funding and study.
3. Androcentric bias in the design and interpretation of experiments so that only male rats or monkeys are used as experimental subjects.
4. Androcentric bias in the formulation of scientific theories and methods so that unicausal, hierarchical theories that coincide with the male experience of the world become the "objective" theories that define the interpretation of the scientific data.

The implication is that because of these practices, attitudes, and perspective science becomes totally a masculine province which excludes females. Rossiter (1982) also claims that this masculinity has made it doubly difficult for women in science: "As scientists they were atypical women; as women they were unusual scientists" (p. xv).

As the statistics compiled by Betty Vetter (1980) of the Scientific Manpower Commission and the National Science Foundation Report (1984) on *Women and Minorities in Science and Engineering* indicate, fewer women entered natural science and engineering in the past two decades than entered fields in the humanities and social sciences. These statistics also demonstrate that those women who entered natural science fields have lower employment and poorer chances for advancement than men in those fields. (This is not true for women in engineering.) Other researchers (Fennema and Sherman 1977; Sherman 1979; 1982) describe the inequalities in the educational process, such as subtle influences of teachers, parents, and media that discourage females from entering science and math in the secondary schools and earlier. Hall and Sandler (1982) in "The Classroom Climate: A Chilly One for Women?" underline faculty assumptions and behaviors at the undergraduate and graduate levels, which steer women away from mathematics and science. Martin and Irvine (1982) document as additional barriers the position of woman in the family and society, where traditionally her career is subordinated to that of her husband and she is burdened with more childcare and housekeeping chores, thus leaving her less time and energy to pursue a scientific career.

How then, if by some accounts science itself is synonymous with a masculine way of viewing the world, can it be changed by a feminist perspective? Is reconceptualization possible? Yes, I think that it is possible and that the first step towards reconceptualization is having more women scientists. Although I am not naive enough to believe that all women in science will become feminists (particularly since we have been trained in the traditional masculine way of thinking about science), I do think that enough women to form a critical mass is important. It was not until a large number of women were working in the other academic disciplines for a lengthy period of time that changes began to occur.

The new scholarship by and about women is transforming the research and teaching curricula of most of the traditional academic disciplines. As more women enter previously male-dominated disciplines, we bring new approaches and methodologies to previously considered questions and explore territories that are new to the traditionally prescribed frameworks and methodologies.

Women have questioned the very foundations and constructs of the disciplines of history, literature, and anthropology. Due to feminist research and perspective, historical periods are being redefined. When women – the other half of humanity – are considered, perhaps political and military events should not be the criteria that define and separate one historical period from another. Other economic or social factors, such as the entrance of women into the work force and advances in reproductive health care, may more accurately depict major changes in people's lives and might be used to mark the periods and thus define the approaches to study (Mitchell 1972; Rowbotham 1972; 1973).

In literature as well, it is being suggested that the chronological periods into which literary production is ordinarily divided, based primarily on writing by men, may need to be revised to take women's writing fully into account. Further, many feminist critics, led by the example of French writers such as Hermann (1976), Leclerc (1974), and Wittig (1969; 1976) point out that literary language, like all language, has been forged in a patriarchal society and thus is inadequate for self-expression by women. Such a stance puts the very basis of literature radically into question.

The work of Leacock (1977), Leavitt (1975), Leibowitz (1975), and other women anthropologists has changed anthropology. From their field work, in which they talked to and studied the women of other cultures, it became apparent that our view of these cultures had been biased. Male anthropologists had produced an androcentric view. At worst, they might have spoken only with men; thus the information they gleaned about women either came from men or from their observation and interpretation of what they saw women doing. At best, they might have been able to communicate with the women. However, the kinds of questions that an American man asks a woman from another culture and the responses she gives might lead to very different interpretations than if a woman had asked the questions. In short, the feminist anthropologists have revolutionized the discipline of anthropology. With their new approaches, which question concepts such as dominance and subordination as the only effective ways to describe complex social relationships among people, anthropology has made much progress. The feminist anthropologists brought about the awareness that alternative approaches and interpretations, which may even run counter to the established assumptions, can yield more information and prove a more complete picture of reality.

As more and more disciplines are changed by the new scholarship on women, it has become possible to chart the developmental phases through which the scholarship progresses. Peggy McIntosh, Director of Faculty Development Programs of the Wellesley College Center for Research on Women, developed a scheme that may be applied to a variety of disciplines across the curriculum. She and others (Schuster and Van Dyne 1984) who developed schemes of this sort are primarily interested in bringing women's studies into the mainstream of traditional curriculum. However, I think that such schemes may provide an interesting tool for people, not particularly interested in mainstreaming, who are concerned about the slow progress towards feminist transformation in the sciences compared to other disciplines. I paraphrase the scheme that McIntosh has developed, using her major example, history, to delineate the five phases of transformation (McIntosh 1984):

Phase I: Womanless History—This is the very traditional approach to the discipline, which is exclusive in that only great events and men in history are deemed worthy of consideration.

Phase II: Women in History—Heroines, exceptional women or an elite few, who are seen to have been of benefit to culture as defined by the traditional standards of the discipline are included in the study.

Phase III: Women as a Problem, Anomaly, or Absence in History — Women are studied as victims, as deprived or defective variants of men, or as protestors, with "issues." Women are at least viewed in a systemic context, since class, race, and gender are seen as interlocking political phenomena. Categories of historical analysis still are derived from those who had the most power.

Phase IV: Women as History — The categories for analysis shift and become racially inclusive, multifaceted, and filled with variety; they demonstrate and validate plural versions of reality. This phase takes account of the fact that since women have had half of the world's lived experience, we need to ask what that experience has been and to consider it as half of history. This causes faculty to use all kinds of evidence and source materials that academics are not in the habit of using.

Phase V: History Redefined and Reconstructed to Include Us All — Although this history will be a long time in the making, it will help students to sense that women are both part of and alien to the dominant culture and the dominant version of history. It will create more usable and inclusive constructs that validate a wider sample of life.

Many, including McIntosh herself (1983), may question whether or not the developmental scheme she posits is the best way to depict the transformation of the disciplines by the new scholarship on women. However, I think that for three reasons it is a useful paradigm to consider applying to the sciences. First, applying her scheme to the sciences should underline the fact that reconceptualizing disciplines, particularly those that have been long-established and presented extreme barriers to women, will only occur after going through other phases. Passing through these phases may take varying amounts of time. I think that it is important to emphasize the accomplishments (phases) already made as well as those still to be reached (reconceptualization). Recognizing that reconceptualization occurs relatively late (phase IV) in this developmental process may make women in science less discouraged about the amount of progress achieved so far. Second, by applying her scheme to as many disciplines as possible, we can determine whether the order of the phases is accurate and whether the notion of a developmental sequence is applicable. For example, if in several disciplines, phase IV preceded phase II, one might question the validity of the order; it is not inconceivable that theoretical changes might have preceded specific examples. Third, it is necessary for scientists to incorporate material from the early phases into their research and teaching. Total reconceptualization is not necessary before utilizing the considerable material already available. Furthermore, use and consideration of that material by many scientists may be important steps towards reconceptualization. For example, if many scientists begin using female rats or monkeys as subjects for hormone experiments, the entire theory regarding steady states versus cyclicity for hormone levels may be revised (Hoffman 1982).

At this point, I would like to develop the application of McIntosh's scheme to biology. Although McIntosh (1984) outlined briefly how her scheme might be applied to biology, I would like to elaborate upon that sketch. My development of her scheme will also deviate from McIntosh's ideas in one major conceptual way: I do not accept her implication that we really have made much, if any, progress in phase IV, the reconceptualization of biology. Although her brief sketch (McIntosh 1983) is ambiguous on this point, many readers might infer from some of her examples and suggestions that more far-reaching theoretical changes have already occurred. It is precisely because such changes have yet occurred that has led, I believe, to the discouragement of many feminists in science.

Biology is the scientific discipline that probably has seen the most activity in terms of the new scholarship on women. Biology is also the science that, according to the statistics of the National Science Foundation (1984), includes more women than any of the other sciences, outside of the social sciences. Undoubtedly, these two factors are linked in a significant way. It was not until a substantial proportion of women were active in the humanities and social sciences that the feminist perspective was felt, and transformations in those disciplines occurred. Thus, it is not surprising that the discipline within the sciences that has the most women is also the discipline in which substantial work is proceeding on feminism and science. However, biology still has substantially fewer women (Vetter, 1981) than the disciplines within the humanities and social sciences, where feminists have had the most impact at the theoretical or conceptual level. We should therefore be neither surprised nor discouraged because reconceptualization has not yet occurred in biology. How then does biology fit into McIntosh's scheme? At what phase are we?

Obviously, many scientists and most courses are in phase I: Womanless Science. Many scientists would deny that their gender influences their theories, data collection, subjects, or questions asked. They suggest that science is "manless" as well as "womanless." However, Thomas Kuhn (1970) and his followers have suggested that all scientific theories are the products of individuals living in a particular historical and social milieu. As such, they are biased by the perspective and paradigms of those individuals. Fee (1981) and Keller (1982) have suggested that the absence of women from the decision-making levels of science has produced a science that views the world from a male perspective and is, therefore, womanless. The failure of scientists to recognize this bias has perpetuated the idea of the "objectivity" of science.

Some scientists have been able to recognize the shortcomings of phase I science. Considerable research is now being done on phase II: Women in Science. In 1983, Vivian Gornick's book appeared under that very title. Historians of science in particular are busy discovering the lost women of science. It is becoming very clear through the work of Evelyn Fox Keller (1983), Margaret Rossiter (1982), and Ann Sayre (1975), to name a few, that women always have been in science. Frequently, their discoveries and roles have been brushed aside, attributed to others, or misunderstood. The new studies of Rosalind Franklin (Sayre 1975) and Barbara McClintock (Keller 1983) provide excellent documentation of the work done by women making important discoveries in biology.

Many teachers have reached phase II in their teaching and make efforts to integrate the work done by women into their discussions of important scientific experiments. It can be rewarding for students to learn of women who succeeded in the traditional scientific establishment and won the Nobel Prize. In some cases, just mentioning the first name of the experimenters, for example, Alfred Hershey and Margaret Chase when discussing the experiments determining that DNA was the genetic component in bacteriophage (Taylor 1965), will break the stereotype that all scientists are male. It is also crucial to convey to students that although the scientific hierarchy is set up so that often only one man wins the prize or heads the laboratory, much of the actual work leading to the important discovery is done by many people, most of whom are women.

Much work has also been done that might be categorized as phase III: Women as a Problem, Anomaly, or Absence in Science. That women are seen very frequently in this context is evident from article titles written by and about women in science:

- "Adventures of a Woman in Science" (Weisstein 1979)
- "Rosalind Franklin and DNA: A Vivid View of What It Is Like to be a Gifted Woman in an Especially Male Profession" (Sayre 1975)

- "Sex Discrimination in the Halls of Science" (Vetter 1980)
- "Women in Academic Chemistry Find Rise to Full Status Difficult" (Rawls and Fox 1978)
- "The Anomaly of a Woman in Physics" (Keller 1977)
- "The Disadvantaged Majority: Science Education for Women" (Kahle 1983)
- "Can the Difference Between Male and Female Science Majors Account for the Low Number of Women at the Doctoral Level in Science?" (Baker 1983)

A further aspect of this phase shows up in the current studies being made with the attempt of attracting more women into science and math, the traditionally "male" disciplines. The National Science Foundation (1984), the Rockefeller Foundation (Berryman 1983), the American Association of Colleges under the auspices of the Carnegie Corporation and the Ford Foundation (Hall and Sandler 1982), and the American Chemical Society (1983), along with other foundations and professional societies, have each issued studies and reports with statistics documenting the lack of women in science and possible "causes and cures."

I believe that this phase is analogous to the woman as victim aspect of phase III described by McIntosh (1984) for history. Frequently, biologically deterministic theories, such as sociobiology and those regarding hormone effects on the brain, have been used to justify women's position in society. I am defining *biological determinism* here as the assumption that a difference between males and females in a biological structure or hormone level at some point in development will lead to a difference in behavior, ability, or performance. The biological deterministic theory is not new, of course. Darwin's (1967) *On the Origin of Species*, originally published in 1859, provided the framework for its current form. In 1875, Antoinette Blackwell made one of the first rebuttals of the theory using scientific information to show that women were not mentally inferior to men, although she accepted that women might have different attributes and interests. During the early part of this century, many well-known women scientists, Calkins (1896), Hollingsworth (1914), Tanner (1896), and Thompson (1903) spent a great deal of time and energy pointing out scientific flaws in the research showing higher intelligence levels in males than females.

Today, the biological determinism question is particularly related to two areas of current research: hormone research and animal behavior.

HORMONE RESEARCH

The prenatal exposure of the developing male's central nervous system to androgens has led many workers to propose that these androgens cause certain effects on brain lateralization and behavior that differ from those found in females. The differing levels of androgens, estrogens, and progestins in postpubertal men and women have also led many researchers to write voluminous works concerning the effects of these levels on visual spatial ability, verbal ability, aggression, and other behaviors in the two sexes.

ANIMAL BEHAVIOR

Some researchers have examined behavior in lower animals in a search for "universal" behavior patterns in males of all species or in all males of a particular order or class, such as primates or mammals. This behavior is then extrapolated to humans in an attempt to demonstrate a biological, or innate, basis for the behavior. The sociobiologists, such as Barash (1977), Dawkins (1976), and Wilson (1975) based their new discipline on biological determinism, stating that behavior is genetically determined and that differences between males and females in role, status, and performance are biologically based.

Today's feminist scientists refute the biologically deterministic theories by pointing out their scientific flaws (Bleier 1979; Hubbard 1979; Lowe 1978; Rosser 1982). Bleier (1979) discussed at length the subtle problems that accompany biochemical conversions of hormones within the body, so that an injection of testosterone may be converted to estrogen or another derivative by the time it reaches the brain. She and others have also repeatedly warned against extrapolating from one species to another in biochemical, as well as behavioral, traits. Feminist scientists have warned sociobiologists about the circularity of logic involved in using human language and frameworks to interpret animal behavior, which is then used to "prove" that certain human behavior is biologically determined, since it was also found in animals.

These refutations and warnings about the problems of biologically deterministic assumptions are necessary. Even a century of women scientists pointing out the unscientific bases of the assumptions has not led to their eradication from current scientific theories. It is, therefore, essential to continue our efforts to expose the inadequacies of such assumptions.

However, women in science must move beyond this phase. As

McIntosh points out for phase III in history, "Phase III work reveals its own limits; we will never make most of ordinary women's experience seem either real or valid if our teaching and research still rest on the categories of historical analysis which were derived from the experience of those who had the most power" (1984, 3). Feminists in science will also be limited as long as we continue to question some of the methods, subjects, or interpretations of traditional science while basically accepting and remaining within its paradigms. We must make a quantum leap to reconceptualize some of the existing paradigms of science before we can have a phase IV or a feminist science.

It is my contention that this leap in reconceptualization has not yet occurred; therefore, I cannot describe it here. I think that much of the language in which we might think about a different approach to science has not yet evolved; that is one of the obstacles to reconceptualization. However, if the current "scientific and objective" structure of science is, in fact, synonymous with a masculine view of the natural, physical world, perhaps a "feminine" view of that world is needed. By this, I do not mean replacing theories such as "man the hunter," which are based on bias and conjecture from a view of power and dominance rather than data, with equally unscientific and speculative theories about "woman the gatherer" (Morgan 1973), which are also based on fantasy rather than data. What I mean by a reconceptualization of science is an expansion of the number and kinds of questions asked, the experimental models and subjects used, and the design and interpretation of experiments. Some recent work by women in science hints at the sorts of changes that might come from phase IV research.

Barbara McClintock is an achieving scientist who is not a feminist. However, in her approach towards studying maize, she indicates a shortening of the distance between the observer and the object being studied and a consideration of the complex interaction between the organism and its environment. Her statement upon receiving the Nobel Prize was that "it might seem unfair to reward a person for having so much pleasure over the years, asking the maize plant to solve specific problems and then watching its responses" (Keller 1983). This statement suggests a closer, more intimate relationship with the subject of her research than typically is expressed by the male "objective" scientist. One does not normally associate words such as "a feeling for the organism" (Keller 1983) with the rational, masculine approach to science. McClintock also did not accept the predominant hierarchical theory of genetic DNA as the "Master Molecule" that controls gene action but focused on the interaction between the organism and its environment as the locus of control.

Models that more accurately simulate functioning, complex biological systems may be derived from using female rats as subjects in experiments. Women scientists such as Hoffman (1982) have questioned the tradition of using male rats or primates as subjects. With the exception of insulin and the hormones of the female reproductive cycle, traditional endocrinological theory predicted that most hormones are kept constant in level in both males and females. Thus, the male of the species, whether rodent or primate, was chosen as the experimental subject because of his noncyclicity. However, new techniques of measuring blood hormone levels have demonstrated episodic, rather than steady, patterns of secretion of hormones in both males and females. As Hoffman (1982) points out, the rhythmic cycle of hormone secretion, as also portrayed in the cycling female rat, appears to be a more accurate model for the secretion of most hormones.

As more women have entered primate research, they have begun to challenge the language used to describe primate behavior and the patriarchal assumptions inherent in searches for dominance hierarchies in primates. Lancaster (1975) describes a single-male troop of animals as follows:

> For a female, males are a resource in her environment which she may use to further the survival of herself and her offspring. If environmental conditions are such that the male role can be minimal, a one-male group is likely. Only one male is necessary for a group of females if his only role is to impregnate them. (p. 34)

Her work points out the androcentric bias of primate behavior theories, which would describe the above group as a "harem" and consider dominance and subordination in the description of behavior.

Even the *New York Times* recognized the fundamental changes occurring in primate research primarily due to the increased number of women scientists in the field in recent years. In an article, "New View of Female Primates Assails Stereotypes—Studies by Women Influencing the Field," the following statements are made:

> We have learned more about primate behavior in the last 10 years than in the previous 10 centuries. . . . An explosion of knowledge about monkeys and apes is overturning long-held stereotypes about sex roles and social patterns among the closest kin to humans in the animal world. . . . Dr. Hrdy believes that improved methodology, the broad

questioning of sexual stereotypes by the women's liberation movement (influencing scientists of both sexes), and the infusion of female scientists have all contributed to the new understanding of primate societies. . . . (Eckholm 1984, C1)

These examples provide glimpses of some aspects that might take place in the reconceptualization of phase IV. I think that it is important not to become discouraged because we cannot yet see the exact form of reconceptualization. It seems likely that developments towards that form may be embedded in the very work we are doing now; we are quite naturally blind to them, since it is difficult to understand the full implications and ramifications of ideas as they evolve. The work of Bleier (1984), Fee (1982), and Hein (1981) suggest central ideas to a feminist science may be the rejection of dualisms, such as subjectivity/objectivity, rational/feeling, and nature/culture, that focus our thinking about the world. Primatologists (Lancaster 1975) and ecologists (Carson 1962) have shown us that the concepts of dominance and hierarchy might be replaced by relationship, interdependence, and contextuality, as more suitable approaches to viewing complex behavior within and among species on the earth. The work of McClintock, as interpreted by Keller (1983), demonstrates the importance of considering multicausal factors and interactions among those factors, rather than a unicausal, hierarchical theory, such as the "Master Molecule," which oversimplifies complicated biological processes in living organisms.

At this point, I am too constricted by my training, the language of science, and its paradigms to suggest other parameters for the reconceptualization of biology. Based on an examination of what has happened in other disciplines, I am confident that the reconceptualization that will emerge will define a new science. From that reconceptualization may develop the roots of phase V: Science Redefined and Reconstructed to Include Us All. Clearly, this would mean for the first time that science would be formulated from a perspective other than that of the white, middle- and upper-class Western men. I can't imagine what that would be like or whether it would occur in our lifetime, but I am sure that it would be a better science. Therefore, I think that it is important to recognize that our current position in the process is likely to be followed by the fundamental theoretical changes for which we are currently hoping and searching. The courses, teaching methods, and syllabi presented in this book demonstrate the impact of the feminist perspective on biology, health, and science education. In these courses, in our continuing

efforts to incorporate new information into them, and in the impact
they will have on the next generation of scientists may be the seeds
for the reconceptualization of science.

REFERENCES

American Chemical Society. 1983. Medalists study charts women chemists'
role. *Chemistry and Engineering* (Nov. 14): 53.
Arditti, R. 1980. Feminism and science. In *Science and liberation*, eds. R.
Arditti, P. Brennan and S. Cavrak. Boston: South End Press.
Baker, D. 1983. Can the difference between male and female science majors
account for the low number of women at the doctoral level in science?
Journal of College Science Teaching (Nov.): 102–107.
Barash, D. 1977. *Sociobiology and behavior.* New York: Elsevier.
Berryman, S. 1983. Who will do science? Minority and female attainment of
science and mathematics degrees: Trends and causes. *Rockefeller Foundation Special Report* (Nov.).
Blackwell, A.B. [1875] 1976. *The sexes throughout nature.* New York: G.P.
Putnam's Sons; reprinted, Westport, Conn.: Hyperion Press, Inc.
Bleier, R. 1979. Social and political bias in science: An examination of
animal studies and their generalizations to human behavior and evolution.
In *Genes and gender II*, eds. R. Hubbard and M. Lowe, 49–70. Staten
Island, N.Y.: Gordian Press Inc.
Bleier, R. 1984. *Science and gender: A critique of biology and its theories on
women.* New York: Pergamon Press.
Calkins, M.W. 1896. Community of ideas of men and women. *Psychological
Review* 3, no. 4: 426–430.
Carson, R. 1962. *Silent spring.* New York: Fawcett Press.
Darwin, C. 1967. *On the origin of species: A facsimile of the first edition.*
New York: Atheneum. Originally published 1859.
Dawkins, R. 1976. *The selfish gene.* New York: Oxford University Press.
Eckholm, E. 1984. New view of female primates assails stereotypes—studies
by women influencing the field. *The New York Times.* (September 18):
C1.
Fee, E. 1981. Is feminism a threat to scientific objectivity? *International
Journal of Women's Studies* 4, no. 4: 213–233.
Fee, E. 1982. A feminist critique of scientific objectivity. *Science for the
People* 14, no. 4: 8.
Fennema, E., and J. Sherman. 1977. Sex-related differences in mathematics
achievement, spatial visualization and affective factors. *American Educational Research Journal* 14: 51–71.
Gornick, V. 1983. *Women in science: Portraits from a world in transition.*
New York: Simon and Schuster.
Hall, R., and B. Sandler. 1982. *The classroom climate: A chilly one for
women?* Washington, D.C.: Association of American Colleges Project on
the Status and Education of Women.
Haraway, D. 1978. Animal sociology and a natural economy of the body
politic, Part I: A political physiology of dominance; and Animal sociol-

ogy and a natural economy of the body politic, Part II: The past is the contested zone: Human nature and theories of production and reproduction in primate behavior studies. *Signs: Journal of Women in Culture and Society* 4, no. 1: 21–60.

Hein, H. 1981. Women and science: Fitting men to think about nature. *International Journal of Women's Studies* 4: 369–377.

Hermann, C. 1976. *Les voleuses de langue.* Paris: des femmes.

Hoffman, J.C. 1982. Biorhythms in human reproduction: The not-so-steady states. *Signs: Journal of Women in Culture and Society* 7, no. 4: 829–844.

Hollingsworth, L.S. 1914. Variability as related to sex differences in achievement. *American Journal of Sociology* 19, no. 4: 510–530.

Hubbard, R. 1979. Have only men evolved? In *Women look at biology looking at women*, eds. R. Hubbard, M.S. Henifin, and B. Fried. Cambridge, Mass.: Schenkman Publishing Co.

Hubbard, R., and M. Lowe. 1979. Introduction. In *Genes and gender II*, eds. R. Hubbard and M. Lowe. New York: Gordian Press.

Kahle, J. 1983. The disadvantaged majority: Science education for women. Burlington, N.C.: Carolina Biological Supply Company. AETS Outstanding Paper for 1983.

Keller, E. 1977. The anomaly of a woman in physics. In *Working it out*, eds. S. Ruddick and P. Daniels. New York: Pantheon.

Keller, E. 1982. Feminism and science. *Signs: Journal of Women in Culture and Society* 7, no. 3: 589–602.

Keller, E. 1983. *A feeling for the organism: The life and work of Barbara McClintock.* New York: W.H. Freeman and Company.

Kuhn, T.S. 1970. *The structure of scientific revolutions.* 2d Ed. Chicago: The University of Chicago Press.

Lancaster, J. 1975. *Primate behavior and the emergence of human culture.* New York: Holt, Rinehart and Winston.

Leacock, E. 1977. Women in egalitarian societies. In *Becoming visible: Women in European history*, eds. R. Bridenthal and C. Koonz. Boston: Houghton Mifflin.

Leavitt, R.R. 1975. *Peaceable primates and gentle people: Anthropological approaches to women's studies.* New York: Harper and Row.

Leclerc, A. 1974. *Parole de femme.* Paris: Bernard Grasset.

Leibowitz, L. 1975. Perspectives in the evolution of sex differences. In *Toward an anthropology of women*, ed. R. Reiter. New York: Monthly Review Press.

Lowe, M. 1978. Sociobiology and sex differences. *Signs: Journal of Women in Culture and Society* 4, no. 1: 118–125.

Martin, B.R., and J. Irvine. 1982. Women in science—The astronomical brain drain. *Women's Studies International Forum* 5, no. 1: 41–68.

McIntosh, P. 1983. Interactive phases of curricular re-vision: A feminist perspective. Working Paper No. 124, Wellesley College, Center for Research on Women, Wellesley, Mass.

McIntosh, P. 1984. The study of women: Processes of personal and curricular re-vision. *The Forum for Liberal Education* 6, no. 5: 2–4.

Mitchell, J. 1972. *Women's estate.* New York: Pantheon Books.

Morgan, E. 1973. *The descent of woman.* New York: Bantam Books.

National Science Foundation. 1984. *Women and minorities in science and engineering*. Report 84-300.

Rawls, M., and S. Fox. 1978. Women in academic chemistry find rise to full status difficult. *Chemical and Engineering News* (Sept. 11).

Rosser, S.V. 1982. Androgyny and sociobiology. *International Journal of Women's Studies* 5, no. 5: 435-444.

Rossiter, M.W. 1982. *Women scientists in America: Struggles and strategies to 1940*. Baltimore: The Johns Hopkins University Press.

Rowbotham, S. 1972. *Women, resistance, and revolution*. New York: Pantheon Books.

Rowbotham, S. 1973. *Woman's consciousness, man's world*. Baltimore: Penguin Books.

Sayre, A. 1975. *Rosalind Franklin and DNA: A vivid view of what it is like to be a gifted woman in an especially male profession*. New York: W.W. Norton & Company, Inc.

Schuster, M., and S. Van Dyne. 1984. Placing women in the liberal arts: Stages of curriculum transformation. *Harvard Educational Review* 54, no. 4.

Sherman, J. 1979. Predicting mathematics performance in high school girls and boys. *Journal of Educational Psychology* 79, 242-249.

Sherman, J. 1982. Mathematics the critical filter: A look at some residues. *Psychology of Women Quarterly* 6, no. 4 (Summer).

Tanner, A. 1896. The community of ideas of men and women. *Psychological Review* 3, no. 5, 548-550.

Taylor, J. 1965. *Selected papers on molecular genetics*. New York: Academic Press.

Thompson (Woolley), H.B. 1903. *The mental traits of sex*. Chicago: The University of Chicago Press.

Vetter, B. 1980. Sex discrimination in the halls of science. *Chemical and Engineering News*, March, 37-38.

Vetter, B. 1981. Degree completion by women and minorities in science increases. *Science* 212, no. 3.

Weisstein, N. 1979. Adventures of a woman in science. In *Women look at biology looking at women*, eds. R. Hubbard, M.S. Henifin, and B. Fried, Boston: Schenkman Publishing Co.

Wilson, E.O. 1975. *Sociobiology: The new synthesis*. Cambridge, Mass.: Harvard University Press.

Wittig, M. 1969. *Les guerilleres*. Paris: Les Editions de Minuit.

Wittig, M., and S. Zeig. 1976. *Brouillon pour un dictionnaire des amantes*. Paris: Bernard Grasset.

2
THE BIOLOGY CURRICULUM

Chapter 2
Transforming Introductory Biology

Including new information about women and the perspective of feminism is crucial in all courses in health and science, but it is particularly crucial in introductory biology. For most students, such courses serve as the introduction to college science generally and to all courses in health and biology that they will subsequently take. Thus, it sets the stage, establishes an outlook, and provides the foundation for further study. Frequently, introductory biology is the course that determines a student's decision to pursue work in science or abandon it.

Traditionally, large numbers of women students have not gone on in the sciences. Women tend to exclude themselves from science because of cultural influences that dictate gender roles, and women also tend to be excluded from science by active discrimination. Even when women choose careers in science, seldom do they reach the theoretical and decision-making levels (Keller 1982). The first task of the biology teacher who wishes to conduct an introductory course that breaks this pattern of exclusion and self-exclusion is to understand the reasons that lie behind it.

If women are not included in science, it is because science is a masculine province. Science is masculine not only in that it is populated by men, but also because it is biased and not objective, as has always been assumed, due to the lack of input by women.

Feminists (Bleier, 1984; Fee 1982; Hubbard 1979) have written critiques of science in which they point out that all investigations are carried out from some perspective. The decision, either conscious or unconscious, regarding what questions are asked, who is allowed to do the asking, what information is collected, and who interprets that information create a particular vantage point from which the knowledge or truth is perceived. However, few scientists candidly acknowledge the current historical and social contexts that influence the basic theories from which their hypotheses emanate. One wonders if the reason that little or no history of science is included in the standard science curriculum is that inclusion of such material would raise questions about the changes that have occurred in scientific objectivity over time. Moreover, science, like all forms of knowledge, is used to serve the dominant political or ideological views, so that those who share those views or have a stake in their perpetuation act in their own self-interest by pretending that objectivity is observed (Hubbard 1979).

Thus, in science, the traditional belief in objectivity makes it difficult for scientists to admit the relevance of perspective and, therefore, even the more obvious perspectives by which their data and theories are influenced. Recognizing the influence of the androcentrism (a recognition that was difficult in the humanities and social sciences, where the concept of perspective in approaching knowledge is more acceptable) is doubly difficult for the scientist. Fee (1981; 1982), Haraway (1978), Hein (1981), and Keller (1982) described the specific ways in which the very objectivity said to be characteristic of scientific inquiry is in fact a masculine way of relating to the world, which specifically excludes women. If the approach to science as it is practiced in the Western world suffers from an androcentric bias, then a feminist perspective is needed to counter that bias and make the scientific description more accurate and inclusive.

From a feminist perspective, we would insist that women be central to the questions and theories of science and that women be studied for their own sake, not as compared to men; only then does one develop accurate understanding that permits valid comparisons. With a focus on women, entirely different questions might be asked. Experiments might be set up using the female body as a model, with female rats or monkeys as the experimental subjects. Alternative and multiple interpretations of data might be encouraged. Thus, females, the other half of humanity, would be included in the scientific descriptions of reality (Minnich 1982).

Recently some feminist scientists have begun to envisage the progress and richness that might develop from including a female perspective in scientific hypotheses, subjects, and theories. Feminist scientists have proposed new theories and models in animal behavior (Hrdy 1981; Lancaster 1975) and hormone research (Hoffman 1982).

Teaching science from a feminist perspective should make young women realize that science is open to them, by setting before all students the examples of great women scientists. This would help dispel the stereotype of scientists as men. Unveiling the stories of other women scientists, such as Rosalind Franklin and Barbara McClintock, may stimulate people to study the history of women in science and to begin to shape a feminist science.

In short, a feminist critique of science aims at making young women and men aware of the deficiencies, lack of objectivity, and androcentric bias of traditional science. The question for the introductory biology teacher then becomes how—at the present time—does one incorporate the nascent scholarship on women and science into the biology curriculum in a manner that will inspire further critiques and theoretical changes? How can one integrate into the standard biology curriculum the considerable, but diffuse, information constituting the contemporary feminist perspective: the critique of biological determinism and androcentric "objectivity," the substantial information about famous and lesser-known women scientists and their discoveries, some remarks about the obvious influence of masculine thinking on the descriptive language of biology, the feminist theoretical changes that have already taken place, and those areas where the theoretical changes are still needed?

The answer to this question will vary depending on the subject matter and level of the course. For example, it is quite feasible to teach an upper level course on Human Reproduction or Biology of Women from a feminist science theoretical basis (Rosser 1985). Enough work has been done in this area to permit a transformation of the traditional androcentric scientific thinking. In contrast, the professor teaching an upper level course in immunology might only be able to integrate the information on women scientists (Franklin, Yalow) who made contributions to the field and to discuss the way in which the warlike terminology of immunology, which describes cellular interaction in theories of competition, inhibition, and invasion, reflects a masculine world view and skews the view of nature and our choice of research avenues. For example, one might speak of cooperation and the dependence of the membrane upon its surrounding environment.

If the degree to which the feminist transformation has affected the fields within biology varies so drastically, how does one integrate this range of transformation into a basic biology course that attempts to introduce the student to all the fields in biology? Of course, the variation will be reflected as one covers different areas.

After an introduction to the scientific method, most introductory syllabi and textbooks attempt to cover the following six broad fields within biology: the scientific method, the cell, genetics, development, evolution and animal behavior, and ecology. I will indicate some issues that might be raised, an activity or reading that students might do, and some background resource material for the professor, which aid in integrating the feminist perspective in each of these areas.

THE SCIENTIFIC METHOD

Most beginning biology courses include a presentation of the modern conception of the scientific method. This provides an ideal opportunity for presenting the feminist critique of the methodology of science, which can then be applied when assessing the research and data presented in individual areas. In the feminist critique of the scientific method, the following issues need to be raised: To what extent are the scientific method and the theories derived from it biased by the particular social and historical context of the scientist? To what extent is the language of scientific theories reflective of a particular social and historical context? Is the scientific method really an objective approach to the world or is it androcentric? If it is androcentric, is this bias reflected in experimental design, use of only male subjects and models for experimentation, and the language and conceptualization of scientific theories?

A means of making the students aware of the effect of previous experience and world view on "objective" reporting of data is to ask them to repeat Kuhn's (1970) experiment. After they are shown a deck of cards with a red ace of spades, which they "see" as a black ace, they have a concrete example of how their hypotheses may influence their data collection. This activity can then lead into a discussion of androcentric and other sociohistorical biases in data collection and theory formation. The journal articles and books listed in the bibliography section entitled "Feminist Critique of Scientific Methodology and History of Science" might aid the professor in thinking about this section of the course.

THE CELL

Cell biology is an area in which virtually no theoretical changes have been proposed by feminist scientists. The integration of a feminist perspective in this area will probably have to be raised in terms of the terminology in which the theories are expressed and the very few female scientists who have worked in this area.

Students might be asked to make a list of the terminology used to describe cells and their interaction. They should then determine which of those terms (e.g., competitive inhibition) are correlated with aggression, war, competition, or other characteristics defined in our society as masculine. This activity can be used to lead students to speculate about how the language might transform the theories if more feminine characteristics were used to describe the cell interactions. The resources that faculty might read in preparation for this section of the course are listed under "The Influence of Language on Science and Cell Biology" in the bibliography.

GENETICS

The study of genetics and DNA provides an excellent locus to raise the issues of the position of women in science and why women are not accepted as "good" scientists. Such questions must be addressed as why, in science, most of the data collection and technical work are done by women while most of the theorizing and decision-making are done by men? Why are hypotheses suggested by women not accepted? One might also ask if the unicausal approach to teaching in genetics, which reflects a reductionist view that understanding the genes means understanding everything about an organism and not taking into account its complex interaction with the environment, is a male approach to the world?

The ideal activity to emphasize the difference between the positions of men and women in science is to ask the student to read *Rosalind Franklin and DNA* by Anne Sayre (1975) and *The Double Helix* by James Watson (1969). This pair of books demonstrates the difficulties that women in science have in being taken seriously and achieving the necessary research positions. Several excellent resources regarding careers and the position of women in science are now available for faculty to consult; they are listed under "The Position of Women in Science and Genetics" in the bibliography.

DEVELOPMENT

The area of developmental biology including endocrinology, for purposes of an introductory course, provides opportunities to begin to raise the issues of how the male models, experimental subjects, and the language used to describe those models are beginning to be transformed by a feminist critique.

The evidence from developmental biology that the initial groundplan for development in most species is female will come as a shock to most students, who are used to the androcentric Western view that the male is primary in all realms and that female is the "other" or secondary (Sherfey 1973). Learning about parthenogenesis and that in development it is the so-called *reacting* (an androcentric turn of phrase?) biological system that is important in egg development rather than what is applied to it (the sperm) reemphasizes the importance of the female (Manning 1983).

The increasing evidence that most hormones operate on a cyclical rather than steady-state basis (Hoffman 1982) raises the question of why male rats and monkeys are used as experimental subjects when females would obviously provide a more accurate model. Students can begin to see that the "cleaner" data derived from male models, due to their noncyclicity, may lead scientists to oversimplified conclusions. Perhaps the "messier" data derived from female models is in fact more reflective of biological complexity. An explanation of the subtle problems that accompany biochemical conversions of hormones within the body, so that an injection of testosterone may be converted to estrogen or another derivative by the time it reaches the brain (Bleier 1979), may lead students to ask questions about proper controls and extrapolating from biochemical to behavioral traits.

The issue, first raised by E.E. Just in the 1930s and recently brought forth by feminist scientists, of the nature of the interaction of the cell surface with the surrounding environment demonstrates a beginning theoretical change due to feminist critique. Standard theory holds that the cell is in a struggle with the environment; the newer theory, influenced partially by feminist critique, suggests that cooperative processes along the cell surface may be more important (Manning 1983).

Perhaps the best way for students to understand the resistance to ideas outside the mainstream of the theories formulated by the white male developmental biologists is to read either *A Feeling for the Organism*, about the white female geneticist Barbara McClintock, or *Black Apollo of Science*, about the black male embryologist E.E. Just. Further background resources for faculty are listed in the bibliography under "Developmental Biology and Endocrinology."

EVOLUTION

The field of evolution with its subdiscipline, animal behavior, provides ample opportunity for a feminist critique of the language, experimental subjects, data collection, and theoretical conclusions drawn. One may begin by questioning the extent to which Darwin's theory of natural selection was biased by the social and historical context of its time. His theoretical language (competition, struggle for existence, survival of the fittest) led to theories of biological determinism as a basis for behavioral differences and abilities, which were used to explain differences in social and economic class, and as the basis for the policy of "social Darwinism" during his time (Hrdy 1981). This probably needs to be pointed out to students. Then many of them will be able to understand the problems of some animal behavior research, in which behavior in lower animals is observed in the search for "universal" behavior patterns in males of all species or in all males of a particular order or class, such as primates or mammals. The problems raised by then extrapolating these patterns to human beings must be addressed. The claims of sociobiologists that behavior is genetically determined and that differences between males in role, status, and performance are biologically based (Wilson 1975) can then be refuted by explaining the alternative theories to the classical andro- and ethnocentric descriptions of animal behavior now provided by feminist scientists (Lancaster 1975).

Viewing a sociobiology film or videotape and reading a feminist critique of sociobiology should provide students with alternative approaches to the theory of biological determinism. The Nova tape "Sociobiology" or the film "Sociobiology: Doing What Comes Naturally" are excellent prosociobiology visual representations. "Sociobiology and Biosociology: Can Science Prove the Biological Basis of Sex Differences in Behavior?" (Lowe and Hubbard 1979) provides a feminist critique of sociobiology. "A Feminist View of Evolution and Sociobiology" in the bibliography includes a partial listing from among the abundant resources available in this area.

ECOLOGY

Ecology is the field within biology where the traditional scientific theory and approach are most in harmony with a feminist approach to the subject. Ecology emphasizes the interrelationships among organisms, including human beings, and the earth. Feminists have also focused on the position of human beings as a part of the environmental network. Both ecology and feminism deplore the position that industrialized Western man has taken, as a superior being who has dominion over the right to exploit the earth and its other living beings, including women. The fusion of feminist and scientific theory in the field of ecology brings together the ultimate goal of the course:

the integration of a feminist perspective into science. It is thus the ideal subject matter on which to end the course.

An activity that helps the students to understand the parallels between feminist and ecological theory is to ask them to make the following four lists: a list of the scientific terms they learned to describe ecological processes; a list of the scientific terms they learned to describe Darwin's theory of natural selection; a list of terms associated with women and/or femininity; a list of terms associated with men and/or masculinity. Presumably terms such as *cooperation*, *dependence*, and *importance of relationships* will appear on lists one and three; whereas terms such as *competition*, *dominant*, and *independent* will appear on lists two and four. Resources for faculty are listed under "Feminism and Ecology" in the bibliography.

In summary, the issues, activities for students, and readings for faculty in the different areas in biology vary in the extent to which the feminist and scientific theory can be smoothly integrated. Taken together, it becomes evident that the inclusion of a feminist perspective leads to changes in models, experimental subjects, and interpretations of the data. Not only should these changes attract more women to science, but the changes entail more inclusive, enriched theories compared to the traditional, restrictive, unicausal theories. These alternative, multidimensional theories generally provide a more accurate description of the realities of our complex biological world which should be integrated into the standard biology curriculum, even and perhaps especially at the introductory level.

0401.110 CONTEMPORARY GENERAL BIOLOGY

Syllabus and Reading List (Fall 1983)

AUGUST

29	Introduction to the course and the scientific method.
31	In what sense is the scientific method "objective"? (1: 1–19)

SEPTEMBER

2	Discussion of Kuhn experiment done in lab. Atoms and molecules. (3: 36–42)
5	Labor Day Recess
7	Macromolecules. (6: 84–94; 16: 284–285)
9	Cells. (4: 50–70)
12	Cells.
14	Cellular transport. (5: 71–73; 75–83)

16	Cellular communication. Discussion of terminology describing cells and their interactions. (14: 221–231)
19	Glycolysis and respiration. (7: 102–104)
21	Glycolysis and respiration.
23	Gas exchange. (16: 292–297)
26	Photosynthesis. (7: 95–102)
28	Photosynthesis.
30	EXAMINATION I: Covers material up to September 23.
OCTOBER	
3	Summary of energy transformations. (7: 115–118)
5	Mitosis and meiosis. (8: 120–140)
7	Mitosis and meiosis—Last day to drop a class
10	Biochemical genetics. (10: 165–178)
12	Biochemical genetics. (11: 179–185)
14	Biochemical genetics. Complete reading of *Rosalind Franklin and DNA*.
17	Gene regulation. (11: 185–191)
19	Patterns of inheritance. (9: 141–147)
21	Patterns of inheritance. (9: 148–164) Complete reading of *The Double Helix*.
24	Human genetics. Discussion of positions of women and men in science as portrayed in *Rosalind Franklin and DNA* and *The Double Helix*.
26	Reproduction: Basic concepts.
28	Reproduction and development in animals. (18: 321–350)
31	EXAMINATION II: Covers material up to October 24.
NOVEMBER	
2	Reproduction and development in animals: The initial female groundplan.
4	Reproduction and development in plants. (23: 426–443)
7	Reproduction and development in plants. Discussion of *A Feeling for the Organism*. (19: 365–367)
9	Evolution: Basic concepts. (2: 20–34)
11	Genetic variation. Videotape "Sociobiology." (25: 468–472)
14	The Hardy-Weinberg principle.
16	Selection. (25: 472–477)
18	Adaptation. Discussion of the article, "Sociobiology and Biosociology: Can Science Prove the Biological Basis of Sex Differences in Behavior?"
21	Speciation. (25: 477–481)

23   Diversification. (21: 394–410)
25   Thanksgiving Recess
28   Ecology. (26: 482–495)
30   Ecology: Interdependence of all organisms. (28: 510–534)

DECEMBER

2   Ecology. (29: 535–538)
7   Discussion of terminology describing ecological processes, Darwin's theory of natural selection, femininity, and masculinity.
9   Examination III: Covers material up to December 7.
12   Review and evaluation of course. Can science be taught from a feminist perspective?
15   FINAL EXAMINATION.

Texts

Starr, C., and R. Taggart. *Biology: The Unity and Diversity of Life.* Belmont, Calif.: Wadsworth, 1981. Reading assignments in parentheses are from this text.

Keller, Evelyn F. *A Feeling for the Organism: The Life and Work of Barbara McClintock.* New York: W.H. Freeman and Company, 1983.

Lowe, M., and R. Hubbard. "Sociobiology and Biosociology: Can Science Prove the Biological Basis of Sex Differences in Behavior?" In *Genes and Gender II*, eds. R. Hubbard and M. Lowe. Staten Island, N.Y.: Gordian Press, 1979.

Sayre, Anne. *Rosalind Franklin and DNA.* New York: W.W. Norton and Company, Inc., 1975.

Watson, James D. *The Double Helix.* New York: Atheneum Publishers, Mentor, 1969.

REFERENCES

Bleier, R. 1979. Social and political bias in science: An examination of animal studies and their generalizations to human behavior and evolution. In *Genes and gender II*, eds. R. Hubbard and M. Lowe, 49–70. Staten Island, N.Y: Gordian Press, Inc.

Bleier, R. 1984. *Science and gender: A critique of biology and its theories on women.* New York: Pergamon Press.

Fee, E. 1981. Is feminism a threat to scientific objectivity? *International Journal of Women's Studies* 4, no. 4: 213–233.

Fee, E. 1982. A feminist critique of scientific objectivity. *Science for the People* 4, no. 4: 213–233.

Haraway, D. 1978. Animal sociology and a natural economy of the body politic, Part I: A political physiology of dominance; and Animal sociology and a natural economy of the body politic, Part II: The past is the contested zone: Human nature and theories of production and reproduction in primate behavior studies. *Signs: Journal of Women in Culture and Society* 4, no. 1: 21–60.

Hein, H. 1981. Women and science: Fitting men to think about nature. *International Journal of Women's Studies* 4, no. 4: 369–377.

Hoffmann, J.C. 1982. Biorhythms in human reproduction: The not-so-steady states. *Signs: Journal of Women in Culture and Society* 7, no. 4: 829–844.

Hrdy, S.B. 1981. *The woman that never evolved.* Cambridge, Mass.: Harvard University Press.

Hubbard, R. 1979. Have only men evolved? In *Women Look at Biology Looking at Women*, eds. R. Hubbard, M.S. Henifin, and B. Fried. Cambridge, Mass.: Schenkman Publishing Co.

Keller, E.F. 1982. Feminism and science. *Signs: Journal of Women in Culture and Society* 7, no. 3: 589–602.

Kuhn, T.S. 1970. *The structure of scientific revolutions.* 2d Ed. Chicago: The University of Chicago Press.

Lancaster, J. 1975. *Primate behavior and the emergence of human culture.* New York: Holt, Rinehart and Winston.

Lowe, M., and R. Hubbard. 1979. Sociobiology and biosociology: Can science prove the biological basis of sex differences in behavior? *Genes and Gender II*, eds. R. Hubbard and M. Lowe. Staten Island, N.Y.: Gordian Press, Inc.

Manning, K.R. 1983. *Black Apollo of science.* Oxford: Oxford University Press.

Minnich, E.K. 1982. A feminist critique of the liberal arts. In *Liberal education and the new scholarship on women: Issues and constraints in institutional change*, 22–38. Washington, D.C.: Association of American Colleges.

Rosser, S.V. 1985. Teaching about sexuality and human reproduction: Attempts to include multiple perspectives. *Women's Studies Quarterly* 7, 4: 31–33.

Sayre, A. 1975. *Rosalind Franklin and DNA.* New York: W.W. Norton & Company, Inc.

Sherfey, M.J. 1973. *The nature and evolution of female sexuality.* New York: Random House.

Watson, J.D. 1969. *The double helix.* New York: Atheneum Publishers, Mentor Paperback.

Wilson, E.O. 1975. *Sociobiology: The new synthesis.* Cambridge, Mass.: Harvard University Press.

BIBLIOGRAPHY

General References on Science and Women

Bleier, R. 1984. *Science and Gender: A critique of biology and its theories on women.* New York: Pergamon Press.

Brighton Women and Science Group. 1980. *Alice through the microscope.* London: Virago.

34   *Teaching Science and Health from a Feminist Perspective*

Gersh, E.S., and I. Gersh. 1981. *Biology of women.* Baltimore: University Park Press.

Hubbard, R., M.S. Henifin, and B. Fried, eds. 1982. *Biological woman— The convenient myth: A collection of feminist essays and a comprehensive bibliography.* Cambridge, Mass.: Schenkman Publishing Co.

Keller, E.F. 1985. *Reflections on gender and science.* New Haven: Yale University Press.

Lowe, M., and R. Hubbard. 1983. *Women's nature: Rationalizations of inequality.* New York: Pergamon Press.

Rose, S., ed. 1982. *Towards a liberatory biology.* New York: Allison and Busby.

Sayers, J. 1982. *Biological politics: Feminist and anti-feminist perspectives.* New York: Tavistock Publications.

Sloane, E. 1985. *Biology of women.* New York: John Wiley and Sons.

Special issues of journals devoted to women and science: *Signs: Journal of Women in Culture and Society.* 4, no. 1, Autumn, 1978.

International Journal of Women's Studies. 4, no. 4, 1981.

Feminist Critique of Scientific Methodology and History of Science

Arditti, R. 1980. Feminism and science. In *Science and liberation*, eds. R. Arditti, P. Brennan and S. Cavrak. Boston: South End Press.

Bleier, R. 1982. Comment on Haraway's "In the beginning was the world: The genesis of biological theory." *Signs: Journal of Women in Culture and Society* 7, no. 3: 725-727.

Bleier, R. 1976. Myths of the biological inferiority of women: An exploration of the sociology of biological research. *University of Michigan Papers in Women's Studies* 2: 39-63.

Fee, E. 1982. A feminist critique of scientific objectivity. *Science for the People* 14, no. 4: 8.

Fee, E. 1981. Is feminism a threat to scientific objectivity? *International Journal of Women's Studies* 4, no. 4: 213-233.

Gould, S.J. 1981. *The mismeasure of man.* New York: W.W. Norton and Company.

Harding, S., and M.B. Hintikka, eds. 1983. *Discovering reality: Feminist perspectives on epistemology, metaphysics, methodology, and philosophy of science.* Boston: D. Reidel.

Hein, H. 1981. Women and science: Fitting men to think about nature. *International Journal of Women's Studies* 4, no. 4: 369-377.

Keller, E.F. 1983. Feminism as an analytic tool for the study of science. *Academe Bulletin of the American Association of University Professors* 69, no. 5: 15-21.

Keller, E.F. 1982. Feminism and science. *Signs: Journal of Women in Culture and Society* 7, no. 3: 589-602.

Keller, E.F. 1978. Gender and science. *Psychoanalysis and Contemporary Thought* 1: 409.

Kuhn, T.S. 1970. *The structure of scientific revolutions.* 2d Ed. Chicago: The University of Chicago Press.

Longino, H., and R. Doell. 1983. Body, bias, and behavior: A comparative analysis of reasoning in two areas of biological science. *Signs: Journal of Women in Culture and Society* 9, no. 2: 206–227.

Rose, H. 1983. Hand, brain, and heart: A feminist epistemology for the natural sciences. *Signs: Journal of Women in Culture and Society* 9, no. 1: 73–90.

Tuana, N. 1983. Re-fusing nature/nurture. *Women's Studies International Forum* 6, no. 6: 621–632.

The Influence of Language on Science and Cell Biology

Fried, B. 1979. Boys will be boys will be boys. In *Women look at biology looking at women*, eds. R. Hubbard, M.S. Henifin, and B. Fried, 37–59. Boston: Schenkman Publishing Co.

Hogsett, A.C., and S.V. Rosser. 1983. Darwin and sexism: Victorian causes, contemporary effects. In *Women's studies and the curriculum*, ed. M. Triplette, 67–75. Winston-Salem, N.C.: Salem College.

Martyna, W. 1983. Beyond the "he/man" approach: The case of nonsexist language. In *Feminist frontiers*, eds. L. Richardson and V. Taylor. Reading, Mass.: Addison-Wesley Publishing Company.

Vetterling-Braggin, M., ed. 1980. *Sexist language: A modern philosophical analysis.* New York: Littlefield, Adams and Company.

The Position of Women in Science and Genetics

Goodfield, J. 1981. *An imagined world.* New York: Penguin Books.

Gornick, V. 1983. *Women in science: Portraits from a world in transition.* New York: Simon and Schuster.

Haas, V.B., and C.C. Perrucci, eds. 1984. *Women in scientific and engineering professions.* Ann Arbor: University of Michigan Press.

Haber, L. 1979. *Women pioneers of science.* New York: Harcourt Brace Jovanovich.

Hubbard, R. 1983. Reflections on the story of the double helix. *Feminist Frontiers.* eds. L. Richardson and V. Taylor, 136–144. Reading Mass.: Addison-Wesley Publishing Company.

Keller, E.F. 1983. *A feeling for the organism: The life and work of Barbara McClintock.* New York: W.H. Freeman and Company.

Keller, E.F. 1977. The anomaly of a woman in physics. In *Working it out: 23 women writers, scientists and scholars talk about their lives*, eds. S. Ruddick and P. Daniels. New York: Pantheon Books.

Malcom, S.M., P.Q. Hall, and J.W. Brown. 1975. *The double bind: The price of being a minority woman in science.* Washington, D.C.: American Association for the Advancement of Science.

Martin, B.R., and J. Irvine. 1982. Women in science—The astronomical brain drain. *Women's Studies International Forum* 5, no. 1: 41–68.

National Research Council. 1979. *Climbing the academic ladder: Doctoral women scientists in academe.* Washington, D.C.: National Academy of Sciences.

National Science Foundation. 1984. *Women and minorities in science and engineering*. Report 84-300.

Rossiter, M.W. 1982. *Women scientists in America: Struggles and stategies to 1940*. Baltimore: The Johns Hopkins University Press.

Sayre, A. 1975. *Rosalind Franklin and DNA*. New York: W.W. Norton and Company, Inc.

Vetter, B.M. 1980a. Opportunities in science and engineering. Scientific Manpower Commission slide-tape presentation produced under National Science Foundation Grant No. SPI-7913025.

Vetter, B.M. 1980b. Sex discrimination in the halls of science. *Chemical and Engineering News* (March): 37–38.

Weisstein, N. 1979. Adventures of a woman in science. In *Women look at biology looking at women*, eds. R. Hubbard, M.S. Henifin, and B. Fried. Boston: Schenkman Publishing Co.

Developmental Biology and Endocrinology

Bleier, R. 1979. Social and political bias in science: An examination of animal studies and their generalizations to human behavior and evolution. In *Genes and gender II*, eds. R. Hubbard and M. Lowe, 49–70. Staten Island, N.Y.: Gordian Press, Inc.

Gordon, S. 1983. What's new in endocrinology? Target: Sex hormones. In *Genes and gender IV*, eds. M. Fooden, S. Gordon, and B. Hughley. Staten Island, N.Y.: Gordian Press.

Hoffmann, J.C. 1982. Biorhythms in human reproduction: The not-so-steady states. *Signs: Journal of Women in Culture and Society* 7, no. 4: 829–844.

Manning, K.R. 1983. *Black Apollo of science*. Oxford: Oxford University Press.

Star, S.L. 1979. The politics of right and left: Sex differences in hemispheric brain asymmetry. In *Women look at biology looking at women*, eds. R. Hubbard, M.S. Henifin, and B. Fried. Boston: Schenkman Publishing Co.

Villars, T. 1983. Sexual dimorphisms in the brain and behavior: Reflections on the concept. In *Women's studies and the curriculum*, ed. M. Triplette. Winston-Salem, N.C.: Salem College.

A Feminist View of Evolution and Sociobiology

Barash, D. 1977. *Sociobiology and behavior*. New York: Elsevier.

Blackwell, A.B. [1875] 1976. *The sexes throughout nature*. New York: G.P. Putnam's Sons; reprinted, Westport, Conn.: Hyperion Press, Inc.

Chasin, B. 1977. Sociobiology: A sexist synthesis. *Science for the People* (May/June).

Dahlberg, F., ed. 1981. *Woman the gatherer*. New Haven, Conn.: Yale University Press.

Haraway, D. 1978. Animal sociology and a natural economy of the body politic, Part I: A political physiology of dominance; and Animal sociology and a natural economy of the body politic, Part II: The past is the contested zone: Human nature and theories of production and reproduction in primate behavior studies. *Signs: Journal of Women in Culture and Society* 4, no. 1: 21–60.

Hrdy, S.B. 1981. *The woman that never evolved.* Cambridge, Mass.: Harvard University Press.

Lancaster, J. 1975. *Primate behavior and the emergence of human culture.* New York: Holt, Rinehart and Winston.

Leavitt, R.R. 1975. *Peaceable primates and gentle people: Anthropological approaches to women's studies.* New York: Harper and Row.

Lowe, M. 1978. Sociobiology and sex differences. *Signs: Journal of Women in Culture and Society* 4, no. 1: 118–125.

Montagu, A., ed. 1980. *Sociobiology examined.* Oxford: Oxford University Press.

Reed, E. 1978. *Sexism and science.* New York: Pathfinder Press.

Rosser, S.V. 1982. Androgyny and sociobiology. *International Journal of Women's Studies* 5, no. 5: 435–444.

Tanner, N.M. 1981. *On becoming human.* New York: Cambridge University Press.

Feminism and Ecology

Griffin, S. 1978. *Women and nature.* New York: Harper and Row.

Griffin, S. 1982. Woman and nature. In *Made from this earth: An anthology of writings.* New York: Harper and Row.

King, Y. 1983. Toward an ecological feminism and a feminist ecology. In *Machina ex dea: Feminist perspectives on technology*, ed. J. Rothschild. New York: Pergamon Press.

McStay, J.R., and R.E. Dunlap. 1983. Male-female differences in concern for environmental quality. *International Journal of Women's Studies* 6, no. 4: 291–301.

Merchant, C. 1983. Mining the earth's womb. In *Machina ex dea: Feminist perspectives on technology*, ed. J. Rothschild. New York: Pergamon Press.

Merchant, C. 1979. *The death of nature: Women, ecology, and the scientific revolution.* New York: Harper and Row.

Nelkin, D. 1981. Nuclear power as a feminist issue. *Environment* 23: 14–20, 38–39.

Pasino, E.M., and J.W. Lousbury. 1976. Sex differences in opposition to and support for construction of a proposed nuclear power plant. In *The behavioral basis of design, Book I*, eds. L.M. Ward, S. Coren, A. Gruft, and J.B. Collins. Stroudsburg, Penn.: Dowden, Hutchinson, and Ross.

Reuther, R.R. 1975. *New women, new earth.* New York: Seabury.

Chapter 3
Biology of Reproduction and Reproductive Technologies

What we have is patriarchal rear-hegemony of technology, information, medicine and facilities affecting female reproduction. And who exactly are these men who dominate female reproductive lives? They are males raised, as we all have been, in a society steeped deep in woman-hatred. Only these men have unique on-the-job opportunities to act out their misogyny. (Dreifus, 1977, xix)

This quotation comes from the Introduction to *Seizing Our Bodies* which was written in 1977. Since that time, even more technologies have been invented, which are imposed more frequently, even routinely, upon women's reproductive lives.

In the Introduction and preceding chapter of this book, we discussed the grounding of modern scientific theories and methods, particularly those of biology, in an androcentric approach to the world. Technologies developed from the application of such theories and methods are also conceived primarily by men limited by the same constricted perspective. These reproductive technologies are used primarily on women's bodies and most directly affect the lives of women and children. The purpose of the course, Biology of Reproduction and Reproductive Technologies, is to explore, from a gynocentric perspective, the extent to which the technologies have invaded various, if not all, aspects of reproduction and the potential negative and positive results that these technologies have for women. This course differs from other courses on the biology of reproduction and/or sexuality in that its major focus is upon the new reproductive technologies. Students must have a good understanding of the biology of sex and reproduction in order to comprehend the mechanisms by which the technologies work and the implications of the technologies for the health of women and children. However, primary emphasis is placed upon critically examining and evaluating the effect of technologies on the reproductive life. The course may differ from other courses dealing with reproductive technologies in that it is taught from a feminist perspective. This means that the benefits and effects on women — rather than men, fetuses, or society as a whole — become the focus for evaluation of these technologies. It also means that freedom of choice and varieties of perspective among women with regard to religion, class, race, able-bodiedness, and sexual preference are considered and explored for all technologies.

In our society, the technologies are not only based in androcentric scientific theories, but the control of those technologies is also primarily in the hands of men (Albury 1984). An evaluation of these technologies from a feminist perspective is essential, since they represent very powerful tools in the continued struggle for men's domination and control over women's bodies.

The source of men's desire for this control is unclear. Some sociologists (Levi-Strauss 1969) have suggested that the desire comes from men's jealousy over women's ability to bear children and their view that marriage is a contract between *men*, in which there is a formalized exchange of women as commodities. Sociobiologists, arguing from the perspective of men's insecurity about paternity, would agree that once men's minor role in reproduction (contribution of the sperm) was understood, men set up all sorts of legal and social conditions to ensure that the child whom they might be protecting or supporting in some way was genetically theirs (Daly and Wilson 1978). Brownmiller (1975) suggests that women accepted some of these sociolegal arrangements, such as monogamy and marriage, as a trade-off for protection against being raped by more than one man. Whatever its sources, in patriarchal societies women (and their offspring) are viewed as the property of the men.

In the past and in other countries today, men often controlled the sexuality and reproduction of their "property" through physical as well as social and legal means: chastity belts (Davis, 1971), footbinding (Daly 1978), and clitoridectomy (still common today in many Moslem countries) (Hosken 1976). In the United States today, forced sterilizations (CARASA 1979), hysterectomies performed too frequently (Centers for Disease Control 1980), lack of Medicaid funding for abortion, and denial of access by lesbians to artificial insemination (Hornstein 1984) are simply examples of the ways women's sexuality and reproduction are regulated by the medical establishment. Not coincidentally, the medical establishment, particularly the decision-making portion dealing with women's reproduction, is strongly dominated by men.

The history of gynecology in the United States has shown a distinct pattern of takeover and control of the childbirth and reproductive procedures by male doctors from female midwives, from the mid-nineteenth century (Ehrenreich and English 1978; Wertz and Wertz 1979) to the present time. Today, 96.5 percent of obstetricians and gynecologists are men (Scully 1980). Considering this history and the current abuses, can we expect that the new reproductive technologies, developed and controlled by a scientific and medical establishment dominated by men, will be completely positive for women? Technologies such as amniocentesis, artificial insemination, and *in vitro* fertilization are heralded by the media as "liberating" women. They permit women who are older, who do not wish to have intercourse, or who have blocked oviducts to bear children. However, upon closer examination, each of these new technologies also has an oppressive side; each may also be used in a way to control or limit women's sexuality or reproductive access. Amniocentesis may be used to abort a child of an unwanted sex, usually female (Roggencamp 1984; Hoskins and Holmes 1984). In most localities, artificial insemination is denied women who are unmarried or open about their lesbianism (Hornstein 1984). *In vitro* fertilization is very expensive, $5000 per insemination with a 23 percent chance of success, and available only to married couples (Gold 1985).

As with most technologies, intrinsically the new reproductive technologies are neither good nor bad; it is the way they are used that determines their potential for benefit or harm. The androcentric scientific and medical establishment creates and controls these technologies. Using our biological knowledge, we must evaluate them from a feminist perspective to begin to appreciate the full implications of these technologies for women before we can assess their benefits or hazards.

CONTENT

In order to assess the double-edged sword of the new technologies, which penetrate ever further into women's reproductive lives, I find it useful to group the technologies by the aspect of women's reproductive life upon which they are used. After a review of the basic anatomy and physiology associated with the particular aspect of the reproductive life, each technology is considered in light of four basic questions:

1. What is the basic biological principle upon which this technology is based and how is it applied to the woman's body?
2. What are the proven and potential biological/health and sociopolitical benefits of this technology for women?
3. What are the proven and potential biological/health and sociopolitical risks or harms of this technology for women?
4. How does a consideration of the varying perspectives of class, race, religion, able-bodiedness, and sexual preference broaden or change the issues or answers to the first three questions?

The example of amniocentesis provides an opportunity to outline the way in which I study the technologies in the course. Amniocentesis is considered in the section of the course dealing with pregnancy. After a review of the biological events of a normal pregnancy, I introduce the various technologies frequently used during pregnancy. I explain the biological principle surrounding amniocentesis (that fetal cells and enzymes secreted into the amniotic fluid may be cultured and tested for abnormalities) and the timing and steps of the actual procedure (insertion of the syringe at the fourteenth to sixteenth week of pregnancy to withdraw amniotic fluid). After reading and discussing the biology and technicalities of the procedure, I move to a consideration of the technology's benefits — ability to detect some 70 abnormalities including Trisomy 21, Edwards' Syndrome, and spina bifida (Ritchie 1984); peace of mind during the latter half of the pregnancy. Then I explore some of its risks — 1.0–1.5 percent increased chance of miscarriage or fetal abnormalities, like clubfoot or dislocated hip, breathing difficulties at birth, and Rh sensitization (Ritchie, 1984); necessity of a second trimester abortion if the woman wishes to terminate the pregnancy after learning the results; physical discomfort of the procedure; psychological discomfort of waiting three to four weeks for the results; and false sense of security due to the assumption that most "defects" may be detected by the procedure. When the students consider amniocentesis from the perspectives of class and religion, they begin to realize that since it may be expensive, at this point, it is restricted mostly to middle-class women whose religious background has limited sanctions against abortion. After some reading (Saxton 1984) and a guest lecture by a physically challenged woman, students broaden their perspective to recognize that the issue of amniocentesis raises questions about what it means to be labelled *abnormal* or defective in our society and about who decides who is "normal," therefore worthy of life, and who is "abnormal," and should be aborted. Women of color point out that other tests of normality (IQ) have often been used to screen out non-whites and represent people of color as inferior (Chase 1980). This point becomes even clearer when we consider that in India (Chacko 1982; Roggencamp 1984), China (Campbell 1976), and probably in some clinics in the United States (Roggencamp 1984), amniocentesis is used to abort fetuses who are female. All women react strongly to the fact that this reproductive technology may be used to define who is worthy of living, and that in many cases, this decision would exclude women. Thus, the technology that has been represented by the media and medical profession as a benefit to women, that allows women to delay childbearing and still guarantee a healthy baby, may also be used to enforce societal restrictions on physical and mental norms and even limit women in subsequent generations.

The other technologies, grouped under the specific areas of the reproductive cycle, may be explored to yield complex discussions similar to those surrounding the example of amniocentesis. For convenience, I have placed the major discussion of a technology under a specific category; however, some of them, such as hysterectomy, might be discussed in more than one section (e.g., sexuality or aging).

History of Obstetrics and Gynecology in the United States

We begin the course with a discussion of the takeover by male physicians of female reproductive care.

1. Forceps
2. Hospital births
3. Caesarean sections
4. Use of medication

Sexuality

Men in patriarchal societies have used a variety of means to control the sexuality of women and their offspring, whom the men view as their property. An examination of access to contraception and abortion and the statistics regarding sterilization reveal the medical means by which the sexuality of heterosexual women is manipulated. Women have fought hard for their reproductive rights: choice of contraception, abortion, and sterilization. However, access to and control of these procedures is in the hands of men, which means that the procedures may also be used to manipulate women's sexuality.

1. Contraception
2. Abortion
3. Sterilization

Conception and Infertility

Most of the new reproductive technologies have been developed for this area of a woman's reproductive life. For some individual women these technologies may be liberating; they permit women to have children who cannot conceive due to blocked oviducts or who do not wish to have intercourse. However, when we consider that these technologies are so often limited only to married women in order to produce "perfect" offspring, we begin to suspect that their usage may be oppressive. We then read that the scientists who developed the technologies describe the women contributing the eggs for *in vitro* fertilization as *egg farms* and *egg factories* (Murphy 1984). They envision a day when, through a combination of supraovulation, *in vitro* fertilization, sex selection, and artificial wombs, women need only be a small percentage of the population (Postgate 1973), which makes evident some scientists' plans to use these technologies to control women.

1. Sex selection
2. Gene manipulation
3. Cloning
4. Supraovulation
5. Sperm banks
6. Artificial insemination
7. *In vitro* fertilization
8. Frozen embryos

Pregnancy

The future development of artificial wombs may free women from pregnancy and permit the development of healthy offspring. As envisioned by Shulamith Firestone in her utopian feminist fantasy (1970), this would only bring about a better world if men were not using the technology to eliminate women and other "defectives." The current use of surrogate mothers has become a clear way in which women's bodies are used to produce the property of men (Ince 1984). The new technologies that currently permit women to increase the chances of having healthy babies place extreme pressure on the individual woman to produce a "perfect piece of property." The information now available about the effects of alcohol, drugs, smoking, disease, and nutrition during pregnancy and the availability of amniocentesis place on individual women the guilt of bearing a child with a "defect." By placing the burden of guilt on individual women, men and society lose sight of their responsibility to care for these children. Although the vast majority of physical and mental disabilities are not due to diseases or abnormalities detectable by amniocentesis or to the maternal environment during pregnancy, the current trend leaves people with the impression that they are. Therefore, society as a whole feels that the woman is responsible for "producing" (or failing to abort) this "defective" child, and so must care for it (Shaw, 1980).

1. Surrogate mothers
2. Artificial wombs
3. Amniocentesis and ultrasound
4. Maternal environment during pregnancy — fetal alcohol syndrome, drugs, smoking, disease, nutrition

Childbirth

Childbirth is an area in which the male scientific and medical establishments have developed and used technologies for over a century. Some of these technologies have greatly benefitted women in their potential to save the lives of both mothers and babies. Once again, the difficulty is in the control and overuse of these technologies by the medical profession to speed normal deliveries, make money, and enhance hospital procedure at the cost of a normal delivery by women who might not have needed medical intervention.

1. Medication during childbirth
2. Caesarean sections
3. Induction of labor
4. Episiotomy
5. Fetal heart monitors

Aging

The medical profession's use of technology in menopausal and aging women further demonstrates the desire of men to control women's sexuality and reproduction. Many doctors advise women past childbearing age to agree to removal of the uterus, since it has the potential to become cancerous (Taylor, 1979). Do doctors ever suggest removing the prostate in men since it too has the potential — much higher than the uterus — to become cancerous?

Although the advantages and disadvantages of estrogen replacement therapy to a woman's health are still being explored, the pharmaceutical ads in medical journals appeal to physicians to put their patients on estrogen replacement therapy to keep the woman looking young. The implication is that, with aging as with other aspects of women's health, women's bodies are manipulated to conform to the standards of society regarding sexuality and reproduction.

1. Hysterectomy
2. Estrogen replacement therapy
3. Menopause counseling

METHODS

The Biology of Reproduction and Reproductive Technologies is a course that deals with controversial, current subjects that evoke intense emotional reactions in many students. After learning the biological principles upon which the technologies are based and exploring the procedures by which the technologies are applied to a woman's body, most of the discussion centers on the benefits and risks of each technology for women. I think that it is crucial to create an atmosphere where choice, openness, and exploration of all ideas, options, and opinions are encouraged. Clearly, there is no right or wrong answer or stand on any of the technologies in all situations. Each student needs to feel that her or his informed opinion will be respected. Through the readings, field work, and class sessions, students explore a variety of perspectives and issues raised by the technologies. Since new technologies will be developed and since usage of the current technologies will change with time, the goal of the course is to aid the students in developing an approach that they may use to gather information from a variety of perspectives (see Chapter 4) to evaluate benefits and risks of these technologies for women.

In creating the atmosphere and developing the approach, I have found some of the following factors to be important:

1. *Course Level and Audience.* As a prerequisite, I require the students to previously have taken a course on the biology of sexuality and/or reproduction (Women and Their Bodies in Health and Disease or Biology and Psychology of Women are ideal). This permits us to focus directly on the complex social, legal, and psychological issues surrounding use of the technology rather than the basic biology of reproduction. I also try to attract students from a wide variety of majors, ages, races, classes, religions, able-bodiedness, and sexual preferences. This variety increases the perspective within the group from which the technologies may be discussed.

2. *Coteaching.* Because the course deals extensively with the social, legal, psychological, and ethical aspects of the technologies, as well as their biological impact, it is important that it be team-taught. The ideal team would consist of someone from the humanities, preferably with training in philosophy; someone from the social sciences, possibly with some legal background; and a biologist. A historian of science or medicine could also bring a needed perspective to the course. In addition, all members of the team need a firm grounding in women's studies to approach the issues from a feminist perspective. In these days of tight budgets and ever-increasing constraints on the time of women's studies faculty members at most institutions, it will probably be necessary to accept less than the ideal team. (See Chapter 4, Teaching about Sexuality and Human Reproduction: Attempts to Include Multiple Perspectives for additional ideas about how to increase perspectives.) However, I think that the course is immensely improved by the perspective of someone in addition to a scientist.

3. *Multiple Avenues for Students to Express Opinions.* Many students will react very strongly on an emotional level to some, if not most, of the issues raised by the new reproductive technologies. Although students are encouraged to discuss these feelings in class, some will not wish to air them in front of the entire group and not all class time can be spent in discussion of feelings. I have, therefore, found it useful to permit students to clarify and express their feelings outside of class discussions. The reaction paper is a mechanism that has proved successful. Students are required to turn in three brief (1–2 page) papers during the semester expressing their reactions to the implications of a current or potential technology. Students are

encouraged to write more reaction papers; in fact four additional papers can substitute for one examination. In addition, teaching techniques such as debates and mock court trials are used to elaborate the advantages and disadvantages of particular technologies. At least once during the semester, each student will be on a debating team or take part in a mock court trial. These techniques allow the student to verbally clarify her or his ideas about the technology. Journals are a third technique that might be equally effective as an avenue through which students can express their feelings. These might be done on an individual basis, each student documenting her or his reactions to issues brought up in reading and in the class. Alternately, the journals might be on a group basis, where each week each student contributes a phrase to a class journal.

4. *Texts.* *Test-tube Women* (Arditti et al. 1984), a book that explores the positive and negative aspects of reproductive technology for women from a feminist perspective, is the obvious text for this course. In addition, *The New Our Bodies, Ourselves* (Boston Women's Health Book Collective 1984) provides the information and diagrams needed for the biological background of the discussions. *Seizing Our Bodies* (Dreifus 1977), although somewhat dated for this rapidly changing technical field, raises many of the basic issues from a variety of perspectives in the area of women's reproductive biology.

5. *Nonacademic Component.* In order to break the image of science fiction and utopian ideas that surrounds the new reproductive technologies in many people's minds, we ask the students to interview someone who has had direct experience with one of the reproductive technologies. Although it is difficult to find someone who has had, or will talk about, *in vitro* fertilization or artificial insemination, many people have had amniocentesis, ultrasound, induction, fetal heart monitors, or Caesarean sections during pregnancy and childbirth. Students report gaining a more realistic perspective on the technologies by talking with a woman who experienced one or more of them.

All of the pedagogical methods of the course must emphasize the general course aim: providing information and approaches by which the students may learn to assess the biological, social, legal, and psychological benefits and risks of the new reproductive technologies for women. These technologies have been developed and used by the scientific and medical establishment, who approach women's sexuality and reproduction from an androcentric perspective. It is time for women to assess and evaluate these technologies from a feminist perspective so that they may begin to understand their full potentiality and implications.

BIOLOGY OF REPRODUCTION AND REPRODUCTIVE TECHNOLOGIES
Syllabus and Reading List

JANUARY

15	Introduction and course rationale. (TTW 11–19)
17	History of obstetrics and gynecology in the U.S. (TTW 23–33; OBO Chapter 24)
22	From midwives to physicians. (TTW 331–355)
24	Forceps, medication, and caesarean sections. (TTW 402–413; OBO Chapter 12)
29	Is technology a means to control women's sexuality? (TTW 356–370) FIRST REACTION PAPER DUE.
31	Contraception: Why are there so many methods for usage on women? (TTW 131–187; OBO Chapter 13)

FEBRUARY

5	Abortion: Equal access for all? (TTW 213–234, 266–278; OBO Chapter 16)
7	Sterilization: Choice and informed consent. (TTW 119–130, 188–212)
12	FIRST EXAMINATION.
14	Conception and infertility: Who is encouraged to have children in the U.S. today? (TTW 54–67; OBO Chapter 21)
19	Sex selection, gene manipulation, and cloning: Changing sex and gene frequency. (TTW 76–98)
21	Sperm banks and artificial insemination: Who has access? (TTW 371–390)
26	Supraovulation, *in vitro* fertilization, and frozen embryos: Women as egg farms? (TTW 68–75)
28	Panel discussion: Technologies regulating conception and infertility. SECOND REACTION PAPER DUE.

MARCH

5	Spring Break.
7	Spring Break.
12	Pregnancy: Do the new technologies provide liberation or loss of power? (TTW 391–396; OBO Chapter 15)

14	Surrogate mothers and artificial wombs. (TTW 99–115)
19	Amniocentesis and ultrasound. (TTW 235–265)
21	Maternal environment during pregnancy: Fetal alcohol syndrome, drugs, and smoking. (TTW 281–297; OBO Chapter 18)
26	Maternal environment during pregnancy: Disease and nutrition. (TTW 298–328)
28	Debate on technologies: Should the state have the right to require every women over 35 or every couple who has given birth to a child with a genetic disease to have amniocentesis? (OBO Chapters 25–26)

APRIL

2	SECOND EXAMINATION
4	Childbirth: Historical perspectives on technological intervention in reproductive processes. (TTW 397–401; OBO Chapter 19)
9	Caesarean sections and forceps birth. (TTW 413–418)
11	Induction, medication, and episiotomies. (TTW 418–426) THIRD REACTION PAPER DUE.
16	Fetal heart monitors. (TTW 427–437)
18	Aging: A final attempt to prolong and control women's reproductive lives. (OBO Chapter 22)
23	Estrogen replacement therapy, hysterectomy, and menopause counseling. (TTW 438–456)
25	Review, evaluation, and debate: How much money should be given to support reproductive technologies after a consideration of their risks and benefits for all women? (OBO Chapter 17)

Texts

TTW: Arditti, Rita, Renate Duelli Klein, and Shelley Minden. *Test-Tube Women: What Future for Motherhood?* London: Pandora Press. 1984.

OBO: Boston Women's Health Book Collective. *The New Our Bodies, Ourselves.* New York: Simon and Schuster, Inc., 1984.

Grades

The final grade will be based on examinations, reaction papers, and oral work in class. The first two examinations will each count 15 percent towards the final grade; the final examination will count 30 percent. The three reaction papers will each count 5 percent; the debate or mock trial will count 15 percent. The other 10 percent of the grade will be based on attendance and class participation. Please note that four additional reaction papers may substitute for one of the first two exams.

REFERENCES

Albury, R. 1984. Who owns the embryo? In *Test-tube women*, eds. R. Arditti, R. Duelli Klein, and S. Minden 54–67. London: Pandora Press.

Arditti, R., R. Duelli Klein, and S. Minden. 1984. *Test-tube women*. London: Pandora Press.

Boston Women's Health Book Collective. 1984. *The new our bodies, ourselves*. New York: Simon and Schuster, Inc.

Brownmiller, S. 1975. *Against our will: Men, women, and rape*. New York: Simon and Schuster, Inc.

Campbell, C. 1976. The manchild pill. *Psychology Today* (August): 86–91.

Centers for Disease Control. 1980. *Surgical sterilization surveillance: Hysterectomy in women aged 15–44, from 1970–1975*.

Chacko, A. 1982. Too many daughters? India's drastic cure. *World Paper* (November): 8–9.

Chase, A. 1980. *The legacy of Malthus*. Urbana: University of Illinois Press.

CARASA (Committee for Abortion Rights and Against Sterilization Abuse). 1979. *Women under attack: Abortion, sterilization and reproductive freedom*. New York: Author.

Daly, M., and M. Wilson. 1978. *Sex, evolution and behavior*. North Scituate, Mass. Duxbury Press.

Daly, M. 1978. *GynEcology: The metaethics of radical feminism*. Boston: Beacon Press.

Davis, E.G. 1971. *The first sex*. New York: G.P. Putnam.

Dreifus, C. 1978. *Seizing our bodies*. New York: Vintage Books.

Ehrenreich, B., and D. English. 1978. *For her own good*. New York: Anchor Press.

Firestone, S. 1970. *The dialectic of sex*. New York: Morrow.

Gold, M. 1985. The baby makers. *Science 85* 6, no. 3 (April): 26–38.

Hornstein, F. 1984. Children by donor insemination: A new choice for lesbians. In *Test-tube women*, eds. R. Arditti, R. Duelli Klein, and S. Minden, 373–381. London: Pandora Press.

Hosken, F.P. 1976. *WIN News*, II no. 3 (Summer).

Hoskins, B., and H. Holmes. 1984. Technology and prenatal femicide. In *Test-tube women*, eds. R. Arditti, R. Duelli Klein, and S. Minden, 237–255. London: Pandora Press.

Ince, S. 1984. Inside the surrogate industry. In *Test-tube women*, eds. R. Arditti, R. Duelli Klein, and S. Minden, 99–116. London: Pandora Press.

Levi-Strauss, C. 1969. *The elementary structures of kinship*. Boston: Beacon Press.

Murphy, J. 1984. Egg farming and women's future. In *Test-tube women*, eds. R. Arditti, R. Duelli Klein, and S. Minden, 68–75. London: Pandora Press.

Postgate, J. 1973. Bat's chance in hell. *New Scientist*, 5: 11–16.

Ritchie, M. 1984. Taking the initiative: Information versus technology in pregnancy. In *Test-tube women*, eds. R. Arditti, R. Duelli Klein, and S. Minden. 402–413. London: Pandora Press.

Roggencamp, V. 1984. Abortion of a special kind: Male sex selection in India. In *Test-tube Women*, eds. R. Arditti, R. Duelli Klein, and S. Minden, 266–278. London: Pandora Press.

Saxton, M. 1984. Born and unborn: The implications of reproductive technologies for people with disabilities. In *Test-tube women*, eds. R. Arditti, R. Duelli Klein, and S. Minden, 298–312. London: Pandora Press.

Scully, D. 1980. *Men who control women's health: The miseducation of obstetrician-gynecologists*. Boston: Houghton Mifflin Co.

Shaw, M. 1980. The potential plaintiff: Preconception and prenatal torts. In *Genetics and the law II*, eds. A. Milunsky and G.J. Annas, 225–232. New York: Plenum Press.

Taylor, R. 1979. *Medicine out of control*. Melbourne: Sun Books.

Wertz, R.W., and D. Wertz. 1979. *Lying-in*. New York: Schocken.

Chapter 4
Teaching About Sexuality and Human Reproduction: Attempts to Include Multiple Perspectives

Until relatively recently, discussion and teaching about female sexuality and reproduction were either forbidden or absent from most college curricula. In most institutions, women's studies provided the first courses in which female sexuality and reproduction are considered in their own right. These topics traditionally have been considered as adaptations of the human species compared to other animals in biology classes or as the sex that doesn't fit the male model in psychology and sociology classes. Male-centered courses too often put the woman student in the position of simply memorizing theories and facts that do not always take them into account. Women's studies courses also present one of the first opportunities for women instructors and students to evaluate theories and facts for themselves, rather than simply learning them from men professors.

Unfortunately, some women's studies classes tend to present sexuality and reproduction only from the perspective of white, middle-class heterosexual women. Many of the facts were gathered from this group, and most of the research is based on them. Quite frequently, given the structure of academia, the instructor is also from this group. As a result, the experiences of only one group of women are held up as the "facts" and models for sexuality. At best, this leaves nonwhite women, lesbians, women of other socioeconomic classes or religions, and physically challenged women feeling that the model does not describe their experiences. They may discount the course as taught from an oppressive, normative viewpoint (Dill, 1983). At worst, women who are not white, middle-class, and heterosexual may instead discount their own experiences. They again realize that they deviate from the standards and wonder why they fail to conform in this area, too.

During the last nine years, I taught courses on the biology of women at both Mary Baldwin College and the University of Wisconsin — Madison. At least two-thirds of the course centers around sexuality and reproduction. As my own consciousness continues to be raised, I have begun to recognize the narrowness of the perspective from which I began teaching these subjects. The first recognition came from personal experiences. I became aware of the bias in my teaching, in which I had assumed a heterosexual viewpoint. Thus, I widened my teaching about sexuality to include the lesbian perspective on all issues involving sexuality and reproduction, rather than segregating lesbianism to a section on alternative lifestyles or leaving it to a guest speaker. I then began to recognize other limitations in my perspective imposed by race, class, religion, age, and able-bodiedness. Realizing that I could not personally represent those perspectives, I sought means to include other viewpoints in both the content and methods of my teaching.

CONTENT

Including perspectives other than that of majority-group women involves rethinking all the issues of the course, not simply adding additional material to what is already said. For example, many instructors approach the birth control issue as if all women came from a heterosexual, white, middle class, able-bodied perspective: it is as an accepted or desired given for all women of reproductive age. This approach also reflects the extent to which the ethos of "compulsory heterosexuality" pervades our patriarchal culture (Rich 1980). The focus of the discussion thus becomes the advantages and disadvantages of the different methods and the choice of which one to use.

A wider focus means more than including discussion of possible complications of birth control methods for different ethnic or religious groups, such as the particular health risks to a black woman with sickle cell anemia of taking the birth control pill (Ammer 1983) or the newer methods of using the cervical mucus to determine the exact time of ovulation to aid in rhythm or natural birth control. The very issue of birth control must become the central focus of the discussion, since it presents itself differently to different groups of women. To many women of color, the testing and forced use of birth control may represent a genocidal attempt of whites to limit other racial groups. Puerto Rican women recall that over one-third of the women on their island were sterilized during the last thirty years without their consent (Vazquez-Calzadar 1973) and that the pill was tested there before it was considered safe to market in mainland United States (Zimmerman 1980). Black women, American Indian women, and Chicanas may feel torn between what their ethnic liberation movements and the women's movement advocate about contraception. To some lower-income women, birth control and forced sterilizations represent further humiliations, suggested to them to "help" them decrease their government support (Rodgers 1973). To many women of the Roman Catholic or fundamentalist religions, birth control may raise a conflict between religious belief and what the "dominant" culture suggests as ideal. To most lesbians, birth control may be a nonissue, except when gynecologists assume the heterosexual norm (Darty & Potter 1984) and insist on prescribing a method. Thus, the central focus of the birth control presentation must be a thorough discussion of the complications of the use and misuse of birth control for women in different situations. After that, the issues concerning particular methods can be addressed.

Sexuality is another area in which each woman's perspective is very different, depending on her race, class, sexual preference, religion, body, and life experiences. I was made acutely aware of this during a discussion. Shere Hite (1976) considered the relative infrequency and longer period of time needed for a woman to achieve orgasm when stimulated by vaginal penetration compared to clitoral stimulation. A black student asked me what I was talking about. She and the other black students made it clear that this information did not correspond to their experience at all. Without recognizing it, I had assumed as the norm the experience of the publicized white female. Other assumptions expressing not only racial but social, religious, age, and sexual preference prejudices underlie most discussions about sexuality. Some of these assumptions become evident from an examination of the content of the information presented and left out; more can be inferred from the order in which the topics are considered, who presents the topics, and how questions are handled.

Since our culture is permeated with "compulsory heterosexuality," most sexuality is taught from this perspective, even when homosexuality is discussed. The timing and method by which material is presented may convey subtly negative messages about lesbianism to the students. If material on heterosexuality is presented first, then heterosexuality becomes the norm. Lesbianism and bisexuality are automatically seen as deviations from the norm, even though the terminology used does not state that directly.

It may be wise to place sexuality on the syllabus before a lengthy section on contraception, pregnancy, and childbirth. This is more in keeping with the sequence of biological development. Presenting the material on lesbianism early in the course should create an atmosphere of respect for women of different sexual preferences, who may not choose to deal with contraception, pregnancy, and childbirth during their lives.

In handling the inevitable question, What do lesbians *do?*, it is important to broaden the answer beyond clitoral stimulation to a discussion of other means of expressing sexuality. Since our culture is dominated by men, as Germaine Greer (1984) stresses, sexuality is defined in male terms. This makes penile insertion and ejaculation the focus of and definition for a sexual act. Considering other means of sexual expression, such as touching, opens the way for a discussion of sexuality in aging and physically challenged people, as well as lesbians.

METHODS

Birth control and sexuality provide two examples of the complex issues that need consideration when class, race, religion, age, able-bodiedness, and sexual preference are included in discussions of sexuality and reproduction. Pregnancy, childbirth, menopause, abortion, diseases of women, lactation, and nutrition are equally complex when viewed from multiple perspectives. One must not underestimate the difficulties of attempting to include these multiple perspectives. Each woman has a unique set of experiences that determines her individual perspective; the lives and experiences of women are shaped by belonging to a particular group. Although there is not a *single*, totally identical racial, ethnic, or religious perspective, some commonalities arise out of such roots and they may be overlooked in our teaching. A person who has not shared those experiences cannot speak for the group, and it would be presumptuous, inaccurate, and potentially insulting for her to assume that she could. Caught between her commitment to include a variety of perspectives and the impossibility of speaking from other than her own viewpoint and experiences on these issues, the instructor may well feel that she is faced with an unsolvable dilemma. Although inadequate, the methods suggested here increase the visibility of these groups, while allowing the women to speak of their own experiences.

With limited budgets, excessive demands placed on ethnic and women's studies faculty, and emphasis on increased student-faculty ratios at most institutions, it becomes very difficult to represent different perspectives in one course. Team-teaching with women who represent the different perspectives is probably the best way to include varying viewpoints on all issues. When team-teaching is not possible, guest lectures may provide perspectives on particular issues. Students in the class may also provide valuable resources for different perspectives. However, it is important to avoid spotlighting the only Chicana in the class, by expecting her to represent the "Chicana viewpoint" on every issue. Diaries and accounts of sexuality and reproduction in literature written by women provide accounts of individual experience, which statistics may distort. Commercial or student-produced films and tapes may provide another alternative to allow women to express their own experiences of sexuality and reproduction.

As another means of broadening the students' view beyond what is presented in the textbook and class, I ask them to interview another woman about a biological event concerning reproduction or sexuality in her life. The woman is to differ as much as possible from the student with regard to class, ethnicity, religion, age, or sexual preference, so that the student can see the effect that the difference may have on the biological event and its interpretation. Students 18–22 years old report that this provides the best opportunity to learn about reproductive or sexual events from another perspective and to see how they affected another woman's life.

SYLLABUS PRESENTATION

The syllabus presented below represents my current attempt to include multiple perspectives in Biology of Women and Its Social Implications. This is an introductory course focusing on sexuality and reproduction. After a brief critique of methodology used in scientific and medical research, the possible biological events of a woman's life are considered in the order of their chronological developmental sequence. I also discuss the interplay between these biological events and their psychological effects. At the end of the course, nutrition, stress, diseases of women, and methods for dealing with the health care system are considered. The course described in the syllabus is taught as an elective for non-biology majors during a fourteen week semester. I have taught a similar course during both four- and eight-week summer sessions and during continuing education courses meeting three hours per week for twelve weeks. Adding some material from endocrinology and biochemistry, I have also taught the course to biology majors. With the help of a grant from the National Science Foundation, the course is now available on a combination of audiotapes, videotapes, and computer for self-instruction for students outside of the classroom and city.

This particular syllabus represents a point in the evolution of my thinking about changing this course to include more perspectives. It is a very different syllabus from the one I first used in 1975, and I welcome the changes that I know will occur in it in the future.

INT5: 121 BIOLOGY OF WOMEN AND ITS SOCIAL IMPLICATIONS
Syllabus and Reading List

SEPTEMBER

7	Is anatomy destiny? Is science only for the white, middle-class male? (Sloane 1–14; T&R 7–8; H&L 7–34)
9	Evolutionary and genetic theories of sex determination. (Sloane 97–138; T&R 13–31; H&L 35–48)
12	Sociobiology vs. a feminist counter to genes determining behavior. Videotape: "Sociobiology." (T&R 51–62, 75–86; H&L 49–70)
14	Biology of sexual differentiation and development. (H&L 70–130)
16	Biology of sexual response. (Sloane 139–149)
19	Sexual preference and behavior. (Sloane 149–161; H&L 131–142)
21	Lesbiansim: Social and legal aspects. Slide-tape Show: "Women Loving Women."
23	Panel of speakers on lesbianism, bisexuality, and hetero-sexuality. Videotape: "The Word Is Out."
26	Anatomy of genitals and reproductive organs. (Sloane 15–53)
28	Birth control: Perspectives of class, race, religion, and sexual preference.
30	Birth control. (Sloane 346–349)

OCTOBER

3	EXAMINATION I.
5	Biology of hormones. (Sloane 54–71, 347–370; T&R 31–50)

7	Cycles of reproduction. (Sloane 71–87; Weideger 148–171)
10	Cycles of reproduction and birth control. (Weideger 17–43, 172–194)
12	Premenstrual syndrome and toxic shock syndrome (Weideger 43–84)
14	Views of menstruation in our society. (Weideger 85–113)
17	Choosing parenthood: Issues of age, race, class, religion, and sexual preference. Movie: *La Operacion.* (Sloane 329–345)
19	Biology of pregnancy. (Sloane 252–291)
21	Biology of pregnancy.
24	Psychological aspects of pregnancy.
26	Childbirth. (Sloane 211–323)
28	Childbirth.
31	*Fall Break.*

NOVEMBER

2	Videotape: "Giving Birth."
4	Psychological aspects of childbirth.
7	Videotape: "In the Way of Our Grandmothers." Postpartum.
9	Lactation. (Sloane 162–170, 323–327)
11	EXAMINATION II.
14	The decision not to have children: Individual, ethnic, and global perspectives. (Sloane 403–416)
16	Abortion: legal and procedural issues.
18	Speaker from abortion clinic in Richmond. INTERVIEW PAPER DUE.
21	Biology of aging and menopause. (Sloane 88–96; Weideger 195–218)
23	*Thanksgiving Break.*
25	*Thanksgiving Break.*
28	Psychological aspects of aging. (Weideger 219–240)
30	Women and nutrition. (Sloane 467–516)

DECEMBER

2	Diseases of women: Venereal diseases. (Sloane 213–233)
5	Diseases of women: Vaginal infections and malignancies. (Sloane 233–251, 170–200)
7	Women and stress.

9   Women and the health care system: Equal access for
      all? (Sloane 417–466, 201–212)
12   Current movements in women's health. Movie: *Taking
      Our Bodies Back.*
14   Discussion and evaluation of the course. (T&R 87–90;
      H&L 143–152)

Required Texts

Sloane, Ethel. *Biology of Women.* New York: John Wiley and Sons, 1980.
This book serves as the basic text for biological and medical information
for the course. Written from a feminist perspective, it emphasizes facts
and descriptions of biological events rather than social, psychological,
and political implications of these events.

Tobach, Ethel and Betty Rosoff (T&R). *Genes and Gender.* Staten Island,
New York: Gordian Press, Inc., 1978. This is the first book of the Genes
and Gender series on hereditarianism and women. It examines the
political and social uses of science to support the white, middle-class,
male establishment.

Hubbard, Ruth, and Marian Lowe (H&L). *Genes and Gender II.* Staten
Island, N.Y.: Gordian Press, Inc., 1979. This is the second in the Genes
and Gender series. The six articles of the volume explore the pitfalls in
research on sex and gender. The authors particularly examine hormone
studies and the feasibility of extrapolating from animal studies to
humans.

Weideger, Paula. *Menstruation and Menopause.* New York: Knopf, 1976.
Although written a number of years ago, in my opinion, it presents the
best discussion of the attitudes and opinions regarding these two major
events in women's lives.

Recommended Texts

Boston Women's Health Book Collective. *Our Bodies, Ourselves. A Book by
and for Women.* 2d Ed. New York: Vintage Books. 1978. This book
serves as an excellent resource for the layperson seeking clear explanations
and discussions on topics dealing with sexuality and reproduction. The
quotations expressing how women with varying perspectives feel about
their own biological experiences give an added dimension to the
information.

Dreifus, Claudia, ed. *Seizing Our Bodies: The Politics of Women's Health.*
New York: Vintage Books. 1978. This book reveals the social and political effects of many current medical practices applied to women. It exposes
the insensitivity of the health care system to women of color and lower
socioeconomic status.

Hubbard, Ruth, Mary Sue Henifin, and Barbara Fried, eds. *Biological Woman—The Convenient Myth: A Collection of Feminist Essays and a Comprehensive Bibliography.* Cambridge, Mass.: Schenkman Publishing Co., 1982. Hubbard et al. explore the ways in which the theory of science, as demonstrated in research, and the application of that theory, as demonstrated in medical practice, often ignore or exploit women. The volume contains an excellent bibliography on women and the health care system.

Lowe, Marian, and Ruth Hubbard. *Woman's Nature, Rationalizations of Inequality.* New York: Pergamon Press, 1983. This book examines the myths about women's nature and how such myths constrain, distort, and limit women's participation in society. The authors bring perspectives from a variety of ethnic and racial backgrounds to show the diversity of claims about woman's nature.

Sayers, Janet. *Biological Politics: Feminist and Anti-feminist Perspectives.* London and New York: Tavistock Publications, Ltd., 1982. Sayers discusses the historical and current use of biological deterministic theories against women. She also explores some ways in which biology may benefit feminism.

Movies and Videotapes

"Sociobiology"—This videotape was a NOVA program on public television. Although it attempts to present both pro- and anti-sociobiology views, the overall thrust of the program favors sociobiology. It provides an excellent starting point for a discussion and feminist critique of sociobiology.

"Women-Loving Women"—This is a synchronized slide-tape that explores common misconceptions or myths about lesbians and clarifies the facts that represent the true situation. The second half of the presentation shows a large variety of lesbians representing different occupational, class, ethnic, and religious perspectives.

"The Word Is Out"—This videotape, based on a book, features lesbians and homosexual men discussing how their sexual preference has affected their lives.

La Operación—This film features the sterilization scandal in Puerto Rico during the last four decades. The film clearly links the manipulative efforts at population control to United States' interests in cheap labor for its industries.

"Giving Birth"—This videotape was a program originally made for public television. Four different portraits of childbirth are shown: forceps delivery in a hospital where the mother is heavily medicated; a Leboyer home birth; a Caesarean section; delivery by a midwife in a birthing clinic. The videotape also features interviews with Margaret Mead, Dr. Leboyer, and Elizabeth Bing.

"In the Way of Our Grandmothers"—This videotape explores the role and tradition of the midwife in different ethnic groups. Two black midwives and two midwives from white ethnic groups discuss their experiences and feelings about helping women to give birth.

Taking Our Bodies Back — This presentation is available either as a film or videotape. A variety of women, in groups and singly, discuss important issues in dealing with the health care system today. They underscore the importance of self-help and women over a physician-based initiative.

REFERENCES

Ammer, C. 1983. *The A to Z of women's health*. New York: Everest House.

Darty, T., and S. Potter. 1984. Lesbians and contemporary health care systems: Oppression and opportunity. In *Women identified women*, eds. T. Darty and S. Potter. Palo Alto, Calif.: Mayfield Publishing Company.

Dill, B.T. 1983. Race, class, and gender: Prospects for an all-inclusive sisterhood. *Feminist Studies* 9, no. 1.

Greer, G. 1984. *Sex and destiny*. New York: Harper and Row.

Hite, S. 1976. *The Hite report: A nationwide study of female sexuality*. New York: Dell Publishing Co.

Rich, A. 1980. Compulsory heterosexuality and lesbian existence. *Signs: Journal of Women in Culture and Society* (Summer).

Rodgers, J. 1973. Rush to surgery. *The New York Times Magazine* September 21: 34.

Vazquez-Calzadar, J. 1973. La esterilización feminina en Puerto Rico. *Revista de Ciencias Sociales* 17, no. 3 (San Juan, Puerto Rico, Sept.): 281–308.

Zimmerman, B., et al. 1980. People's science. In *Science and Liberation*, eds. R. Arditti, P. Brennan, and S. Cavrak, 299–319. Boston: South End Press.

Chapter 5
Women in Science: History, Careers, and Forces for Change

"Confronted with the reality of a male-oriented world, how can women retain their love for science and technology and still work successfully within their fields?" (Hynes 1984, 47). The purpose of Women in Science: History, Careers, and Forces for Change is to increase women students' awareness of the difficulties faced by women who choose careers in science and to equip them to work successfully in the scientific field that they love.

Janice Raymond, a medical ethicist and feminist writer, suggests in her forthcoming book, *Female Friendship*, that the biggest aid for women scientists may be to "find other women who have gone before them and who are going their way." The first aim of the course is to acquaint students with the history of women in science. Most students (both male and female) will not have learned much history of science in the standard science curriculum. With the exception of Marie Curie, they are unlikely to have heard anything at all about the history of women in science. Very few students can list more than one of the seven women who have won the Nobel Prize in science or medicine. As feminist scholars have begun to find, there have always been women in science (Kien and Cassidy 1984) and they made valuable contributions and discoveries in the fields in which they worked. However, all too frequently, one of four possible fates has befallen these contributions.

1. Often the contribution is brushed aside. For example, James Watson treated Rosalind Franklin's work on X-ray diffraction as if it were not critical for the elaboration of the double helical structure of DNA (Watson 1968). Our curriculum pays constant homage to Socrates and his pupil Plato; however we rarely, if ever, hear of Socrates' teacher, Aspasia, a woman (Arditti 1980).

2. Sometimes the discovery is attributed to a man. In some cases, in the past, this occurred because women were specifically excluded

from scientific societies (Arditti 1980) so a male relative or friend would read the paper and be credited with, or take the credit for, the discovery. Even Marie Curie was refused membership in the French Academy of Science at the height of her career (Arditti 1980). Today, women in the United States are still denied membership in the elite Cosmos Club (for prestigious scientists) in Washington, D.C. In other situations women were afraid to apply for patents, so that Eli Whitney (an employee) rather than Catherine Green (Haber 1979) became the inventor of the cotton gin. In more recent times, the structure and funding of scientific research is set up so that the head of the laboratory, usually a man, receives credit for any work done in that laboratory.

3. The work of even a well-established woman scientist may be described in such a way as to undercut its importance. In an article in *Realities*, the distinguished French physicist Louis Leprince-Ringuet characterized Pierre Curie as a "creator" and a "genius," while Marie Curie was described as "patient, tenacious, and precise" (Hynes 1984). From this description, who would guess that it was she, not he, who received two Nobel Prizes?

4. Sometimes the work of a female scientist is misunderstood and not taken seriously. Of course, this may happen to male scientists too, although one wonders if it would have taken as long for the groundbreaking work of Barbara McClintock (Keller 1984) or Rachel Carson (1962) to be accepted had that work been proposed by a man. Rossiter (1982) documents the systematic underrecognition by prize and selection committees of the work of American women scientists.

Just now, a great deal of scholarship is trying to recover lost women of science and explore the lives of individual women scientists. Within the last few years, several excellent works have appeared: Margaret Rossiter's *Women Scientists in America: Struggles and Strategies to 1940* (1982); Vivian Gornick's *Women in Science: Portraits from a World in Transition* (1983); and Evelyn Fox Keller's *A Feeling for the Organism* (1983). The older works by Anne Sayre, *Rosalind Franklin and DNA* (1975), Lynn Osen, *Women in Mathematics* (1974), Louis Haber, *Women Pioneers of Science* (1979), and H. J. Mozans, *Woman in Science—1913* (1974) provide further valuable insights regarding the past contributions of women in science. It is imperative that students become aware of the women scientists who preceded them. Not only will the students feel less alone, but they can learn strategies to apply to their own careers.

A second aim of Women in Science: History, Careers, and Forces for Change is to explore the discrimination and obstacles facing women who choose careers in science and to suggest successful methods to reduce and overcome those barriers. Four categories of information are explored in an attempt to create an awareness of the problems and provide strategies:

1. The students are given the best statistical data available about the present employment situation and predicted future employment opportunities for women in science. In 1983 and 1984, the National Science Foundation (1984), the Rockefeller Foundation (Berryman 1983), and the Carnegie Corporation and Ford Foundation (Hall and Sandler 1982) issued reports with substantial statistical data on job opportunities for women in science. Some professional societies (American Chemical Society 1983) have also issued job forecasts for men and women in their fields. The slide-tape show put together by Betty Vetter (1980a) of the National Science Foundation provides excellent displays comparing employment, salary, and promotion data for women and men in science, the social sciences, and the humanities. Although students may find the data somewhat discouraging, most of them ultimately express relief at knowing the reality of the situation and may plan careers in some of the growth areas or prepare for months of job hunting in the nongrowth areas.

2. I present the theory and data from the psychological research on women's motive to avoid success (Horner 1969) and fear of success (Shaver 1976). Then I discuss the particular implications of this theory to women in science. Using "The Classroom Climate: A Chilly One for Women?" (Hall and Sandler 1982), I discuss barriers in the educational system that further reinforce the social and psychological barriers which women who choose any career, but particularly one in a "masculine" field such as science, may face. Directly confronting and overtly discussing some of these barriers and discriminatory practices, which most students have already encountered on some level, provide the initial steps for producing strategies to overcome the obstacles.

3. I invite women scientists in government, industry, and academia to talk to the class about their lives and careers. Students can ask them directly about strategies for achieving career goals. More than any theoretical discussions or statistical data, these women scientists provide the students with the most practical knowledge about career realities. They hear from first-hand experience about the obstacles, exclusions, pitfalls, and triumphs of being a woman in science.

4. Evelyn Fox Keller (1982) has delineated four levels by which

women are excluded, or exclude themselves, from science: unfair employment practices that prevent women from reaching the theoretical and decision-making level of science; androcentric bias in the choice and definition of problems studied, so that subjects concerning women such as menstrual cramps, childbirth, and menopause receive lower funding and less study; androcentric bias in the design and interpretation of experiments, so that only male rats or monkeys are used as experimental subjects; androcentric bias in the formulation of scientific theories and methods so that unicausal, hierarchical theories that coincide with the male experience of the world become the "objective" theories that define the interpretation of the scientific data. The implication of this exclusion is that, because of these practices, attitudes, and perspective, science becomes totally a masculine province that excludes women at all levels.

From considering these levels of exclusion, students begin to realize that, with women working at all levels, science as we know it might be changed radically. With women in the theoretical and decision-making levels of science, different topics might be funded and studied, using different experimental subjects and methods. This in turn might lead to broader, multicausal theories that would include the female experience of the world and, thus, be more accurate. Students then begin to explore the third area of the course. They realize that they and other women have a unique contribution to make to science. Without them, science is likely to continue to view the world from its androcentric perspective. With increasing numbers of women in science, new subjects can be explored from different perspectives. Through this, a feminist science or a gender-free science might emerge. Surely, this would be a better science, a dream worth working for. I hope that Women in Science: History, Careers, and Forces for Change will provide the mechanisms necessary to overcome the barriers and begin to make the dream a reality.

CONTENTS

Women in Science: History, Careers, and Forces for Change is the only course at the institution where I teach that attempts to deal with pragmatic problems of careers, the history of women scientists, or the changes that might occur in traditional scientific theory if considered from a feminist perspective. Although some large institutions have history of science programs, containing courses or sections of courses devoted to women, rarely are considerations of career strategies and the ultimate changes in theories included in these courses. I suspect that most institutions would have only one course dealing with these matters, if they have any at all. This means that a very broad area of content must be considered in a single semester. The history, career strategies, and potential of women as forces for change in all of the physical and biological sciences, mathematics, computer science, and medicine include a huge spectrum of information. (I do not consider engineering because we do not have an engineering program at the institution where I teach; however, a growing base of data is being gathered on women in engineering.)

The course needs enough breadth to include the common patterns of the obstacles, choices, successes, and experiences of women in these different fields. Thus, students begin to recognize that the difficulties and barriers are not unique to a particular field or individual. They become sensitized to the social roles and expectations that may reinforce the obstacles for women in science. At the same time, each field needs to be explored in sufficient depth to give the students concrete information about career options and demands in a particular field.

I begin the course with a discussion of issues shared by most fields:

1. *The Early History of Women in Science:* After some introductory remarks explaining factors (attributing achievements to others, misunderstanding of their research, great *men* of history theory) that may have led to the erasure of most of the history of women in science, I present what is known about the history of women in science before 1900. Since some of the scientific disciplines did not become separate fields until shortly before or after that time, 1900 is a useful demarcation point in the course.

2. *General Statistical Information on Employment Opportunities:* Much of the statistical information compiled by Betty Vetter for the government (1980b; 1981), the data in the National Science Foundation's report on Women and Minorities in Science and Engineering (1984) and reports of other foundations include information on all the fields in science. Presenting the data on all of the fields at once allows students to compare current employment patterns and future forecasts for the various disciplines.

3. *Research Data from Psychology and Sociology:* A considerable amount of data has now been gathered on general factors influencing women and their careers. I explore the research on the avoidance or fear of success, careers and mental health, sexual harassment, careers and marriage, and careers and motherhood. Some research either

directly examines or is relevant to women in scientific careers. This would include the implications for a woman's self-image of perceiving science as a "masculine" field (Baker 1983), the importance of role models and mentors (Kahle 1983), the difficulties of being a minority or token (Keller 1977) and reactions to on-the-job discrimination (Rawls and Fox 1978).

4. *Feminist Perspectives on Science:* As I indicated in the introduction to this volume, I do not think we have as yet developed the theoretical reconceptualizations necessary for a feminist science. However, many feminist scientists and historians have written critiques of traditional science; some (Bleier 1984; Fee 1982; Hein 1981) suggested ways in which a feminist science might differ from the current view of science. After discussing this, I consider the examples of Barbara McClintock (genetics), Ellen Swallow (home economics and environmental science), and Rachel Carson and Lois Gibbs (ecology). Each of these women overcame the barriers of traditional science — often receiving shabby, if not scornful, treatment — to champion her ideas, which ran counter to established scientific theory.

After establishing a common base of knowledge and discussing obstacles that women may face in any discipline, I turn to an examination of each individual field. I follow essentially the same pattern for each of the six fields under investigation (chemistry, physics, mathematics, computer science, biology, and medicine): First, a brief look at the history of women in that field, particularly since 1900. The major emphasis then turns to career patterns, obstacles, and options. These are explored by guest speakers, who represent different career options within a given field and different life patterns. Finally, students are encouraged to discuss how the feminist perspective would change the current scientific theories and employment patterns in that particular field. Throughout the exploration of varying fields, the focus is upon balancing and integrating the information that students learn from texts and class discussion with the practical experience of women who worked and lived with a career in that discipline.

METHODS

The unusual approach of Women in Science: History, Careers, and Forces for Change centers around discussions with women in scientific careers. Since these women are the source of pragmatic information regarding life choices and decision making, they must be carefully chosen to reflect the greatest possible variety of careers and lifestyles. In addition, the students need sufficient educational and personal development to take full advantage of these opportunities for discussion. I found the following factors crucial to maximal learning in this format:

1. *Course Level and Department:* I think that this should be an upper level course in one of the traditional science departments. Some science departments may not be willing to include such a course in their listings. Two techniques help overcome this problem: a course description that reflects the theoretical aspects of the course, and first trying out the course as a special topics elective. In many institutions, special topics courses need not initially be approved by the curriculum committee; after the course is successfully established, it may fare better before such a committee. In my opinion, this course should not be taught in women's studies programs unless it can be cross listed with a science department, where it is more likely to attract women science majors. Although students who are not science majors may take the course, it really is the women science majors who will face these career obstacles and can profit most from the practical suggestions for overcoming the barriers. Perhaps, with some warnings and suggestions, these women will be able to stay in science and aid in the radical feminist transformation we are seeking.

2. *Student Involvement:* Student involvement is crucial to the success of the discussions led by the women already in science. In order to develop an atmosphere that involves students from the very beginning, I try to consider the class composition and interest when developing the syllabus. For example, if most of the class majors in chemistry but no one majors in physics, I invite more chemists to speak and fewer physicists. Before the guest speakers participate in the course, each student is required to lead a brief (10–15 minute) discussion of some aspect in the history, psychological or sociological research, or feminist theory of women in science. This prepares the entire class for active involvement in each session. Students are encouraged to invite women scientists they know to be speakers in the course.

3. *Choice of Outside Guests:* Women who chose careers in science share their experience in the real world with the class. I try to find women who represent as great a variety as possible with regard to sector (industry, academia, government), educational background (B.A., M.S., Ph.D., or differing professional degrees), lifestyle (sin-

gle, married, divorced, with or without children), and career pattern (continuous, interrupted for a period of time, begun at a later age) within each field. Obviously, I cannot always include enough people to represent this great variety of factors for each discipline; however, I seek as much diversity as possible.

4. *Texts:* Increasing numbers of books, which might serve as texts for the course, appear each year. Originally, when I began teaching the course, only Haber's *Women Pioneers of Science* (1979), Osen's *Women in Mathematics* (1974), Mozans' *Women in Science — 1913* (1974), and Sayre's *Rosalind Franklin and DNA* (1975), were available. I supplemented these with journal articles. Now, several excellent works are also available: Rossiter's *Women Scientists in America* (1982), Gornick's *Women in Science* (1983), Goodfield's *An Imagined World* (1981), and Keller's *A Feeling for the Organism* (1983). Last year, I successfully used the Haber book as a general text, with the Gornick and Keller books providing individual portraits. In addition, I used journal articles or *Science and Liberation* (Arditti, Brennan, and Cavrak, 1980) for their feminist critiques of traditional science. Bleier's *Science and Gender* (1984) or *Alice Through the Microscope* (Brighton Women and Science Group 1980) may also serve this purpose.

5. *Use of Professional Organizations:* I have used the women's caucuses or chapters of scientific professional organizations in several ways. Many of the organizations (American Chemical Society 1983; American Women in Science 1984; National Science Foundation 1984) have published reports or statistics documenting the employment figures for women in the different fields. Some (American Chemical Society) have produced slide-tape shows or movies discussing career options for women in their profession. Naturally, the societies are a major source of speakers for the course. However, probably the most effective and long-lasting use of the societies has been to provide contacts and networks for the students. I encourage the students to join, attend, and present papers at the meeting of the professional society affiliated with their probable career choice. In some cases, this active involvement has resulted in contacts that eventually led to jobs. In all cases, student involvement with women in scientific professional organizations follows the advice given to women seeking successful careers in science: "find other women who have come before them and who are going their way" (Hynes 1984, p.38).

BIOLOGY 383: ADVANCED STUDY IN BIOLOGY.
WOMEN IN SCIENCE: HISTORY, CAREERS,
AND FORCES FOR CHANGE

Syllabus and Reading List (Spring 1984)

JANUARY

11	Introduction and course rationale. (S&L 1–13; 15–33)
18	Early history of women in science (Greeks to 1900). (WPS Foreword; 3–11; S&L 350–358)
25	History of American women scientists (1900 to present). (S&L 369–382)

FEBRUARY

1	Employment opportunities for women in science: statistical data and slide-tape show from the Scientific Manpower Commission. (S&L 215–256)
8	Social and psychological barriers to achievement for women seeking careers: Fear of success, careers and mental health, sexual harassment, careers and marriage, and motherhood. (S&L 283–350)
15	MIDTERM EXAMINATION.
22	Particular social and psychological barriers to achievement for women in science: Perceptions of "masculine" field, role models and mentors, tokenism, and discrimination. (S&L 358–369; Gornick, *Women in Science)*

MARCH

1	Feminist perspectives on science: Women who have challenged androcentric scientific theory: McClintock, Swallow, Carson, and Gibbs. (Keller, *A Feeling for the Organism)*
8	*Spring Break*
15	Women in chemistry. (S&L 257–266; WPS 63–72)
22	Women in physics. (WPS 41–51; 83–96; 105–116)
29	Women in mathematics. (S&L 63–75; 191–214)

APRIL

5	Women in computer science. (Osen handout)
12	Women in biology. (WPS 73–82; 141–154)
19	Women in medicine. (WPS 12–29; 30–40; 97–104; 117–140)
26	Commonalities in the history and careers of women in science: Future forces for change.

MAY

2	FINAL EXAMINATION.

Texts

Arditti, Rita, Pat Brennan, and Steve Cavrak. eds. *Science and Liberation.* Boston: South End Press, 1980.
Haber, Louis. *Women Pioneers of Science* (WPS). New York: Harcourt Brace Jovanovich, 1979.
Keller, Evelyn Fox. *A Feeling for the Organism.* New York: W.H. Freeman and Company, 1983.
Gornick, Vivian. *Women in Science: Portraits from a World in Transition.* New York: Simon and Schuster, 1983.

Requirements and Grades

The final grade in the course is based on performance and completion of the following requirements: 20 percent of the grade is based on the midterm examination; 30 percent of the grade is based upon an oral report given on an aspect of the history, careers, or theoretical changes of a woman in science (this might be a biographical study of a historical or contemporary woman scientist; alternatively, it might be an investigation of career opportunities and barriers for women in a particular area of science); 30 percent of the grade is based on the final examination (the final will be cumulative and include material presented in student reports and guest speeches); 20 percent of the final grade is based on class participation (since much of the material for the course comes from guest speakers and student reports, attendance and active involvement in class discussions are essential).

REFERENCES

American Chemical Society. 1983. Medalists study charts women chemists' role. *Chemistry and Engineering* (Nov. 14): 53.
American Women in Science. 1984. *AWIS Newsletter* 8, no. 2, pp. 7–8.
Arditti, R. 1980. Feminism and science. In *Science and liberation*, eds. R. Arditti, P. Brennan, and S. Cavrak. Boston: South End Press.
Arditti, R., P. Brennan, and S. Cavrak. 1980. *Science and liberation.* Boston: South End Press.
Baker, D. 1983. Can the difference between male and female science majors account for the low number of women at the doctoral level in science? *Journal of College Science Teaching* (Nov.): 102–107.
Berryman, S. 1983. Who will do science? Minority and female attainment of science and mathematics degrees: Trends and causes. *Rockefeller Foundation Special Report* (Nov. 1983).

Bleier, R. 1984. *Science and gender: A critique of biology and its theories on women.* New York: Pergamon Press.

Brighton Women and Science Group. 1980. *Alice through the microscope: The power of science over women's lives.* London: Virago.

Carson, R. 1962. *Silent spring.* New York: Fawcett Press.

Fee, E. 1982. A feminist critique of scientific objectivity. *Science for the People* 14, no. 4: 8.

Goodfield, J. 1981. *An imagined world: A story of scientific discovery.* New York: Penguin Books.

Gornick, V. 1983. *Women in science: Portraits from a world in transition.* New York: Simon and Schuster.

Haber, L. 1979. *Women pioneers of science.* New York: Harcourt Brace Jovanovich.

Hall, R., and B. Sandler. 1982. *The classroom climate: A chilly one for women?* Washington, D.C.: Association of American Colleges, Project on the Status and Education of Women.

Hein, H. 1981. Women and science: Fitting men to think about nature. *International Journal of Women's Studies* 4: 369–377.

Horner, M. 1969. Fail: Bright women. *Psychology Today,* 3 (Nov.): 36–38ff.

Hynes, H.P. 1984. Women working: A field report. *Technology Review* (Nov./Dec.): 38ff.

Kahle, J. 1983. The disadvantaged majority: Science education for women. Burlington, N.C.: Carolina Biological Supply Company. AETS Outstanding Paper for 1983.

Keller, E. 1977. The anomaly of a woman in physics. In *Working it out,* eds. S. Ruddick and P. Daniels. New York: Pantheon.

Keller, E. 1982. Feminism and science. *Signs: Journal of Women in Culture and Society* 7, no. 3: 589–602.

Keller, E. 1983. *A feeling for the organism: The life and work of Barbara McClintock.* New York: W.H. Freeman and Company.

Keller, E. 1984. Women and basic research: Respecting the unexpected. *Technology Review* (Nov./Dec.): 45–47.

Kien, J., and D. Cassidy. 1984. The history of women in science: A seminar at the University of Regensburg, FRG. *Women's Studies International Forum* 7, no. 4: 313–317.

Mozans, H.J. 1974. *Woman in science—1913.* Cambridge, Mass.: MIT Press.

National Science Foundation. 1984. *Women and minorities in science and engineering,* Report 84-300.

Osen, L.M. 1974. *Women in mathematics.* Cambridge, Mass.: MIT Press.

Rawls, M., and S. Fox. 1978. Women in academic chemistry find rise to full status difficult. *Chemical and Engineering News* (Sept. 11).

Rossiter, M.W. 1982. *Women scientists in America: Struggles and strategies to 1940.* Baltimore: The Johns Hopkins University Press.

Sayre, A. 1975. *Rosalind Franklin and DNA: A vivid view of what it is like to be a gifted woman in an especially male profession.* New York: W.W. Norton & Company, Inc.

Shaver, P. 1976. Questions concerning fear of success and its conceptual relatives. *Sex Roles* 2: 305–320.

Vetter, B. 1980a. Opportunities in science and engineering. Scientific Manpower Commission slide-tape presentation produced under National Science Foundation Grant No. SPI-7913025.

Vetter, B. 1980b. Sex discrimination in the halls of science. *Chemical and Engineering News* (March): 37–38.

Vetter, B. 1981. Degree completion by women and minorities in science increases. *Science* 212, no. 3.

Watson, J.D. 1969. *The double helix.* New York: Atheneum Publishers, Mentor Paperback.

3
WOMEN'S STUDIES COURSES BASED ON BIOLOGY AND HEALTH

Chapter 6
Women and Their Bodies
in Health and Disease

The purpose of Women and Their Bodies in Health and Disease is to rectify the version of biology based on studies of men. A primary aim of the course is to educate women in the language and information needed for knowledge about and control of their own bodies. A secondary purpose is to present biology and health from a women's studies perspective. This means that women become the central focus; women's bodies, health, disease, and the health care system are examined from a gynocentric perspective. Our patriarchal society traditionally examines these issues from an androcentric perspective. This is evident in the low level of funding for study of such health issues as menstruation, contraception, and menopause, issues that are of primary interest to women. The traditional biology and health curricula also reflect androcentrism and the priorities of the society at large. In Women and Their Bodies in Health and Disease, women are the focus of the content and methods of study for these biology and health-related issues. In order to discuss these issues, we must learn and develop a language that will allow us to comprehend traditional scientific theories and transform them to a feminist perspective.

Many scientists take the view of Donald Symons (1979), a self-styled Darwinian psychologist, who recently claimed that language is of secondary interest in development of theories and constructs, brought into play only after perception is in place. He suggested that the writer consciously chooses whatever words suit her or his purpose. I disagree with Symons. I think that our language, which is a part of our cultural, social, and historical context, very much determines our construction of theories and the way we think about ideas. Some feminists (Spender 1980; Nilsen et al. 1977) have suggested that, since our social, cultural and historical context is patriarchal, our language and the theories and ideas constructed in that context are patriarchal. On this basis, some feminist writers (Daly 1984; Wittig 1969; Wittig and Zeig 1976) have rejected this patriarchal language and sought to create a new feminist language from which new theories might eventually originate.

The science created by our Western patriarchal society is an especially masculine province. The statistical evidence (National Science Foundation 1984; Vetter 1981) documents the dearth of women scientists. The language and theories of science further demonstrate the exclusion of women (Keller 1982) or the representation of women in roles that reflect men's perceptions of stereotyped, passive female social roles (Longino and Doell 1983).

A clear example of the influence of language on the formulation of scientific theory occurs in Darwin's *On the Origin of Species* (1859). Darwin's primary agent of change was natural selection, a paradigm laden with the values of nineteenth-century England. As Rose and Rose (1980) suggest, "its central metaphors drawn from society and in their turn interacting with society were of the competition of the species, the struggle for existence, the ecological niche, and the survival of the fittest" (p. 28). These metaphors reflect Victorian society and were acceptable to it because they, and the social Darwinism quickly derived from it, seemed to ground its norms solidly in a biological foundation (Ruse 1979). When Darwin depicts the fittest as the individuals who pass on their genes to the greatest number of offspring, one thinks of the importance of passing on property in that society. One can hardly overlook an upper-class perspective and appeal when, in the *Descent of Man* (1871) Darwin implores that "both sexes ought to refrain from marriage if they are in any marked degree inferior in body or mind; . . . All ought to refrain from marriage who cannot avoid abject poverty for their children, for poverty is . . . a great evil . . . " (p. 618). The upper class of Victorian England had self-serving reasons for finding his theory attractive; it gave a biological rationale for its very position in society.

In like manner, the theory of sexual selection reflected and reinforced Victorian social norms regarding the sexes. By this theory Darwin set out to explain a phenomenon still not fully understood, that of secondary sex characteristics. He claimed that "when the males and females of any animal have the same general habits of life, but differ in structure, colour, or ornament, such differences have been mainly caused by sexual selection" (*Origin of Species*, 89). Expanding considerably on the theory first presented in the *Origin*, Darwin specifies, in the *Descent of Man*, how the process functions and what roles males and females play in it.

> The sexual struggle is of two kinds: in the one it is between the individuals of the same sex, generally the males, in order to drive away or kill their rivals, the females remaining passive; whilst in the other, the struggle is likewise between the individuals of the same sex, in order to excite or charm those of the opposite sex, generally the females, which no longer remain passive, but select the more agreeable partners. (p. 64)

According to the theory, the males who triumph over their rivals will win the more desirable females and will leave the most progeny, thereby perpetuating and increasing, over numerous generations, those qualities that afforded them victory. The females who succeed in being chosen will also procreate best and pass on their characters. As a result, by the time evolution has produced modern man and modern woman, the two are considerably different, men being superior to women both physically and mentally. They are not only "taller, heavier, and stronger than women, with squarer shoulders and more plainly pronounced muscles: but also they attain to a 'higher eminence' in whatever they take up" (p. 564). The theory reflects the Victorian age, with its depiction of active males competing and struggling with each other for passive females. That depiction of male-female interaction would have seemed quite obvious to most segments of Victorian society and its grounding in scientific fact most reassuring.

Today, the sociobiologists hark back to Darwin and his theories of natural and sexual selection as their source of the idea of innate biological differences. Their language also leads me to believe that their theories are heavily influenced by the current social and political views of gender differences. They suggest that there are genes governing "maternal instinct" and "aggressiveness." Barash states that "Sociobiology relies heavily upon the biology of male-female differences and upon the adaptive behavioral differences that have evolved accordingly. Ironically, mother nature appears to be a sexist" (Barash 1977, 283).

E. O. Wilson writes, "It pays males to be aggressive, hasty, fickle, and undiscriminating. In theory it is more profitable for females to be coy, to hold back until they can identify males with the best genes. . . . Human beings obey this biological principle faithfully" (Wilson 1978, 125).

And Barash explains further, "The evolutionary mechanism should be clear. Genes that allow females to accept the sorts of mates who make lesser contributions to their reproductive success will leave fewer copies of themselves than will genes that influence the females to be more selective. . . . For males, a very different strategy applies. The maximum advantage goes to individuals with few inhibitions. A genetically influenced tendency to 'play fast and loose' — 'love 'em and leave 'em' — may well reflect more biological reality than most of us care to admit" (Barash 1979, 48).

Biology as it is taught in the academy further reflects the exclusion or representation of women in roles that reflect the patriarchal culture's view in its language and theories. As is the case with most of the other disciplines in academia, biology is another example of men's studies (Hubbard 1981). Perhaps the most blatant examples of the male bias in language and theories can be found in courses and research in ethology or animal behavior. In animal behavior, some researchers have observed behavior in lower animals in a search for "universal" behavior patterns, which occur in males of all species or in all males of a particular order or class such as primates or mammals. This behavior is then extrapolated to human beings in an attempt to demonstrate a biological, or innate, basis for the behavior. Feminist scientists (Bleier 1979; Hubbard 1979; Rosser 1982) warned against extrapolating from one species to another in behavioral traits. They warned the sociobiologists about the circularity of logic in using language and frameworks to interpret animal behavior that is then used to "prove" certain human behavior to be biologically determined, since it has also been found in animals. This is particularly dubious, since, until recently, many of the species chosen for extensive observation by animal behaviorists were chosen precisely because that species' societal structure seemed to more closely simulate the human social structure (Hrdy 1981). Dagg (1984) further documents six ways in which sexual bias entered the literature of the social behavior of animals:

1. internal contradictions in reports, with generalizations contradicting primary data
2. inadequate experimental design in behavioural studies so that female behaviour was largely ignored
3. biased collection of data so that information showing females as sometimes dominant, often aggressive, and active in mating (anti-stereotypes for women) was not adequately collected
4. misinterpretation of observations, with females seen as possessions of and inferior to males
5. misleading presentation of data in popular works and textbooks so that males are seen as preeminent to females

    6. misinformation, with sociobiologists actually changing observed
field data so that they would fit in with their theories of sociobiology. (p. 118)

The courses in ethology and segments of introductory courses on
animal behavior may provide the most blatant examples of exclusion
and distortion of female roles and behavior in the biology curriculum. What is perhaps more surprising and undermining to women is
the extent to which data on females are absent, under-represented, or
distorted in other courses such as human anatomy and physiology.
For example, many of the terms applicable to the female body and
physiology, such as the clitoris, are frequently not mentioned or discussed in courses. (Who ever heard of an anatomy course in which
the penis was left out?) Even in a course called *Human Reproduction*, where clearly the woman has a major, if not the central role,
textbooks and professors often describe the male anatomy first, then
female anatomy in terms of how it deviates or differs from the male
norm. As the amusing piece, "A Patriarchal Society Writes Biology"
(Hershberger 1948/1970), underscores, opinion is often represented
as fact by animating the male portion of the reproductive process
while deanimating the female portion of the process. "The male cell
acts, voluntarily, yet with a teleological sense of destiny, while the
female reacts, involuntarily, taking her cues from him" (p. 71). This
exclusion and distortion of women, so prevalent in the science curriculum, robs women of the language and information needed for control of their bodies. It thus perpetuates the male control over women's
bodies and the androcentric theories about women's roles in life
processes.

CONTENT

The content of Women and Their Bodies in Health and Disease
centers on changing the locus of control in scientific language and
theory to women. A major focus of every topic considered and every
lecture is to help students learn the terminology and information necessary to understand their bodies and current medical theories of
health and disease. Science and medical terminology are frightening
and inaccessible to many people in our society because of the heavy
usage of jargon and technical terms. In women, the accessibility is
made more difficult by the emphasis placed on the male body and
theories based on male physiology. Yet, every day, women are asked

to make decisions about health issues, such as contraception, that will affect their lives and possibly those of their children. Decisions on contraception have some of the most profound effects on a woman's life of any decisions she'll make. If a woman cannot control when—or if—she gets pregnant, this affects her choice of careers, choice of whether she has sex and with whom—all of which lead to the stereotypical coy, undereducated woman with no personal wealth or standing outside the home, totally dependent on men. How can women make responsible decisions without knowledge of their bodies? For example, women cannot really understand how the contraceptive pill prevents ovulation without an elementary understanding of hormones, the hypothalamus, the adenohypophysis, the ovaries, and the theories of negative feedback systems. It is, therefore, extremely important to return control over their bodies to women by teaching them the names of body parts and their functions.

A second focus of every lecture is consideration of the current medicosocial view of a health issue under a male-dominated scientific and medical establishment. Then, the focus turns to how that issue might be changed—in terms of priorities, emphasis, funding, and access to care—if women, not men, were central to the thinking about that issue. To demonstrate the negative effects resulting from the current male-dominated system, it is sometimes helpful to ask students to imagine how an issue, such as contraceptive research, would have developed had women been in control but behaved as men have behaved on this issue. The fantasy might develop in the following way: With women as the controlling figures, most contraceptive methods developed would be for males since it is easier to interfere with the male cycle because it is biologically more delicate. Possible side effects of a male pill such as increased risk of cancer in the male reproductive tract, occasional impotence in a few individuals, and development of excess fat deposits in the chest and hip regions would be seen as minor. Although it would be considered desirable to have testing on more than 132 males without informed consent in Puerto Rico (Zimmerman 1980) for twelve months before putting the pill on the market in mainland United States (Seaman 1977), it would be deemed financially unfeasible. Besides, the few complaints that arose during the testing period were discordant with medical theories of the functioning of the male cycle and, therefore, dismissed as hysterical. The best method for determining the long-term effect of the pill would be to assess its effects in the large numbers of poor men who would be coerced into taking the pill through medical assistance, in order to receive checks to feed their children.

After thinking about the above fantasy, which very closely parallels the history of the contraceptive pill for women, most students can see the difficulties with the current patriarchal approach to medical issues. They can then begin to consider changes in the system that would be more favorable to women.

After establishing the importance of the female perspective for examining issues of health and disease, it is important to broaden that perspective to account for variations among women. A health care issue such as contraception may be viewed very differently by individual women, depending on age, racial or ethnic background, religion, sexual preference, class, and physical condition. Chapter 4 discusses the multiple dimensions from which women may view the issue of contraception. A third focus of the course becomes a consideration of how the different aspects of each health care issue vary depending on the individual woman. Applying each of the three foci to each issue, the topics in the course may be placed under four major groupings:

1. *Introduction and Rationale: The "Unwoman" in Science and the Health Care System:* This introduces the problem of an absence of women in the language, theories, and priorities of science and the health care system.
2. *Female Sexuality and the Reproductive System:* This, the largest segment of the course, consists of what might be called *gynecological issues.* The terminology and information about women's bodies, to which they have been denied access, and many of the issues over which they interact with the health care system are developed here: genetic and evolutionary determination of sex; anatomy of the female reproductive system; hormones and reproductive cycles; contraception and abortion; menstruation; infertility; pregnancy and childbirth; lactation and the postpartum period; and sexuality.
3. *Nongynecological Health and Disease:* Language and theories of women's health and disease issues that may interact with but are not directly related to the genitals or reproductive organs are considered in this portion of the course: exercise; nutrition and diet; stress and mental health; aging; cancer and the immune system; the cardiovascular system and associated diseases; and the nervous system and drugs and alcohol.

4. *The Health Care System:* The concluding portion of the course examines very briefly the traditional health care system and its impact on women. The focus then turns to alternative health care systems, particularly the women's self-health and women-centered systems, and examines their potential for returning to women the power and control over their bodies.

METHODS

The goal of Women and Their Bodies in Health and Disease is to help women regain control over their bodies through learning the language and understanding the theories of science and health. Scientists and health care professionals in the United States are often in positions of authority, omniscience, and decision making on health care issues that engenders in all people, but most particularly in women, a sense of loss of control and responsibility for their own bodies. The methods used in this course must aid the students in developing the confidence, based on knowledge and understanding of body functions, to become informed health care consumers.

Women and Their Bodies in Health and Disease is an introductory course without any prerequisites. For most students it may be their first and only college-level science or health course; frequently women students take this course to fulfill their natural science requirements because they are too afraid of a "regular" science course. For many students, it may also be their first women's studies course. In brief, this course is likely to attract a group of students who feel very unsure about their science ability, very unwilling to question authority, and rather fearful of talking about these issues. These factors make it vitally important to consciously include mechanisms that will make the students feel comfortable and be able to develop confidence. I found some of the following strategies to be useful:

1. *Use of Discussion Sections:* Ideally, this course should be taught to small groups to enable discussion. However, most often, this is not the case, since the course is very popular and it would be expensive to provide enough faculty to lead small group discussions. If it is taught as a lecture course to a large group, the format itself may alienate students and induce fear on their part. With a lecture format, it is essential to insist on small group discussion sections meeting at least once a week. In these sections, students have the opportunity to ask

questions, voice their opinions, and use the language and terminology they are learning. Teaching assistants will serve as additional resource people, so that the lecturer does not become the sole authority in the course.

2. *Use of Outside Speakers:* Another way to break the stereotype of the lecturer as the authority is to invite outside speakers to give some of the lectures. Since I am trained as a biologist, I invite health science professionals to present material on the health care system. This also allows the students to develop awareness of varying perspectives on science and the health care system.

3. *Choice of Topics:* Before theories can be discussed, students must learn a certain amount of anatomy and physiology. However, some of the topics, particularly those on which discussions are centered (toxic shock, midwifery, cancer recovery) may be chosen by the students. Students may also decide how the topics in the section will be presented (outside speakers, student reports, student panel). Giving students the choice of topics returns some control over their lives to them.

4. *Pace of the Course:* Although a great deal of terminology and factual information must be covered, I find it especially important to avoid the route chosen by many basic science and preprofessional health courses: cramming as much material as possible into a short period of time. Few, if any, of these students will be premedicine majors, so they have no need to cope with this pedagogical technique. One reason some students will have been previously "turned off" to science is this technique. In my opinion, it is preferable to leave out some topics, rather than overwhelm students with material, thus engendering further feelings of lack of control.

5. *Approach to Concepts and Terminology:* With students who are apprehensive about medical terminology and concepts, I find it helpful to begin with everyday examples that they or their friends may have experienced. Then I introduce the concept, without using scientific language. Only after they have understood the concept, do I tell them the scientific terminology that describes the process. For example, in introducing the concept of the negative feedback between the ovaries and hypothalamus (and adenohypophysis) during the menstrual cycle, I begin by asking the students to describe how a thermostat in a house regulates the furnace. After they have described that, I draw the analogy between the thermostat and furnace and the hypothalamus and ovaries. Only at the end, do I refer to the entire process by name.

6. *Textbook:* I think that it is important to choose a textbook that is readable but contains enough terminology and detail to be a reference guide. When I first began teaching the course, I used *Our Bodies, Ourselves* (Boston Women's Health Book Collective 1976) because it is very readable and, at that time, was the only text available. Although I still think *Our Bodies, Ourselves* is the most personable and accessible text, in recent years, I have used Ethel Sloane's *Biology of Women* (1980) because it has more complete information on anatomy and biological processes. Usually, the teaching assistants use readings from a variety of sources (Dreifus, *Seizing Our Bodies*, 1978; Richardson and Taylor, *Feminist Frontiers*, 1983; journal articles) for the basis of discussion sections.

7. *Use of Body Journals:* Students are asked to keep a daily body journal, in which they write down their awarenesses of, and changes they perceive in, their own bodies. They are encouraged to use the terminology that they are learning to describe their perceptions and to discuss their encounters with the health care system during the semester. Although the teaching assistants and lecturer read the journals, they comment upon their entries rather than grade them. The students report that the journals are really helpful in making explicit the connections between what they learn and what happens to their bodies on a daily basis.

8. *Avoiding the Development of False Confidence:* Occasionally, a student or students will develop an attitude of false confidence at a particular point in the course. They will say something like, "I really know what's happening with my body now and there is no way another doctor or health care practitioner is ever coming near me again" or "Based on this course, I've been able to advise all of my friends in the dorm about birth control." Although rare, this attitude arises occasionally, particularly in a woman who has had previous negative encounters with the traditional health care system. Obviously, this is not a realistic approach and represents confidence based on an inadequate understanding of the complexity of the human body and a misunderstanding of the limited knowledge that the course has given to deal with that complexity. False confidence of this sort does not empower women and give them more control over their bodies. It undercuts them and may lead to unfortunate, if not fatal, decisions regarding their bodies and health care. Clearly, this is not the kind of confidence and control that is the goal of Women and Their Bodies in Health and Disease. The course is designed to pro-

vide women with the language and basic concepts of anatomy and physiology and a feminist perspective on women's health issues to enable them to make responsible, informed decisions about their bodies and health care needs.

WS 103: WOMEN AND THEIR BODIES IN HEALTH AND DISEASE

Syllabus and Reading List

JUNE

13 Introduction and rationale for the course: The "unwoman" in science and the health care system. (Chapter 1)

14 Genetic and evolutionary determination of sex. (Chapter 5) Anatomy of the female reproductive system. (Chapter 2, Chapter 8)

15 Contraceptive devices that work by placement in the anatomy. (Pages 346–349; 370–390; 395–402) Hormones and reproductive cycles. (Chapter 3)

16 Menstruation; contraception methods related to the hormonal cycle. (Pages 349–370; 390–395; 402–403; 411–414) BODY JOURNALS DUE.

20 The decision to parent: Infertility; abortion. (Chapter 11, Pages 403–411)

21 Pregnancy and childbirth. (Pages 252–299)

22 Childbirth; lactation, and postpartum. (Pages 299–323; 323–326)

23 MIDTERM EXAMINATION.

27 Sexuality. (Chapter 6)

28 Women and exercise. (Pages 508–515)

29 Nutrition and diet. (Pages 467–508)

30 Stress and mental health: The nervous system, drugs, and alcohol. BODY JOURNALS DUE.

JULY

5 Aging and menopause. (Chapter 4)

6 Diseases of women: Cancer and cardiovascular disease in women. (Chapter 9; Pages 80–82; 174–199)

7 FINAL EXAMINATION. BODY JOURNALS DUE.

TSH–D

Text

Sloane, Ethel. *Biology of Women.* New York: John Wiley and Sons, 1980. A packet of xeroxed articles will be provided as readings upon which the discussions in section will be based.

Course Requirements

Two (noncumulative) examinations, each is 33 percent of the grade; body journal counts for 17 percent of the grade; attendance and participation in discussion section counts for 17 percent of the grade; discussion sections will meet all *four* weeks.

REFERENCES

Barash, D. 1977. *Sociobiology and behavior.* New York: Elsevier.
Barash, D. 1979. *The whisperings within.* New York: Harper and Row.
Bleier, R. 1979. Social and political bias in science: An examination of animal studies and their generalizations to human behavior and evolution. In *Genes and gender II,* eds. R. Hubbard and M. Lowe, 49–70. Staten Island, N.Y: Gordian Press Inc.
Boston Women's Health Book Collective. 1978. *Our bodies, ourselves: A book by and for women.* 2nd ed. New York: Simon and Schuster.
Dagg, A.I. 1984. Sexual bias in the literature of social behaviour of mammals and birds. *International Journal of Women's Studies* 7, no. 2: 118–135.
Daly, M. 1984. *Pure lust: Elemental feminist philosophy.* Boston: Beacon Press.
Darwin, C. [1859] 1967. *On the origin of species: A facsimile of the first edition.* New York: Atheneum.
Darwin, C. 1871. *Descent of man.* London: Murray.
Dreifus, Claudia, ed., 1978. *Seizing our bodies.* New York: Vintage Books.
Hershberger, R. 1970. *Adam's rib.* New York: Harper and Row. (Original work published 1948)
Hrdy, S. 1981. *The woman that never evolved.* Cambridge, Mass.: Harvard University Press.
Hubbard, R. 1979. Have only men evolved? In *Women look at biology looking at women,* eds. R. Hubbard, M.S. Henifin, and B. Fried. Cambridge, Mass.: Schenkman Publishing Co.
Hubbard, R. 1981. The emperor doesn't wear any clothes: The impact of feminism on biology. In *Men's studies modified the impact of feminism on the academic disciplines,* ed. D. Spender. New York: Pergamon Press.
Keller, E. 1982. Feminism and science. *Signs: Journal of Women in Culture and Society* 7, no. 3: 589–602.
Longino, H., and R. Doell. 1983. Body, bias, and behavior: A comparative analysis of reasoning in two areas of biological science. *Signs: Journal of Women in Culture and Society* 9, no. 2: 206–227.

National Science Foundation. 1984. *Women and minorities in science and engineering.* Report 84-300.

Nilsen, A.P., H. Bosmajian, H.L. Gershuny, and J.P. Stanley. 1977. *Sexism and language.* Urbana, Ill.: National Council of Teachers of English.

Richardson, L., and V. Taylor. 1983. *Feminist frontiers.* Reading, Mass.: Addison-Wesley Publishing Company.

Rose, H., and S. Rose. 1980. The myth of the neutrality of science. *Science and Liberation.* Boston: South End Press.

Rosser, S.V. 1982. Androgyny and sociobiology. *International Journal of Women's Studies* 5, no. 5: 435–444.

Ruse, M. 1979. *The Darwinian revolution.* Chicago: The University of Chicago Press.

Seaman, B. 1977. The dangers of oral contraception. *Seizing our bodies,* ed. C. Dreifus. New York: Vintage Books.

Sloane, E. 1980. *Biology of women.* New York: John Wiley and Sons.

Spender, D. 1980. *Man-made language.* London: Routledge and Kegan Paul.

Symons, D. 1979. *The evolution of human sexuality.* New York: Oxford University Press.

Vetter, B. 1981. Degree completion by women and minorities in science increases. *Science* 212, no. 3.

Wilson, E.O. 1978. *On human nature.* Cambridge, Mass.: Harvard University Press.

Wittig, M. 1969. *Les guerilleres.* Paris: Les Editions de Minuit.

Wittig, M., and S. Zeig. 1976. *Brouillon pour un dictionnaire des amantes.* Paris: Bernard Grasset.

Zimmerman, B., et al. 1980. People's science. *Science and liberation,* eds. R. Arditti, P. Brennan, and S. Cavrak, 299–319. Boston: South End Press.

Chapter 7
Biology and Psychology of Women

Rather than use a dualistic approach to problems, considering them from the perspective of as many disciplines using as many different methodologies as possible is likely to be more fruitful. Recognizing the shortcomings of the dualistic approach, most women's studies courses and research utilize an interdisciplinary focus on topics and issues that do not traditionally "fit" into a single discipline and use a variety of methodologies, some of which may not be found in any traditional academic discipline. Biology and Psychology of Women is such a course. The course looks at the variety of biological and psychological events of a woman's life and undertakes a critical examination of theories and research findings in the fields of biology, psychology, sociology, and medicine that are relevant to the development and evolution of women's roles and behavior. Its emphasis is on breaking down the dichotomy between the psychology and biology to recognize that both interact to produce women's roles and behaviors. The course is interdisciplinary, not only in its content but in its methodological approach as well. It is team-taught and accepts both research findings and the personal experiences of women (students, professors, outside speakers) as valid descriptions of events in women's lives.

Our Western patriarchal society is strongly dualistic or dichotomous. We tend to divide the parts of the world into extremes: nature/nurture; mind/body; rational/feeling; objective/subjective; academia/real world; and masculine/feminine. Scholars have come up with varying ideas for the origin of this dualistic approach to the world. Some (McIntosh, personal communication, 1985) suggest that it is a reflection of the bilaterally symmetrical arrangement of our bodies, which results in two of many body parts, two eyes, two ears, and two hands. Simone de Beauvoir (1949) implies that the dichotomy originates from the fact that the human species is divided into two sexes: the male perceived as the norm and the female as the other. Recently, feminist historians and philosophers of science (Fee 1982; Hein 1981) argued that this dualistic thought process is a particularly masculine approach to the world. The work of Gilligan (1982) reinforces the notion that women (at least those in the very restricted group from which her sample was derived) may not use a dualistic, hierarchical method of problem solving.

Although opinions may differ as to the source of and reasons for the dualistic approach, it is evident that this approach shapes our perceptions of issues; thus we polarize the relevant points into sides that are pro and con. In our teaching methods, beginning at the preschool level, we emphasize separation into different groups and categories and, in the organization of academia, knowledge is divided into separate departments, which represent categories for study.

Each department is usually restricted to the study of only one side of a dichotomy using methods that are categorized as being on a particular side of another dichotomy. For example, the faculty in the sciences, particularly in the biology department, study the nature and body halves of the nature/nurture and mind/body dichotomies. Since most scientists are men, they use methods that are classified as rational, objective and masculine in their study. The faculty in the social sciences, particularly psychology and sociology, study the nurture and mind halves of the same dichotomies. As the statistics of Betty Vetter (1981) and the National Science Foundation (1984) demonstrate, many more women (34.6 percent) are in the social sciences than in the sciences and engineering (10.7 percent); the social sciences are, therefore, perceived as softer and more feminine (Kahle 1983). Although the current trend is to emphasize research methods in the social sciences that are more scientific (i.e., objective and rational), the methods of the social sciences are traditionally considered to be more subjective and intuitive.

Many scientists (Lewontin, Rose, and Kamin 1984), including feminists (Hubbard 1985; Longino and Doell 1983), point out the difficulties of this dualistic approach in the study of most complex problems. Several shortcomings of dichotomous thinking about these issues may be enumerated:

1. In thinking dichotomously, one often fails to recognize the interrelationships between the two poles of the dualism. This leads to reductionism and less-than-accurate descriptions of reality. An example of this is the controversy over whether intelligence is determined by biology or environment (nature/nurture) or, as it is sometimes phrased, what percentage of intelligence is determined by biology and

what percentage by environment. (I once taught from a genetics text [Crow 1976] which stated that I.Q. had a heritability of 80 percent.)

It really is not possible to separate the contribution of biology from that of the environment, since it is now evident that the two interact and determine each other in an inseparable way. Recent experimental evidence (Bleier 1984) demonstrates that the prenatal and postnatal environments may actually influence the number of axons, dendrites, synapses, and neurons. If a fetus is exposed prenatally to particular dosages of certain drugs, alcohol, malnutrition, or viruses, fewer dendrites, axons, synapses, and brain cells will form and thus directly change its biology. As Bleier states, "Normal development of neurons and the brain not only is guided by genetic influences but also requires interaction with a range of particular environmental influences" (1984, 63). Similarly, although environmental stimulation can greatly influence the development of intellectual achievement, biological constraints such as Trisomy 21 or brain damage may limit those achievements. Thus, the dualism of nature/nurture really does not accurately describe so complicated a phenomenon as the development of intelligence. One must consider the interaction between the two poles of the dichotomy, or perhaps even more accurately "insist on the essential oneness of the organism-in-its-environment" (Lewontin, Rose, and Kamin 1984).

2. A second pitfall of dichotomous approaches is that they tend to be correlated with ranking and hierarchies. Although this need not be the case, once one has begun to think in the either-or method associated with dualisms, there is a tendency to think of one pole of the dualism as being superior and the other as inferior. If half of the dualism is associated with men or as masculine, it is frequently ranked as the superior half. An example that demonstrates the inferior ranking associated with the feminine is the research done on brain laterality and visuospatial ability. The research in this area has been riddled with flaws and criticized on several bases (Star 1979). Two opposing theories have been proposed by different research groups. One, the Buffery-Gray Hypothesis (1972), finds that women's brains are more lateralized; the other, the Levy-Sperry Hypothesis (Levy 1972), holds that women's brains are less lateralized. Both groups, however, conclude that women are inferior on visuospatial tasks.

3. A third difficulty with dualisms is that the theoretical framework they provide may lead to a search for technologies that reinforce the dualistic model. This point is somewhat speculative and

certainly could not be proven. However, one facet of the controlling nature of the new reproductive technologies is the way in which they seem to reduce motherhood, which is normally a continuous process from contribution of egg, through pregnancy, childbirth, and child-rearing, to a more dichotomous process similar to fatherhood. The term *to father a child* normally means simply to contribute the sperm. In contrast, the term *to mother* traditionally includes and even emphasizes the nurturing aspect of motherhood. The new reproductive technologies make it possible for mothering to be divided and thus more be similar to fatherhood. Due to *in vitro* fertilization, a woman can now "mother" a child simply by contributing the egg, while another "surrogate" mother carries the fetus during the pregnancy and gives birth to the child. I am not suggesting that the only impetus for reproductive technologies comes from dualisms. How-ever, I suggest that a motivating factor behind men's desire to control women's reproduction may be to make it more similar to their less continuous experience of fatherhood.

4. A final difficulty with dualisms is that they lead to a search for unicausal (and perhaps unidirectional) factors as "the cause" of prob-lems that, in reality, have multiple interactive causes. The fascination of the American public (and for a long time the American medical establishment) with *the* cause for cancer and the search for *a* cure for cancer provides an example of this type of thinking. We now know not only that there are many kinds of cancer, but also that their man-ifestation or causes in any one individual are due to the interaction of complex biological and environmental interrelationships.

CONTENT

Since Biology and Psychology of Women focuses on the inter-related biological and psychological events of women's lives, the sub-jects that can be explored are virtually limitless. Taking into consideration the varieties and pluralities of experience that individ-ual women have with those events, it becomes extremely difficult to select particular topics to be covered in a one-semester course. After teaching the course for ten years, colleagues and I have found a pos-sibility that partially alleviates this difficulty. Certain topics (critique of research methods, development, sex differences, sexuality, men-struation, pregnancy, childbirth, mental health, and menopause) are always included in the course. This provides a body of information that all students who have taken the course will hold in common and satisfies college catalogue and curriculum committee requirements. From all of the other relevant topics (critique of sociobiology, brain lateralization, eating disorders, abortion, motherhood, work, stress, rape, domestic violence, incest, pornography, and the health care system) that might be included, students and faculty members select four or five to consider that semester. This provides some flexibility in the course to fit the group needs and interests, while limiting the subjects to allow coverage in some depth.

We usually begin the course with a critique of traditional biological, medical, and psychological research. After a discussion of possible sources of bias in the researcher (gender, race, class, training as Ph.D. or M.D.) and in research methods (use of animals, patients, case studies, random samples, improper controls), the students are introduced to the idea of a perspective from which research and teaching may be carried out. They become more aware of the limits of the research in each field and the problems of using a dichotomous, disciplinary approach to the study of an area as interwoven as the biology and psychology of women. It quickly becomes evident that research from many disciplines gathered by a variety of methods needs to be brought to bear on this complicated topic. This introduction sets a tone of open questioning, examination, and comparing with experience, which may be applied to all of the reading, lectures, movies, and discussions in the course. Although most students are relieved by this recognition and the admission that research findings and professors may be biased, some are uneasy at the absence of an authoritative, definitive source. Usually, this discomfort passes as the student develops more confidence in her own ability to evaluate research and results and becomes more familiar with the course format.

After experimentation with several different formats, we have found that a good approach is to arrange the topics that are always included chronologically as they might occur during a woman's life:

1. The Prenatal Period: Differentiation and Development
   a. Genetic, hormonal, and environmental determinants in sexual differentiation and development
   b. Hormonal and environmental determinants in differentiation and development of the nervous system.
2. The Child: Research on Sex Differences — Contributions of Biology and Learning

    a. Aggression
    b. Visuospatial ability
    c. Verbal ability
3. The Adolescent: Sexuality
    a. Sexual identity
    b. Menstruation
4. The Adult: Biological and Psychological Options and Pressures
    a. Pregnancy and childbirth
    b. Women and work
    c. Mental health
5. The Older Woman: Realities of the System
    a. Menopause
    b. Aging

The topics chosen for a particular semester usually do not fit into a chronological scheme, since they are relevant throughout a woman's life; they may be dispersed somewhat arbitrarily (sociobiology critique under Prenatal Period; brain lateralization and learning theories under The Child; eating disorders, abortion, rape, and incest under The Adolescent; motherhood, stress, and domestic violence under The Adult; and pornography and the health care system under The Older Woman), with care being taken to consider the varying implications of the issue for different stages of the life cycle. For example, abortion might be considered during the section on The Adolescent but has different, complicating factors (economic, marital, and health status) for a teenager, a woman in her early thirties, or a woman beginning or past menopause.

METHODS

The methods used to teach Biology and Psychology of Women need to reflect a non-dualistic approach that breaks down divisions among disciplines and between academia and real-life experiences. We have found it helpful to convey the interdisciplinary nature of the course by team-teaching and through careful decisions regarding the level of the course, the choice of text, and the integration of academic and experiential learning.

Since this is an interdisciplinary course, ideally, it should be team-taught. It was originally conceived by a biologist, a psychologist, and a medical historian. Really all three individuals should be involved in each session of the course with the discussion interwoven among the three of them. This avoids isolated presentations such as the biology of childbirth in one class followed by the psychology of childbirth in the next and the medical history of the childbirth in a third. Students can much more clearly see the interrelationship of the biological, psychological, and historical factors that shape the experience of childbirth when the professors integrate the information they give about an event. Unfortunately, with tight budgets and over-committed women's studies faculty, most institutions are not willing to commit the resources for three professors to teach one course. This has led to having the course taught by just a biologist and a psychologist and, occasionally, by just a biologist with some training in psychology. Obviously, the students and professors lose a great deal of the interdisciplinary perspective in this situation and must struggle to avoid the dualistic mode.

In order to examine the research critically, to benefit most from the interdisciplinary perspective, and to understand the pitfalls of dualistic thinking, we require the students to have had previous exposure to elementary biology and psychology. These prerequisites give the students the basic knowledge and terminology regarding the human body and psychological development that will free them to consider the interactions between mind and body. As a prerequisite, we also require that students have taken a women's studies course. Students who have not previously had a women's studies course are often so absorbed by the pedagogical methods of women's studies and disoriented by the women-centered focus of the course that it detracts from their ability to deal with the complex issues presented. Despite, or perhaps because of, all of the prerequisites, the course is very stimulating and each semester has a huge list of students eager to take it.

Since most textbooks are written to appeal to the disciplinary market, it is difficult to find an appropriate text for an interdisciplinary course. Although women's studies texts often are interdisciplinary, less work has been done in psychology, medical history, and biology than other areas of women's studies; certainly, no textbook currently combines these three areas. (This needs to be pointed out to students as one negative effect of the disciplinary approach to knowledge and the dearth of women's studies in the traditional disciplines.) In general, we use two or more books plus supplementary readings to cover the vast array of topics. Often, we ask the class to read a piece of contemporary literature, for example, Alice Walker's *The Color Purple* (1982), which presents these issues in a woman's own voice. The inclusion of a literary work, usually not included in social science or natural science courses, underlines the need to search for resources outside the traditional ones.

The pedagogical techniques used in the course should also demonstrate the continuity, as opposed to dichotomy, between the academic information being taught and the "real world" experiences of women. As discussed previously, asking students to help decide on topics to be covered in the course immediately makes it more relevant to them. Many students will have had first-hand experience with some of the topics (for example, anorexia) and may lead part or all of the discussion or serve as resource people for that topic. Several other techniques may help to break the dichotomy between academic and experiential learning:

1. We ask students constantly to compare and contrast what they read and learn about menstruation, sexuality, and work with their own experiences and those of friends and family.
2. We try to use guest speakers from advocacy groups in the community, such as the rape crisis center, battered women's shelter, Lamaze group, and incest survivors support group. Sometimes, a student becomes upset by what she views as a biased or overly personal presentation by a guest speaker. This can provide an opportunity to discuss the difference between advocacy presentations and academic presentations, which give the appearance of being less biased and personal although, in fact, they may not be so.
3. Whenever possible, we encourage people of a variety of ages, racial, ethnic, religious, and class backgrounds to sign up for the course. Although not even an available option at most institutions, the best classes I have ever taught included a mixture of community women taking the course for "fun" along with the traditional college students taking the course for credit.
4. As part of a term paper or project, students may choose from or create a variety of options. However, all options must include both a traditional academic and an experiential component. Thus, a student doing a paper or project on rape might read several papers and books on the topic and interview a rape crisis counselor. Information from both must be included in the paper or project presentation.

Students and professors usually become more involved with the course and learn more when they feel a breakdown of the dichotomy between their lives and what they are learning. Maggie Anderson, chairperson of women's studies at the University of Delaware, told me (personal communication, 1985) that one of the most satisfying comments she had ever heard came from a student at MIT. The student was very upset because, in her women's studies course, unlike all of her other courses, she couldn't distinguish what she was learning in school from what she was learning in the rest of her life. That is the experience that both the students and professors should have in the Biology and Psychology of Women.

WS 430: BIOLOGY AND PSYCHOLOGY OF WOMEN

Syllabus and Reading List

JUNE

17   Introduction. Sex differences and the view of women in biological and psychological research. (Bleier Chapter 1; Unger Chapters 1 and 4)

18   Genetic and environmental determinants in differentiation and development. Critique of sociobiology. (Bleier Chapter 2; Unger Chapters 5 and 6)

19   Anatomical and psychological theories of sexual differentiation and development. (Unger Chapters 7 and 8)

20   The brain: Biological and psychosocial theories of differentiation. Hormonal mechanisms. (Bleier Chapter 3)

24   Biology and psychology of menstrual cycles. (Bleier Chapter 4; Unger Chapter 9)

25   EXAMINATION I: Biology of aggression.

26   Psychological theories of aggression. Violence against women: Rape and domestic violence. (Bleier Chapter 6; Unger Chapter 3)

27   Biology of the sexual response. Development of sexual identity: Bisexual, heterosexual, and lesbian. (Bleier Chapter 7; Unger Chapter 10)

JULY

1   Biology, psychology, and the law: Abortion and incest. (Unger Chapter 15)

2   EXAMINATION II: Biology and psychology of pregnancy and childbirth. (Unger Chapter 12)

3   Women and work: Motherhood; work outside the home. (Bleier Chapter 5; Unger Chapters 11 and 13)
4   *Holiday.*
8   Biology and psychology of aging. PROJECT OR PAPER DUE.
9   Women and mental health. Eating disorders. (Unger Chapter 14)
10   Women in health and disease: Understanding the alternatives. (Bleier Chapter 8; Unger Chapter 16)
11   Women and stress. EXAMINATION III.

Textbooks:

Bleier, Ruth. *Science and Gender: A Critique of Biology and Its Theories on Women*. New York: Pergamon Press, 1984.
Unger, Rhoda K. *Female and Male Psychological Perspectives*. New York: Harper and Row, 1979.
Both texts are available only at Room of One's Own Bookstore.

Grades

Each examination counts 25 percent towards the final course grade. The project or paper also counts 25 percent towards the final grade. Attendance and participation in class discussion may be considered in determination of the final course grade, particularly in borderline cases.

REFERENCES

Bleier, R. 1984. *Science and gender: A critique of biology and its theories on women*. New York: Pergamon Press.
Buffery, W., and J. Gray. 1972. Sex differences in the development of spatial and linguistic skills. In *Gender differences: Their ontogeny and significance*, eds. C. Ounsted and D.C. Taylor. Edinburgh: Churchill Livingstone.
Crow, J.F. 1976. *Genetics notes*. 7th ed. Minneapolis, Minn.: Burgess Publishing Company.
de Beauvoir, Simone. 1949. *Le deuxieme sexe I. Les faits et les mythes. II. L'experience vecue*. Paris: Gallimard.
Fee, E. 1982. A feminist critique of scientific objectivity. *Science for the People* 14, no. 4: 8.
Gilligan, C. 1982. *In a different voice*. Cambridge, Mass.: Harvard University Press.
Hein, H. 1981. Women and science: Fitting men to think about nature. *International Journal of Women's Studies* 4: 369–377.

Hubbard, R. 1985. Putting genes in their place. *The Women's Review of Books* II, no. 4: 7–8.

Kahle, J. 1983. The disadvantaged majority: Science education for women. Burlington, N.C.: Carolina Biological Supply Company. AETS Outstanding Paper for 1983.

Levy, J. 1972. Lateral specialization of the human brain: Behavioral manifestations and possible evolutionary basis. In *The biology of behavior*, ed. J.A. Kiger. Corvallis: Oregon State University Press.

Lewontin, R.C., S. Rose, and L. Kamin. 1984. *Not in our genes: Biology, ideology, and human nature.* New York: Pantheon Books.

Longino, H., and R. Doell. 1983. Body, bias, and behavior: A comparative analysis of reasoning in two areas of biological science. *Signs* 9, no. 2: 206–227.

National Science Foundation. 1984. *Women and minorities in science and engineering.* Report 84–300.

Star, S.L. 1979. Sex differences and the dichotomization of the brain: Methods, limits and problems in research on consciousness. In *Genes and gender II. Pitfalls in research on sex and gender*, eds. R. Hubbard and M. Lowe, 113–130. Staten Island, N.Y.: Gordian Press, Inc.

Vetter, B. 1981. Degree completion by women and minorities in science increases. *Science* 212, no. 3.

Walker, A. 1982. *The color purple.* New York: Washington Square Press.

4
CHANGING PEDAGOGICAL METHODS

Chapter 8
USING FEMINIST PEDAGOGICAL METHODS IN THE SCIENCE CLASSROOM

In *Learning Our Way: Essays in Feminist Education*, Barbara Hillyer Davis (1983) describes the conflict she feels between her role as professor at a traditional university and her conviction as a feminist, which leads to a very different model of teaching:

> The university has taught us well how learning should be done. Because I do "know more" than most of my students, I am easily persuaded that I should impart knowledge for their reception. The institutional pressure to do so is reinforced by the students' well-socialized behavior. If I will tell them "what I want," they will deliver it. They are exasperated with my efforts to depart from the role of dispenser of wisdom.
>
> On the other hand, what I know about feminist process makes me feel an obligation to renounce the professional role, to serve instead as a role model for sisterhood, disclaiming any stance of superiority and presenting myself as one who learns instead of teaching. Struggling to maintain myself between these conflicting pressures, I work out a role as teacher which leans toward a peer relationship but includes enough of the professor to reassure those students who feel comfortable in a more traditional classroom. (p. 91)

Davis' description closely reflects my own inner conflict and the pedagogical position I evolved in my teaching. In a chapter focussed on pedagogical methods, I think that it is crucial for an honest discussion of the subject that I reveal my own stance on pedagogical methods and indicate some possible sources of my particular perspective.

I received a traditional scientific undergraduate and graduate education at a large research-oriented midwestern university. My B.A. (1969) and Ph.D. (1973) were both granted during a time of major student unrest and institutional response to student demands for course relevance and examination of the power structure of the university. Nevertheless, the basic pattern of classroom interaction between professor and students was one of traditional professorial authority and control. The professor delivered knowledge using a lecture format to large numbers of students. Few, if any, questions, other than those of clarification, were permitted due to constraints of time and numbers. The smaller laboratory and discussion sections were headed by graduate-student teaching assistants. Although students were encouraged to ask questions about the lab and the problems we could not solve or material we did not understand, the teaching assistant had assumed from the professor the authority to dispense knowledge. This hierarchical model of classroom education with the professor as authority of knowledge was the one by which I was taught as a student and which I sought to replicate when I began teaching, during my last year of graduate school and first two years as a post-doctoral fellow.

During my third year as a post-doctoral fellow, I began teaching in a nascent women's studies program. For the first time, I thought consciously about my teaching style and classroom methods and the discrepancy between them and my thoughts about feminist processes. At the same time, other women teaching in this first year of the women's studies program were struggling with sharing authority in the classroom, rejecting the notion of a grading system, and making the learning process relevant to the content of the material and equally important. In those early years, all of us in the program experimented with methods that were appropriate to the content of the courses we taught within the setting of the university and yet that did not violate aspects of the feminist process we deemed invaluable, although these processes were quite absent from the college-level teaching in most parts of the institution. Some of those experiments were very successful; others created so much tension and insecurity in the students that they probably hindered learning, certainly in the short run. I also learned that some methods, which worked well for my women's studies colleagues teaching in other disciplines, were less suitable for the experimental and information-based biology and health courses.

After twelve years of teaching both women's studies and science courses, I am evolving some pedagogical methods that seem to help the learning process and with which I am comfortable. Certainly, these methods encourage more sharing of authority and student involvement in determining the structure and methods of the course than most science courses. However, I do retain the power to structure the courses so that students will have access to all of the information given in a traditional science course. The goal of the pedagogical methods for which I am searching is to attract to science students who will be competent in their knowledge of traditional science but who share a feminist perspective, with which to criticize that science and provide the roots of a reconceptualization of that science to include us all.

GENERAL SCHEMES OF FEMINIST PEDAGOGY

Some feminists (Bunch 1983; McIntosh 1983) have written about the ways in which they attempted to include feminist processes and content in their teaching. The written material describing feminist pedagogical methods may be divided into three general areas: the approaches that should be included in a course transformed by the feminist perspective; a consideration of the language that should be used in teaching, so that bias regarding roles and stereotypes of gender, class, and race are not transmitted as part of the curriculum; and approaches to classroom interaction that incorporate feminist processes.

In order to describe each area in this chapter, I chose a representative scheme or description from the literature. I describe, using one or two examples, the ways in which I have adapted or interpreted the methods of that scheme for the sciences. Although the specific examples I use for illustration are drawn from my classes in biology and women's studies, most of them might easily be adapted for other science, health, or science education classes. Some of the general schemes of feminist pedagogy are not as appropriate to the science disciplines as to other disciplines. In addition, the sciences lend themselves to some unique adaptations not found in schemes meant to apply to the social sciences or humanities. In the last part of this chapter, I discuss my view of the particular opportunities and difficulties of using feminist pedagogy in science classes.

Approaches to Consider

Schuster and Van Dyne (1984), in "Placing Women in the Liberal Arts: Stages of Curriculum Transformation," propose eight elements that characterize a transformed course.

We have intentionally included the teacher's and students' relationship to the changed subject matter and to each other as crucial ingredients. A transformed course would:

— be self-conscious about *methodology* — use gender as a category of analysis, no matter what is on the syllabus (even if all males);

— present changed content in a *changed context* — awareness of all knowledge as historical and socially constructed, not immutable;

— develop an *interdisciplinary perspective* — the language of discourse, assumptions of a field, and analytical methods are made visible by contrast with other fields;

— pay meaningful attention to intersections of *race, class, and cultural differences within gender* — avoid universalizing beyond data;

— study new subjects in their *own terms* — not merely as other, alien, non-normative, non-Western — encourage a true *pluralism;*

— *test paradigms* rather than merely "add on" women figures or issues — incorporate analyses of gender, race, and class by a thorough reorganization of available knowledge;

— make the student's experience and learning process part of the explicit content of the course — reaffirm the transcendent goals of the course;

— and recognize that, because *culture reproduces itself in the classroom*, the more conscious we are of this phenomenon, the more likely we are to turn it to our advantage in teaching the transformed course. (p. 428)

Many scientists claim that the science they practice and the courses they teach are gender-free and objective. Thus, they assert that using gender as a category of analysis is not relevant to science research or courses. Although pure, good scientific research may be gender-free (Gornick 1983), most science courses are not. What passes for gender-free and objective in many science and health courses is in fact synonymous with a masculine view of the world (Keller 1982). It appears objective to most men because it puts men in the center or as the norm; most women feel excluded. Using gender as a category of analysis raises the question, What information would we study if women, not men, became the focus of this issue? Suddenly, there is such a wealth of material that entire courses, such as Women and Their Bodies in Health and Disease (Chapter 6) and Biology and Psychology of Women (Chapter 7), are created to include the material excluded from traditional health and biology courses. As Elizabeth Minnich (1983) pointed out, courses titled American Writers or European History usually mean American White Men Writers or European White Men's History. In the academic world, we add prefixes, such as women or black, when a course includes others besides white men. Similarly, the development of biology and health courses focussing on women's issues exposes the androcentric bias of the traditional courses.

Awareness of the androcentric bias is closely linked with, or perhaps preceded by, the recognition of the historical and social construction of all knowledge. Although historians of science (Kuhn 1970) pointed out the evolution of specific scientific paradigms within particular social and historical settings, most scientists accept reluctantly, if at all, the notion that theories constructed from data collected by the scientific method might not be value-free and objective. Viewing issues from an interdisciplinary perspective may expose the more subjective and value-laden theories of science. Certainly coteaching with psychologists and medical historians has helped me to see the changing scientific and health paradigms over time. However, many scientists view the analytical tools of science and the scientific method as superior to the methods of analysis of other fields. It is not unusual to find scientists who accept the idea of changing theories based on different historical and social contexts as relevant to the social sciences and humanities, but fail to recognize its validity to the sciences. Without this recognition, a scientist will not have the freedom to reflect critically on how science, the scientific establishment, and the health care system might differ if women or people of different races, classes, religions, sexual preferences, or ablebodiedness were the central components of those establishments.

Even when women do become the central focus, there is a tendency to universalize beyond the data from a limited sample without questioning whether or not that sample truly reflects the whole universe of women's backgrounds and experiences. As discussed in Chapter 4, conscious efforts must be made to allow women of differing backgrounds to speak about how social and historical factors shaped their perspective on particular science and health care issues.

The scientist who truly accepts that all knowledge, including scientific theories, evolved in a social and historical context comprehends the importance of perspective. Recognition of the importance of perspective leads directly to examining science and health from as many perspectives as possible: gender as a category of analysis, an interdisciplinary perspective, and differing race, class, and cultural perspectives. Quite naturally then, the professor begins to reorganize thoroughly the available knowledge and search for new knowledge that tests the "old" paradigms and creates new paradigms, which include the pluralism that diverse perspectives impart.

In my own teaching development, the first step was recognizing that Darwin's theories of evolution reflected an upper-class British Victorian capitalistic man's viewpoint (Rose and Rose 1980). I then began to think about whose theories were reflected in current twentieth century science and health care practice and why I felt so distant from those theories. Shortly after that, I began teaching women's studies, even though my colleagues in the lab made fun of my "nonscience" courses. It was not terribly difficult for me, as a woman, to realize what I had not learned, and was not teaching, in my traditional science courses that I desperately wanted and needed to know: all about my own body; why no contraceptive methods were satisfactory; why I had felt so out of control during my first pregnancy and childbirth; and why I could not relate to the dominant population's ideas about sexuality. It was only after several years of research and teaching this information that I grew aware that women from backgrounds different from my own viewed these issues and questions very differently from me. I began to seek ways to include the perceptions of women who represented those perspectives. Simultaneous with this evolution of content and awareness of perspective, I continually examined my language and approaches to classroom interaction to try to avoid bias and stereotyping of gender, class, sexual preference, and race so that the students would not find in the classroom a reproduction of the stereotypes and biases of the surrounding culture.

Considerations of Language

A substantial amount of research has been done on language and how it may transmit bias regarding roles and stereotypes of gender, class, and race. Martyna (1978) demonstrated that when generic terms such as *he* and *man* are used, people rarely visualize women. Generic use of masculine terminology also implies that the male is the norm in society. Usage of masculine generic terms makes women feel excluded from the discussion. Gender referencing ("the doctor gives his patient"; "the nurse gives her patient") permeates classroom language and transmits stereotypes of occupational, social, and gender roles. Labelling has traditionally been used as a subtle form of discrimination against women and people of color ("boy" or "girl" for an adult; "credit to your race"). Nonparallel terminology ("men and ladies" or "the dentist and his doctor wife were in Hawaii") also conveys differential status.

Stereotyping encompasses a broad range of issues including age, gender, race, handicaps, and sexual preference. It includes stereotypes of roles (all women as housewives), occupations (all truckdrivers as men), personality characteristics (stoic men; passive women), and physical, mental, and emotional characteristics (mathematical men and verbal women). Stereotyping that assumes a heterosexual and/or able-bodied norm ("When, in your first sexual encounter, he inserts his penis into your vagina") may exclude nonheterosexual and/or physically challenged individuals. Paternalism is a subtle form of stereotyping and racism that conveys surprise that a person of color succeeded in a certain situation ("Dr. Jane Wright, a black woman who rose to the position of Associate Dean of the New York Medical College").

Publications in education (U.S. Department of Health Education and Welfare, Office of Education 1978) and social sciences (Jenkins 1983) include excellent guidelines for student-faculty communication. Most of these guidelines are also appropriate for health and science courses. However, I would like to discuss a couple of problems or special adaptations that might be more appropriate for the natural sciences. Because the sciences have fewer women (Vetter 1981) and people of color (National Science Foundation 1984) than either the social sciences or humanities, I think that it may be advisable to employ particular techniques to break stereotypes and emphasize contributions of women and people of color. The usual custom is to refer to scientists who have made important discoveries or carried out significant experiments by their last names (Watson and Franklin's work on DNA). Use of last names only in referring to work of both men and women scientists is parallel treatment. However, the picture in most people's minds upon hearing a last name is that of a male scientist, since most scientists in our society are men. Similarly, the use of initials rather than forenames in lists of references provides parallel treatment for both men and women. Nevertheless, Johnson-Gazzam (personal communication 1984) found that the overwhelming majority of students in education classes assumed that when initials were used, they stood for a male forename. Therefore, the parallel treatment that may be more helpful in breaking the stereotype of all scientists as male is the use of full forenames and surnames for all experimenters (James Watson and Rosalind Franklin).

It is unparallel treatment to compare the work done by "black scientist E. E. Just (Manning 1983) and scientist R. M. Auerbach." Prefacing Just's name with "black scientist" while not using "white scientist" before Auerbach's name assumes white as the racial norm. It may be effective and parallel to mention everyone's race and gender when talking about individual contributions: "The black female physician Susan McKinney Steward and the white male physicist Albert Einstein." This technique emphasizes the contributions of women and people of color while placing parallel prefixes before the names of white male scientists. Students inevitably begin to think about why most of the scientists are white men. The use of language provides a subtle, yet powerful form of breaking biases and stereotypes of gender, class, and race so that the dominant cultural environment is not replicated in classroom interactions.

Classroom Interaction

In addition to attention to language, the incorporation of other feminist processes may directly improve classroom interaction. In "Feminist Values: Guidelines for Teaching Methodology in Women's Studies," Nancy Schniedewind (1983) describes five basic process goals for classroom interaction: development of an atmosphere of mutual respect, trust, and community in the classroom; shared leadership; cooperative structures; integration of cognitive and affective learning; and action.

Each professor naturally develops different techniques for applying these goals, depending upon the content area, students, and course level. I would like to share my interpretations of the goals and techniques I found appropriate for applying these goals to the science classroom.

Atmosphere of Mutual Respect, Trust, and Community

Building an atmosphere of mutual respect, trust, and community in the classroom is partially entangled with some of the language issues discussed previously. However, it goes beyond use of language to areas of interaction, such as classroom participation, verbal and nonverbal interaction, and use of humor. The atmosphere created is based not only on professor-student interaction, but also on student-student interaction. Research results indicate that there are differences in classroom participation based upon gender and race (Kramarae 1980). Women talk less in class, although are perceived as talking more (Kramarae 1980), are given less time than men to respond to questions (Sadker and Sadker 1979), are called upon less often than men (Karp and Yoels 1976), and are less likely to have issues raised by them pursued by the faculty (Thorne 1979) or other students. "The Classroom Climate: A Chilly One for Women" (Hall and Sandler 1982) includes being asked "lower order" questions, coached less often towards a full answer, and being taken less seriously than males as factors that further discourage women from participating in class. Forms of verbal interaction, such as knowing and addressing the male students more frequently by name and interrupting female students more frequently than males, may be unconscious behaviors on the part of faculty that discourage female participation. Humorous or teasing references to physical or sexual characteristics (more frequently applied to females) or humorous treatment of serious topics such as rape, lesbianism, or mental illness are likely to be offensive to women and make them feel uncomfortable in the classroom interaction.

Other studies have demonstrated that Asian and black students feel ignored or put down by faculty (Noonan 1980). Clearly, these types of behaviors by the faculty, although often unconscious or unintentional, do not create an atmosphere of mutual trust and respect between faculty and students. In science classes, where women and people of color generally comprise a small percentage of the class, these behaviors create further barriers to participation and increase the chances of being ignored. The facts that most faculty in science departments are white men and that science fields are perceived as "masculine" disciplines further exacerbate and alienate all women and men of color.

Faculty in the science classroom need to evaluate critically their verbal and nonverbal communication with students, to ascertain whether or not their classroom behavior discriminates on the basis of gender or race. Since most of us are relatively blind to our own behaviors, it might be helpful to ask a colleague from another department—women's studies would be ideal—to evaluate several classes solely from the perspective of faculty-student interaction. Videotaping class sessions provides another approach to examining these behaviors.

Because of the power differential, faculty-student interactions provide a crucial factor in establishing an atmosphere of trust, mutual respect, and community. However, student-student interaction may be equally important. Not only do white men talk more in class, they exert further conversational control by interrupting women more (Zimmerman and West 1975), referring to women's appearance and sexuality, and taking up more space by using more forceful gestures

(Henley 1977). Male speech patterns, which tend to be more forceful ("I know"; "the fact is"), are more highly valued, so that the information they state using those patterns is more likely to be perceived as credible than the same information expressed in female speech patterns ("I think that"; "perhaps a factor"). Due to these patterns, women students as well as women faculty members, have more difficulty establishing credibility in the classroom (Jenkins and Kramarae, 1978). In science, where women students are rare and women faculty are even rarer, this problem is more severe.

Because of their awareness of the inhibition of full female participation when males are present, many feminist groups outside the university and some women's studies programs within colleges and universities have insisted upon women-only classes (Members of the Women's Studies College, State University of New York at Buffalo 1983). This restriction definitely yields increased participation by women. In most institutions, barring men from women's studies classes is not permitted and would never even be an issue in science classes. In the absence of this restriction, the professor and students need to develop ways to ensure participation by all, without allowing one or a few individuals to dominate the class. Schniedewind (1983) suggests devoting some class time to dealing with process skills throughout the semester. She teaches the students to use *I-messages*.

> *I-messages* offer women a means for giving positive or constructively critical feedback to each other in a supportive way. The format for an I-message is: "When you (behavior), I feel (feeling) because (consequence)." For example, "Sue, when you dominate the class discussion, I feel annoyed because I'm interested in hearing the thoughts of everyone here." This enables a person to tell another how a particular behavior makes her feel without generalizing about her. It doesn't demand, but gives the receiver the choice to change her behavior. I-messages are easy to learn, can be shared among peers and between students and instructor, and are very effective in producing an honest classroom atmosphere. (p. 263)

She also consciously discusses the various function-roles people may play in groups—organizer, devil's advocate, includer, clarifier, withdrawer—and asks them to take turns playing those roles. Students, and faculty, in science courses may have had few, if any, social sciences courses where these process issues are discussed. They may, therefore, be totally unfamiliar with group dynamics and need more time and conscious effort to develop these skills.

Shared Leadership

Developing and using process skills that encourage full class partic-ipation are ways for the professor to share the leadership role. In the atmosphere of mutual trust and respect that has been created, I have taken steps towards sharing the authority that traditionally is that of the professor. As I discussed in Chapters 6 and 7, some of the topics on the syllabus may be selected by the students. I usually have certain topics (about two-thirds of the course) that are required; the other third of the topics may be selected. Both the students and professors contribute to a list of potential subjects; we then decide by mutual consensus (sometimes by an actual vote) which will be included that particular semester.

Another way that I enjoy sharing the leadership role is by coteach-ing with individuals from other disciplines. Although coteaching may take more time than teaching alone, it is definitely more rewarding for both students and faculty, since issues can be explored in greater depth and complexity and from more perspectives. Bringing in guest speakers (see Chapter 5) and asking students with expertise on spe-cific topics to lead the presentation permit further diversity and shar-ing of authority. Scientists who have different areas of specialization, training (M.D. or Ph.D.), or occupational sector (government, clinic, or academia) may have widely differing perspectives on a particular issue in health science. A student who has had a disease (for example, bulimia) and extensive interactions with the health care system may provide a vivid first-hand account of its surrounding issues.

Cooperative Structures

A further extension of shared leadership and an atmosphere of mutual respect and trust are provided by cooperative structures, which facilitate interaction and interdependence among students. Schniedewind (1983) states that "an activity has a cooperative goal structure when an individual can complete it successfully if, and only if, all others with whom she is linked do likewise. The group sinks or swims together" (p. 266). I experimented less with this aspect of femi-nist process than some of the others. In the institutional setting of the university, which encourages competition, I found it difficult to build cooperative structures into my courses. For example, I never insisted that students take the course pass/fail or used the contract method of grading. On a more limited scale, I used cooperative structures in the science classroom. Students are strongly encouraged to give joint panel reports and to devise group projects in Biology and Psychology of Women. The group as a whole receives one grade for the panel or project, which is recorded as the same grade for each individual in the group for that portion of the final grade. If one person does not do the work or attend the meetings, that will be reflected in the group grade. Thus, it becomes the responsibility of all to ensure that each individual becomes a functioning member of the group.

Integration of Cognitive and Affective Learning

Since feminism is premised on valuing each woman's personal experience and recognizing that the personal is political, integration of cognitive and affective learning is basic to most women's studies courses. Based on premises of rationality and objectivity, integration of cognitive and affective learning is quite foreign to most science courses. Thus, the approaches I tried to make the content relevant to women's experiences are methodologies prevalent in women's studies but quite adaptable to the sciences.

For example, in The Biology of Reproduction and Reproductive Technologies, students are asked to write papers that express their feelings about the controversial technologies we discuss in class. In Women and Their Bodies in Health and Disease, students are asked to keep a daily body journal throughout the semester. In their body journal, they record, using the terminology of the course, changes they note in their bodies and psychological states correlated with menstrual cycles, nutrition, exercise, stress, and disease. In Biology and Psychology of Women, students are asked to interview women who are as different as possible from themselves—different class, age, race, religion, or sexual preference—about a biological event studied in the course—childbirth, menopause, hysterectomy. The student is to explore the event's biological and psychological ramifications for the woman interviewed. Both in that course and in Sexuality and Human Reproduction, works of fiction are employed to make sexual and reproductive events less clinical and convey different women's experiences. Using outside speakers, as I do in all my courses but particularly in Women in Science, increases the students' awareness of the varieties of personal options and barriers to women in science.

Action

A final tenet of the feminist process, which further involves the students on a personal level with the material that they are learning, is action-oriented field work. Frequently, the projects (a study of the abortion methods or the counseling techniques of an abortion clinic, methods used for training rape crisis counselors, surveys of attitudes towards sexuality at a women's college compared to a coeducational institution, or surveys of contraceptive methods used among the students) involve the students in interactions in the college and surrounding community. In some cases, students obtained internships and full-time jobs based on contacts initiated by the projects. In Women in Science, students are strongly encouraged to become involved with the professional societies affiliated with their probable scientific career choices. The network and contacts resulting from this involvement have been invaluable for the students, college, and professional societies.

PEDAGOGICAL DIFFICULTIES UNIQUE TO THE SCIENCES AND PROBLEMS NOT ADDRESSED BY THE FEMINIST PROCESS

Incorporating feminist processes, removing bias and stereotypes from language, and approaching courses from the feminist perspective expand both the content and the methods for learning in all courses in all disciplines. I found that conscious usage of these methodologies has improved my teaching of science as well as women's studies courses. As I began to apply the methodologies first evolved in women's studies to my science courses, I discovered some difficulties or issues unique or especially problematic for the sciences. These issues could not be remedied by applying the women's studies methodologies, which had been developed primarily for use in the humanities and social sciences. For some of these difficulties, I found partially satisfactory solutions; for others, I found no real answers. However, these are issues that need to be faced if we hope to attract more women to science and reconceptualize the discipline.

The first issue I find particularly problematic, although not unique to science, is the training that most scientists have had. Our training supposedly embodies a rational, objective, neutral approach to the study of problems, which in fact denies the existence of much of the emotion and subjective basis upon which scientific data are collected and theories are constructed. Earlier in this chapter, I discussed the importance of recognizing that all knowledge and theory, even scientific theory, are constructed by people who view the world from a particular perspective, which is shaped by a variety of social, historical, political, and economic forces. However, most forces in the education and training of scientists—and indeed the scientific method itself—make it difficult for scientists to accept the subjectivity of knowledge. Even when able to do so in general, we usually have a great deal of difficulty recognizing our own perspective or bias on a particular scientific issue and admitting that perspective to ourselves and the class. If the scientist is unable or unwilling to discuss the issue of perspective and admit that perspective to the class, the information will be presented in a way that discourages the subtle, complex analysis that is critical for challenging and transforming traditional theories. The analysis should ask, is there another way to ask this question? Should a different set of experimental controls have been used? Who benefits from approaching this health care problem in this fashion?

Another difficulty in the training of most scientists is the lack of education in the dynamics of group process, power, and relationships. The German model of the Herr Doktor Professor is still used for much science training in the United States. Thus, it is very difficult, and totally foreign to our conception of education, for many scientists to employ some of the feminist processes of shared leadership, cooperative structuring, an atmosphere of mutual respect, and integration of cognitive and affective learning, which may be inherent in the training of sociologists, psychologists, and other social scientists. Even discussions following a format standard to traditional humanities courses may be alien to many scientists. Many scientists consider attention to group process and discussion too "touchy-feely" and not appropriate for the college classroom. Colleagues in other disciplines or faculty development seminars may help scientists to recognize how classroom interactions may inhibit learning, particularly in women, people of color, or those who are put off by the "objective, rational" approach to the world.

The second major and continuing problem in the sciences is the scarcity of women in the discipline. Women students find very few role models in women faculty. Primarily due to the small numbers of women, scientific fields are perceived as "masculine" (Kahle 1983) and women choosing scientific disciplines question—and are questioned about – whether they can truly be both feminine and scientists. In addition, the dearth of women faculty and students in sciences exaggerates a number of problems that women traditionally have had in the university. Men on the faculty, by conscious and unconscious behaviors (Hall and Sandler 1982), make the few women students feel uncomfortable or excluded; the few women on the faculty, in attempts to gain credibility with male colleagues and students, often assume classroom behaviors that appear just as discriminatory and exclusionary as their male colleagues. Women faculty members may be so caught up in the system that they are unable to avoid reinforcing stereotypes and using methods that exclude other women from science. For example, instead of structuring laboratory work so that women are paired with other women, or some other device that ensures that the women will work with the instruments, women faculty members may be oblivious to the dynamics of male-female lab partnerships in which the man inevitably works with the equipment while the woman records the data. This structure does little to increase a woman's ability to handle instruments and equipment. She may never gain the confidence necessary for subsequent laboratory experiences and begin to feel excluded from laboratory work in science. Arranging same-sex pairs as laboratory partners may help to overcome this difficulty.

Until more women teach and study science, women will need courage to risk being scientists at all and a tremendous amount of courage to try to be feminists in their approach to science. Many women science professors fear, and justly so, that too much involvement with women's studies in their teaching or research will detract from their image as serious scientists and cost them tenure or promotions.

Those who attempt to combine women's studies and science must be aware of the very real dangers not only for themselves but also for their students. Many careers in science involve passing some test or licensing examination upon the completion of undergraduate education. The Graduate Record Examination, Medical Catalogue Examination, and the examinations for licensing medical technologists, radiologists, nurses, and other allied health personnel assume a traditional science program. It does not do women a service to attract them to science careers using feminist methods without providing them the skills and information they will need for competence in their field as defined at this point by traditional examinations. This means that, at this point, many science courses must continue to cover the traditional information. However, that information can be presented from a feminist perspective and criticized when the theories and practices exclude women and people of color. It is my conviction that we are at the phase in development where we must emphasize attracting women to science and providing them with the skills and information necessary to understand, make critiques of, and enter careers in traditional science. We must walk the tightrope of awareness and understanding of traditional science, while using our feminist knowledge to remain outside of the system. Only then can we criticize it, avoid falling prey to its exclusive limitations, and attract other women to its study. After substantial numbers of women have worked for a lengthy period of time in science, some of us will be able to use our feminist tools for the reconceptualization of science to include us all.

REFERENCES

Bunch, C. 1983. Not by degrees: Feminist theory and education. In *Learning our way: Essays in feminist education,* eds. C. Bunch and S. Pollack, 248–260. Trumansburg, N.Y.: The Crossing Press.

Davis, B.H. 1983. "Teaching the feminist minority. In *Learning our way: Essays in feminist education*, eds. C. Bunch and S. Pollack, 89–97. Trumansburg, N.Y.: The Crossing Press.

Gornick, V. 1983. *Women in science: Portraits from a world in transition.* New York: Simon and Schuster.

Hall, R., and B. Sandler. 1982. *The classroom climate: A chilly one for women?* Washington, D.C.: Association of American Colleges Project on the Status and Education of Women.

Henley, N.M. 1977. *Body politics: Power, sex and nonverbal communication.* Englewood Cliffs, N.J.: Prentice-Hall.

Jenkins, M.M. 1983, *Removing bias: Guidelines for student-faculty communication*, a part of the series *Sex and gender in the social sciences: Reassessing the introductory course.* Annandale, Va.: Speech Communication Association.

Jenkins, M.M., and C. Kramarae. 1978. Small group process: Learning from women. *Women's Studies International Quarterly* 1: 67–84.

Kahle, J. 1983. The disadvantaged majority: Science education for women. Burlington N.C.: Carolina Biological Supply Company. AETS Outstanding Paper for 1983.

Karp, D.A., and W.C. Yoels. 1976. The college classroom: Some observations on the meanings of student participation. *Sociology and Social Research* 60: 421–439.

Keller, E.F. 1982. Feminism and science. *Signs: Journal of Women in Culture and Society* 7, no. 3: 589–602.

Kramarae, C., ed. 1980. *The voices and words of women and men.* London: Pergamon Press.

Kuhn, T. 1970. *The structure of scientific revolutions.* 2d ed. Chicago: The University of Chicago Press.

Manning, K.R. 1983. *Black Apollo of science: The life of Ernest Everett Just.* New York: Oxford University Press.

Martyna, W. 1978. What does "he" mean? Use of the generic masculine. *Journal on Communication* 28: 131–138.

McIntosh, P. 1983. Interactive phases of curricular re-vision: A feminist perspective. Working Paper No. 124, Wellesley College, Center for Research on Women, Wellesley, Mass.

Members of the Women's Studies College, State University of New York at Buffalo. 1983. All-women classes and the struggle for women's liberation. In *Learning our way: Essays in feminist education*, eds. C. Bunch and S. Pollack, 59–77. Trumansburg, N.Y.: The Crossing Press.

Minnich, E. 1983. Friends and critics: The feminist academy. In *Learning our way: Essays in feminist education*, eds. C. Bunch and S. Pollack, 317–330. Trumansburg, N.Y.: The Crossing Press.

National Science Foundation. 1984. *Women and minorities in science and engineering.* Report 84–300.

Noonan, J.F. 1980. White faculty and black students: Examining assumptions and practices. Paper available from the Center for Improving Teaching Effectiveness, Virginia Commonwealth University, Richmond.

Rose, H., and S. Rose. 1980. The myth of the neutrality of science. In *Science and liberation*, eds. R. Arditti, P. Brennan, and S. Cavrak, 17–32. Boston: South End Press.

Sadker, M., and D. Sadker, 1979. Between teacher and student: Overcoming sex bias in the classroom. Unpublished report of the Non-Sexist Teacher Education Project of the Women's Educational Equity Act Program, U.S. Department of Health, Education and Welfare, Office of Education.

Schniedewind, N. 1983. Feminist values: Guidelines for a teaching methodology in women's studies. In *Learning our way: Essays in feminist education*, eds. C. Bunch and S. Pollack, 261–271. Trumansburg, N.Y.: The Crossing Press.

Schuster, M., and S. Van Dyne. 1984. Placing women in the liberal arts: Stages of curriculum transformation. *Harvard Educational Review* 54, no. 4.

Thorne, B. 1979. Claiming verbal space: Women, speech and language in college classrooms. Paper presented at the Research Conference on Educational Environments and the Undergraduate Woman (13–15 September), Wellesley College, Wellesley, Mass.

U.S. Department of Health Education and Welfare, Office of Education. 1978. *Taking sexism out of education.* The National Project on Women in Education, HEW Publication No. (OE) 77-01017.

Vetter, B. 1981. Degree completion by women and minorities in science increases. *Science* 212, no. 3.

Zimmerman, D.H., and C. West. 1975. Sex roles, interruptions and silences in conversation. In *Language and sex: Difference and dominance*, eds. B. Thorne and N. Henley. Rowley, Mass.: Newbury House.

Chapter 9
Adapting Courses for Use Outside of the Traditional Classroom Setting

The Boston Women's Health Book Collective, in publishing *The New Our Bodies, Ourselves*, state that one of their original goals was "To reach as many women as possible with tools which will enable them to take greater charge of their own health care and their lives, deal with the existing medical system and fight whenever possible for improvements and changes" (1984, xiii). In our society, women have been denied information about their bodies. Part of this exclusion comes from the scientific establishment and the medical profession, which have actively kept people ignorant of their bodies in an attempt to have economic and political control over us. Part has come from remnants of Victorian moral standards, which held that it was improper for a woman to touch or discuss or know too much about her body. Some of the exclusion comes from a lack of communication among women of their knowledge and experience with their bodies.

One of the driving forces behind the women's movement and a major focus uniting all women has been the need to know and control their bodies. All women need basic information about their anatomy and physiology and the structure of the current health care system, in order to make responsible decisions regarding their health and to feel better about themselves as human beings. The response to books such as *Our Bodies, Ourselves* and courses such as Women and Their Bodies in Health and Disease or Biology and Psychology of Women, described in this volume, demonstrates the hunger of women for such knowledge.

All women need, and deserve, access to this information. However, as long as the courses conveying the information are confined to the traditional university classroom, very few women will actually have access to the knowledge. The traditional academic classroom is available to only a select group of women: those whose age, money, time, and previous training allow them to enter a college or university. Since all women have bodies and have the right to the medical and scientific information that will help them make decisions regarding the care of their bodies, it became important to me to devise methods to take this information where it would reach women of all ages in various situations. The methods and changes that I tried, in an attempt to reach more women and women in differing situations, are just beginning steps. By and large, they represent the most feasible steps, given the composition and restrictions of the institution where I teach and its surrounding community. Since the institution is a small private women's college in a southern town surrounded by rural farmlands, these steps are very different than those one might take in a large metropolitan community. I have also limited my outside teaching to women's studies courses, Women and Their Bodies in Health and Disease, and Biology and Psychology of Women. My hope is that, as more women become knowledgeable about their bodies and health, their knowledge will generate interest and demand for more biology, health, and science education courses outside of the traditional classroom.

The changes I made to allow greater access to the course may be grouped into three broad categories: segmenting and changing the time format of the course; using audiovisual tapes and equipment to provide individualized, self-instruction materials; and developing materials suitable for particular audiences. Although many of the changes are interlocking (for example, developing a particular segment of a course often also makes it suitable for a specific audience), it seems simpler to separate them into these categories for purposes of discussion.

SEGMENTING AND CHANGING THE TIME FORMAT

Segmenting and changing the time format of the course is probably the easiest adaptation. Beginning with a traditional semester-length course, the material may be divided in various ways. For a course that is still offered for three semester hours of credit, I tried two basic formats. The first format is most appropriate for a four-week summer-school session that meets daily or a continuing education evening session that meets weekly for an entire semester. Each session lasts three hours, and the students are presented with all of the information and discussion that they would get from a one semester course meeting three times each week. Compressing the material for a full week into one three-hour session means that each session must be planned very carefully. I try to complete a single large topic or several smaller, related topics in each session, in order to have a more cohesive unit. I also try to build variety into the methods by which the information is conveyed within each session. Three hours of lecture-discussion are deadly; I make sure that each session includes a film, a panel of speakers, or student reports to break the routine.

For more advanced students and students used to independent study, I have occasionally used a second format. The students meet as a class only four times during the course. During these four three-hour segments, which are interspersed throughout the duration of the course, I focus on two major topics. Initially, I discuss the subject that the students have studied independently for the latest segment of the course; then I introduce the next major topic, which will be the center of study for the next three weeks and give the detailed, scientific explanations that provide a background for their independent study of the topic. The students' independent work includes reading, watching the films and videotapes, conducting interviews, as well as writing papers and exams. In addition, each student meets privately with me twice during the semester to discuss questions and focus on topics for research papers. I found the format of independent study combined with four class meetings to be particularly successful for adult students returning to school to complete an undergraduate degree. The more flexible schedule suits their other career and family demands, yet the classroom meetings provide opportunities for discussion and sharing of experiences.

If the course is not being offered for three semester hours of credit, time and segmentation can be approached in an entirely different manner. This opens up diverse options, including credit and non-credit mini-courses centered around larger topics within the traditional semester-long course. Pregnancy and childbirth, aging and menopause, diseases of women, sexuality, the anatomy of the reproductive system and contraception, the hormones of the reproductive system and menstruation, and women and stress are each topics that may be presented in several hour-long sessions, two or three three-hour sessions, or one eight-hour session (for example, at a weekend college). These sessions may be offered for one or two credits or not for credit, depending upon readings, papers, and examinations.

Adaptation of the topics from a semester-long course to a mini-course is not particularly difficult. However, I have found a few problems that may result from the transition. The mini-courses are more likely to attract a less varied audience or, at least, a group of individuals with a similar interest in the topic of the course. For example, a course on pregnancy and childbirth is most likely to attract a group of younger individuals who are pregnant or contemplating pregnancy. This means the loss of considerable diversity in perspective and experience compared to the variety of ages and experiences usually represented in a semester-long course. I try to encourage discussion and use films to retain the varying perspectives.

A second difficulty arises when topics from a semester-long course are treated as mini-courses. Inevitably, the context and relationship of each topic to others in the course is lost. Each of the subjects has its own history, anatomical and physiological bases, and unique issues and problems within the health care system. However, each topic is, of course, intimately related to almost every other one on the syllabus, since the functioning of one part of a woman's body is interrelated with the functioning of other parts. I find it more difficult to convey this complex interrelationship in a mini-course. I continually struggle to create some of the context that evolves naturally in a semester-long course. I also try to devote some time in each mini-course to provide the theoretical framework for understanding of the position of women vis à vis the medical and scientific establishments. It is more difficult for students to grasp that the particular difficulties surrounding the issues of pregnancy and childbirth (or whatever is the topic of the mini-course) represent part of a larger pattern of difficulties that the health care system presents for women.

I further adapted many of the topics of the course to be given as brief (30–60 minute) lecture-discussions. Very frequently, student groups and organizations within the community wish to sponsor a program on a particular aspect of women's health. Ideal topics for brief discussions include toxic shock syndrome, premenstrual syndrome, venereal disease in women, the "unwoman in science," and the biological reasons for changes during menopause. I really need a longer time frame to discuss in any depth topics such as sexuality, stress, contraception, aging, and menstruation. However, I have given 45-minute presentations followed by discussions on each of those topics to high school groups, women's clubs, and church organizations. Clearly, these brief presentations are even more difficult to set in the context of other women's health issues and show the topic's relationship to the health care system. However, after hearing a brief presentation, many individuals have been inspired to read more about the subject and other issues in women's health. Some have requested to take a mini-course or the semester-long course as a group or as individuals.

USE OF AUDIOVISUAL TAPES AND EQUIPMENT
FOR SELF-INSTRUCTION

Using audiovisual tapes and equipment to provide individualized, self-instruction materials provides a means of bringing the course to individuals whose time, geographic, or physical constraints do not permit them to attend classes. As the popularity increased of Women and Their Bodies in Health and Disease and Biology and Psychology of Women, and as more people became interested in women's health issues after a presentation of a specific topic, I began to receive many requests to teach the course on an individualized basis. I sought and received a grant from the National Science Foundation* to create an individualized, self-instruction version of the course. The basis of the course is a series of 39 audiocassettes, which contain the lectures and discussions of a semester-long session of the course. The audiocassettes are supplemented by ten videotapes of guest lectures and purchased movies (see Table 9.1), to visually demonstrate many of the topics discussed. In addition, a self-paced homework program of fifteen to twenty questions, based on each audiocassette, is available via computer so the student can check her or his understanding of the lectures. (Some students have successfully completed the course using only the audiocassettes; the videotapes and computer package are

Table 9.1. List of Videotapes

"Taking Our Bodies Back"

"The Sexes: Breaking the Barriers"

"Domestic Violence: Breaking the Cycle"

"Woman-Loving Women"

"In the Way of Our Grandmothers"

"Rape/Crisis"

"Through Young People's Eyes"

"Romance, Sex, and Marriage"

"A Woman's Place Is in the House"

"Giving Birth: Four Portraits"

*National Science Grant #SER-8160817: Self instructional materials for the biology of women project from the Local Course Improvement Program (LOCI); September 1981–February 1984.

Figure 9.1. Syllabus and Reading List

Biology of Women and Its Social Implications, to be used
in independent study with audiocassettes

Tape
1. Is anatomy destiny? "The unwoman in science." (Sloane 1–14)
2. Evolutionary and genetic theories of sex determination. (Sloane 97–138)
3. Sociobiology.
4. The unwoman in psychological research. (Williams Chapter 2)
5. Theories of femininity. (Williams Chapter 3)
6. Anatomy of reproduction. (Sloane 15–53)
7. Anatomical methods of birth control. (Sloane 346–349)
8. Birth control. (Sloane 370–403)
9. Biology of hormones. (Sloane 54–71, 347–370)
10. Cycles of reproduction. (Sloane 71–87)
11. EXAMINATION I.
12. Cycles of reproduction and birth control.
13. Psychological aspects of cycles and birth control. (Williams Chapter 4)
14. "The curse."
15. Choosing parenthood. (Sloane 329–345; Williams Chapter 10)
16. Biology of pregnancy. (Sloane 252–291)
17. Biology of pregnancy.
18. Psychology of pregnancy. (Williams Chapter 9)
19. Childbirth. (Sloane 211–323)
20. Childbirth.
21. Psychology of childbirth.
22. Childbirth movie.
23. Postpartum.
24. Lactation. (Sloane 162–170, 323–327)
25. The decision not to have children. (Sloane 403–416)
26. Abortion.
27. Discussion of abortion.
28. EXAMINATION II.
29. Biology of aging. (Sloane 88–96)
30. Psychology of aging. (Williams Chapter 12)
31. Women and mental health. INTERVIEW PAPER DUE.
32. Anorexia and bulimia.
33. Women and nutrition. (Sloane 467–516)
34. Diseases of women: VD. (Sloane 213–233)
35. Diseases of women: Vaginal infections and malignancies. (Sloane 233–251, 170–200)
36. Women and stress.
37. Women and the health care system. (Sloane 417–466, 201–212)
38. Current movements in women's health.
39. Discussion and evaluation of the course.
    FINAL EXAMINATION.

Text
Sloane, Ethel. *Biology of Women.* New York: John Wiley and Sons, 1980.
Williams, Juanita. *Psychology of Women.* New York: W. W. Norton & Co., 1977.

Evaluation
Most questions on the exams may be answered in several words or sentences. The first and second examinations will each count 25 percent of the grade; the final exam, which will be comprehensive, will count 35 percent. The interview paper, which is explained in a separate handout, will count 15 percent towards the final course grade.

Figure 9.2. Outline of Lecture on Hormonal Mechanisms,
Biology and Psychology of Menstrual Cycles

I. Mechanisms of hormone action
   A. Definition of a hormone
   B. Negative feedback mechanism
   C. Pituitary
      1. Neurohypophysis
      2. Adenohypophysis
      3. Hypothalamus
II. Hormones of menstruation
   A. Hypothalamus
      1. FSH-RF
      2. LH-RF
   B. Adenohypophysis
      1. FSH
      2. LH
   C. Ovary
      1. Estrogen
      2. Progesterone
III. Other cycles
   A. Ovarian cycle
   B. Endometrial cycle
   C. Cervical cycle
IV. Toxic shock syndrome
   A. Symptoms
   B. Probable cause
   C. Possible preventive measures
V. Mind-body interactions during the menstrual cycle
   A. Relationship of reproductive and sexual cycles
   B. Secondary amenorrhea
   C. Break-through bleeding
   D. Dysmenorrhea
   E. Menstrual synchrony
   F. Premenstrual syndrome (PMS)
      1. Benedek and Bardwick's work on mood cycles
      2. Dalton's theory
      3. Possible causes and preventives
VI. Conclusions regarding relationship between mind and body cycles

attractive additions but not necessary for grasping the material.) Each student receives a course syllabus (Figure 9.1), an outline of each audiocassette lecture (Figure 9.2), an explanation of the interview paper (Figure 9.3), and a learning contract (Figure 9.4). At the indicated points in the syllabus, the student requests the written examinations, which are sent and returned by mail.

Figure 9.3. Interview Project Guidelines

Your project is to interview one woman with a different life experience or status from your own. Obviously, this will vary depending on your situation, but one kind of person you may *not* choose is a college student. You may want to interview

an older woman	a single parent
a pregnant woman	(or use your imagination)
a housewife and mother	

Plan to spend at least one hour with the woman you interview, and go to the interview with a prepared set of questions. Don't expect to be able to "wing it."

Since one purpose of this project is to get you to think outside of your own experience, we will not suggest specific questions for you to use. The interview should focus either on the effects that a particular biological event (pregnancy, childbirth, menstruation, menopause, abortion) had on her feelings about herself or on the way in which her psychological feelings affected a biological experience. The quality of the questions that you generate will be taken into account in evaluating your project.

You might include questions about

significant life problems
what makes her happy
relationships with women or men or both
feminism
sex roles

Try to link at least some of your questions to subjects we have discussed in class.

Your write-up should be about 2–3 pages—not room enough for a lengthy discussion. Be sure to organize your thoughts before you write. At the end of your report, also include the questions you used.

Thus far, more than 30 students have completed their three semester hours in Women and Their Bodies in Health and Disease using the individualized instruction package. Their grades have been comparable—and usually a bit better—than those of students taking the course in the classroom. Most of the students would have been unable to attend classroom lectures, which was the impetus for them to take the individualized course. Students from as far away from Virginia as Puerto Rico and Louisiana have taken the course using this method and report that they would not have had access to the material without the individualized approach. Others report liking

Figure 9.4. Learning Contract

Adult Degree Program   Independent Study with MBC Faculty Member

To be Typed and Submitted to Academic Counselor

Name: _____   *I. D. Number:* _____

Address: _____   *Contract Beginning Date:* _____

_____   *Contract Completion Date:* _____

Telephone: _____   (4 months after beginning date)

Tutor: _____   *To Be Recorded:* ___ Fall 19 ___

Address: _____   ___ Spring 19 ___

_____   *Academic Counselor:* _____

Telephone: _____   Check One: ___ Directed Study

                                           ___ Nondirected Study

I.   *Title of Learning Contract:* Category _____ Discipline _____

    Level (check one): ___ 199, ___ 299, ___ 399. Semester Hours _____

    Exact Title of this Learning Experience (for transcript): _____

    _____

II.   *General Description of Activity:*

III.   *Reason(s) for Including in Degree Program:*

IV.   *Specific Learning Objectives* (specify learning outcomes in detail):

V. *Learning Activities: (describe methods of study, list resources to be used):*

Methods of study:

Resources:

Texts: Sloane, Ethel, *Biology of Women.* New York: John Wiley & Sons, 1980.
Williams, Juanita. *Psychology of Women.* New York: W. W. Norton &
Co. 1977.

VI. *Evaluation:*

Who will evaluate Learning Contract? _____

How will learning outcomes be evaluated? (For example, tests, exams, papers, etc.)

Gradient Option (check one): _____ P/NC

_____ Letter Grade

VII. *Signatures:*

Student: _____   *Academic Counselor:* _____

Date: _____   *Date:* _____

Tutor: _____   *ADP Director:* _____

Date: _____   *Date:* _____

the audiocassette format so well that they would like most of their courses in this format.

Other, unexpected advantages resulted from having the course available in this format. It allowed students and others not enrolled in the course, who had an interest in a topic, to listen to the tape at their convenience. Students who are enrolled in the class, but miss a lecture or have difficulty with a topic, may also replay the tape as often as desired. Clearly, this format would also make the course available to physically challenged women and women in institutions (prisons, nursing homes, mental hospitals), who do not have access to classes.

The major difficulty with the audiovisual method of self-instruction is its expense, the money and time needed to produce the initial audiocassettes and produce or purchase the videotapes. Some money and time are also required for routine maintenance and replacement of the cassettes. Because of the time and money, I would not recommend undertaking the preparation of such a course using cassettes without some grant or institutional support.

Students become frustrated when they have technical difficulties with the tapes. Also they report missing the interaction of classroom discussions. However, the overwhelming reaction of the students to the individualized self-instruction package has been positive. The package provides access to the course for many women who are not able to attend a traditional classroom.

DEVELOPING MATERIALS FOR PARTICULAR AUDIENCES

Developing materials suitable for particular audiences is an additional way of reaching women, beyond the traditional college-aged student, with the information about their bodies and health. As I suggested previously, mini-courses or lectures to groups on topics such as pregnancy and childbirth will attract individuals of a certain age and interest. Subjects such as menopause and contraception tend to appeal to older and younger women, respectively. The factors in a topic such as stress, an issue not limited to women of a specific age or situation, may be isolated and discussed for women in a particular situation. Some businesses and industries are eager to have their employees discuss those factors in their work environment that create and add to their stress levels. When speaking to such a group of employees, I emphasize factors and choose examples particular to their work environment to illustrate the points I am making about stress. When talking to a group of women whose primary work is done at home, caring for young children all day, I choose very different examples of probable sources of stress in their lives. Discussing a topic with a particular audience can be very rewarding, since the entire group tends to have a strong interest in the subject and has chosen to explore it in depth. The danger, however, is that the group will begin to see its view of the issue as representative of all women. It becomes a constant struggle to include a variety of perspectives on the health issue, especially those of women not represented in the group.

In the future, I hope to devise newer methods to reach increasing numbers of women from different backgrounds and experiences. In the community where I live and work, I hope to make more contacts with women who are in nursing homes, the state mental hospital, and the state prison. By working with people from social service agencies and support groups, I try to learn more about the physically challenged women in the community and modify the course to include their experiences.

People teaching courses similar to this in other communities undoubtedly will think of new and different ways to reach more women. Clearly, a first step in many communities would be to translate or have the course taught in languages other than English. Only when all women have access to knowledge about their bodies and the health care system can they really hope for control over their own bodies. With knowledge and control may come the insights that would lead to the transformation of science and the health care system.

REFERENCE

Boston Women's Health Book Collective. 1984. *The new our bodies, ourselves.* New York: Simon and Schuster, Inc.

5
CONCLUSION

Chapter 10
Positive Rewards from Teaching Science and Health from a Feminist Perspective

The purpose of *Teaching Science and Health from a Feminist Perspective: A Practical Guide* is to provide courses that meet the needs of women currently enrolled in the science and health disciplines and to attract more women to pursue careers in science. My long-term goal, and the goal of many feminists in science today, is to attract enough women into science to build a base large enough to challenge the exclusive, androcentric theories and methods of science and the health care system. Ultimately, this may lead to a reconceptualization of science and health care to include us all — women and people of color, as well as white men.

As I admitted in the Introduction, the length of time that it will take to build that critical mass of women in science and to re-envision scientific theory will most certainly exceed one, if not many, life-times. The forces of resistance to this change are powerful; they dominate the decision-making positions in health and science. Because the people holding these decision-making positions in science and health are overwhelmingly white Western men, the science they have created reflects their perspective. Their responses to challenges to that perspective often attack the gender of the challenger or the "unscientific" (often seen as synonymous with gender) nature of the challenges.

Women scientists and health practitioners who challenge the current methods, theories, and hierarchies run many risks: They are told that they are not really scientists; pure science is "objective" and is not biased by issues such as gender, race, or limited access. They are told that one reason for the lack of any great women scientists is that women in science have often been distracted by these sorts of ancillary interests, which detract from basic research. They are told that in order to survive in the scientific world at all, since they are women, they must work harder and concentrate only on traditional scientific research. They must choose between having a family and having a scientific career, and that they certainly should avoid any involvement in women's studies or the women's movement. They are also aware that it is difficult for a woman in science to receive tenure; they have seen the statistics. They are shown individual examples of women scientists whose work in women's studies was either ignored or counted against them in the struggle for tenure. In short, being a scientist seems to be synonymous with accepting the masculine perspective of the world, so that they are faced with the classic dualistic choice between being a woman and being a scientist.

Why then, if the risks are so great and if one's femininity is placed in direct conflict with one's career choice, should any women in science or health try to teach from a feminist perspective and combine women's studies with science? Women in other disciplines, in the humanities and social sciences, have enumerated the benefits they found from women's studies and research and teaching from a feminist perspective:

1. The interdisciplinary nature of women's studies necessitates learning different methodologies, examining theories, and talking with colleagues from other disciplines, who view issues from varying perspectives. They recall that what originally attracted them to graduate study and academia was the opportunity to learn different methodologies and explore new ideas. However, during their graduate study and particularly since they became professors, they have been increasingly confined in the approaches they use, the subjects they study, and even the colleagues with whom they talk in their own disciplines. Many women report a renewed understanding of old issues and ideas to explore in new subjects as a direct result of the interdisciplinary study and interaction engendered by women's studies.

2. Women in some disciplines in the social sciences and the humanities report that women's studies and the feminist perspective have been on the growing edge of the new breakthroughs in their disciplines. For example, in literature, some of the finest and most respected work is being done by the feminist critics. Feminist theory is seen by many to be the latest in a series of approaches (structuralist, deconstructionist) to the study of a text. In science, for reasons discussed numerous times in this book, the point has not yet been reached where the feminist perspective has this impact. However, my prediction is that when the sciences are reconceptualized from a feminist perspective, the tremendous breakthroughs will rival,

if not surpass, those in molecular biology during the latter half of the twentieth century.

3. Women's studies scholars in the social sciences and humanities discuss the tremendous pleasure and satisfaction they feel from finally reaching the women students with information and theories that include them and are relevant to their lives. The mammoth influx of women students into courses entitled Women in Literature, Women in History, and Psychology of Women demonstrates the hunger of women for knowledge about themselves and their past, which they are not finding in the traditional androcentric curriculum. My experience with teaching courses in health and science also indicates that women have a tremendous desire to know about their bodies and the world in a way that they are not taught in other science and health care courses.

4. Most of the women's studies scholars today were originally trained in traditional disciplines and did their early teaching and research from the androcentric perspective inherent in the usual approach to their discipline. Many of these women report having felt a division between themselves and the material they loved, studied, and taught and, most certainly, between their personal and professional lives. For most women, teaching and doing research from a feminist perspective has been the unifying force that ended that separation.

For example, a colleague, who received her Ph.D. in eighteenth-century French literature in 1960, reports that she perceived herself as never being as interested in Diderot, Voltaire, Rousseau, and Montesquieu as the men in her class. Although she did very well in graduate school, she always felt that she viewed the texts differently from the male professor and felt more distant from the literature. It was not until the 1970s, after some involvement with the women's movement, that she began to think about studying an eighteenth-century female writer (all of the great ones had been men, of course). The woman writer was difficult to read, but she recognized that many of the woman writer's so-called problems were due to the fact that she had always been judged by male standards of excellence and writing style. In understanding the reasons for the writer's choice of words, subject, and style, my colleague became intensely interested in her subject. She no longer felt the distance between herself and the subject nor the conflict within herself as to how this professional work related to her personal life. She recognized that the writer faced many of the same personal and professional obstacles — different education, family expectations, and life experiences from men — that women face today. From the feminist perspective, my colleague was able not only to evolve a different reading and interpretation of the eighteenth-century author, which made the work of Germaine de Stael more understandable, but she was also able to integrate the different forces in her own life.

All of the reasons for teaching and carrying out research from a feminist perspective given by women's studies scholars in the humanities and social sciences would also benefit women who combine women's studies and science. However, for women in science I think that the last reason, the potential to end the division between one's personal and professional lives, is more than a benefit. I believe that for women in science and health care it is an absolute necessity. As long as science is perceived as masculine or unfeminine, women in science have an inherent, difficult division between their personal and professional lives. It is also my contention that an "unfeminine" science will never meet the needs of most individuals. In *Women in Science: Portraits in Transition* (1983), Vivian Gornick documents repeatedly how many women scientists today report that feminism is the one factor that helped them to survive and succeed professionally. With a feminist analysis, women scientists can begin to comprehend why they feel continually discriminated against, frustrated, and divided. Even with few, if any, role models and under the continued pressure to practice science from a masculine viewpoint (their professional life), which may be antithetical to the way they see the world as women (their personal life), many women scientists can begin to cope with the system if they approach it from a feminist perspective. Some, it is true (Gornick 1983) want no more to do with science once their feminist perspective has revealed the deep androcentrism of the current science and health care professions. Most, however, find that the feminist perspective gives them the basis and strength to challenge the current view of science and its methods. A few may even find the roots to begin the reconceptualization of science to include us all. This is the new science that the welfare of women demands and upon which a beneficial role for science and technology in the world of the future may well depend.

REFERENCE

Gornick, V. 1983. *Women in science: Portraits from a world in transition.* New York: Simon and Schuster.

APPENDIX

Course Syllabi

This book was written because I am convinced that there are Science and Health courses being taught from feminist perspectives, but that these courses are unfamiliar to the majority of educators and students. Out of a desire to make information on such courses available, I tried to obtain information on these curricula. I believe that the responses will show that *real* courses are being developed and taught.

The chairpersons of all women's studies programs listed in the *Women's Studies Quarterly* (Fall 1984) were sent a questionnaire and a request for a course syllabus. Responses were returned for 54 courses taught at 36 different institutions. This constitutes an 8.3% response from the 434 institutions to which the questionnaire was sent. Eleven of these courses were from the graduate program in Women, Health and Healing at the University of California, San Francisco. This appears to be an excellent program and the only graduate program in the country dealing with these issues. However, all other responses and syllabi were for undergraduate courses; therefore, the eleven courses from the program in Women, Health and Healing were not included in this survey. Of the remaining 43 responses, 31 were complete (including both the syllabus and questionnaire) and were for science and/or health-related courses (rather than courses in sociology or religion). These 31 courses, from 26 different institutions, make up this appendix. Undoubtedly, those heading some women's studies programs offering courses in science, health, and technology did not respond to the questionnaire; however, a tremendous variety of the types and locations of institutions responded. These responses verify that feminist curricula are being developed and utilized.

Quite a variety of styles and lengths of the syllabi were received. In the interest of creating a uniform and consistent appendix, some information was omitted or edited.

Course Title: Biology and Gender, Women's Studies 530

Credits: 3.

Institution name: University of Wisconsin–Madison.

Name(s) and departmental affiliation(s) of individual(s) teaching this course: Cynthia Cowden, Women's Studies Program, Zoology Department.

Specific information regarding the course:
  Department(s) in which the course is listed: Women's Studies Program.
  Course level and audience for whom it is intended: Advanced.
  Prerequisites: WS 103 – Women's Bodies in Health and Disease; or WS 430 – Biology and Psychology of Women; *and* Introductory Biology or Zoology course.
  Method of instruction: Analysis of books and articles. Emphasis on discussion, like a seminar.

Texts:
  Bleier, Ruth. *Science and Gender.*
  Bulkin, Elly, Minnie Bruce Pratt, and Barbara Smith. *Yours in Struggle.*
  Davis, Angela. *Women, Race, and Class.*

Methods of evaluation: Regular attendance and preparation for class discussions. Attendance at and a written analysis of the Feminist Science Symposium, April 11–12, 2:30–4:30 and 7:30–9:30. Two take-home essay exams.

Brief course description: While sex and sex differences can be biologically described and defined, gender and gender differences are complex social constructs, influenced by one's cultural milieu and history, one's personal history, and by biological factors. Biological and behavioral sciences actively investigate questions of sex and gender differences, and have produced a number of important and influential theories that attribute differences in the economic, political and social positions and accomplishments of the two sexes/genders to differences in evolutionary selection factors and to differences in their brains, hormones, or genes. This course will critically examine the theories and methodologies of the relevant research areas in biology and animal behavior that underlie biological determinist theories and will explore alternative approaches, theoretical constructs and interpretations. This semester our collective effort will be to
  – clarify the interconnectedness of all forms of biological determinism.
  – locate biological determinism in biological and feminist theory and practice.
  – evaluate environmental determinism, codeterminism, and indeterminancy as alternatives to biological determinism for biology and for feminism.

Syllabus

A radical feminist critique of science
    Jan. 22: Introduction
    Jan. 24: *Science and Gender*, Bleier (ch. 1–4)
    Jan. 29: Bleier (ch. 5–8)
Feminist perspectives on racism and antisemitism
    Jan. 31: *Yours in Struggle*, Bulkin, Pratt, Smith (1–87)
    Feb. 5: Bulkin, Pratt, and Smith (91–193)
Racism and classism in the women's movement
    Feb. 7: *Women, Race, and Class.* Davis (ch. 1–7)
    Feb. 12: Davis (ch. 8–13)
Group differences in scientific analysis
    Feb. 21: From sociobiology to sociology, Wilson (reader)
    Feb. 26: IQ: the rank ordering of the world, Lewontin et al. (reader)
              TAKE HOME ESSAY EXAM IS DUE
    Feb. 28: Science and social values, Bleier (class handout)

Analysis of primary literature
    Mar. 5: Aggressivity (reader)
    Mar. 7: Lateralization and cognitive functioning (reader)
    Mar. 12: Testosterone, left-handedness, and math ability (reader)
    Mar. 14: Alternative hypotheses (reader)
           SPRING BREAK
    Mar. 26: Sociobiology, mind and culture (reader)
    Mar. 28: Gene, organism and environment (reader)
    Apr. 2: Determinism in ecology (reader)
    Apr. 4: Metamorphosis in sand dollars: an example (reader)
Feminist science symposium
    Apr. 9: Haraway, Hrdy and Fee (reader)
    Apr. 11: Rose and Hammonds (reader)
           SYMPOSIUM: APRIL 11 AND 12 (2:30–4:30 and 7:30–9:30)
    Apr. 16: Discussion of symposium
    Apr. 18: WRITTEN ANALYSIS IS DUE
Student reports: April 18, 23, 25, 30, May 2, 7
Final summary: May 9 TAKE HOME ESSAY IS DUE

*   *   *   *   *

Course Title: Biology and Gender, US 219

Institution name: Colgate University.
Name(s) and departmental affiliation(s) of individual(s) teaching this course: Vicky
    McMillan, Women's Studies Program, University Studies Division.
Specific information regarding the course:
    Department(s) in which the course is listed: Women's Studies Program (University
    Studies Division).
    Course level and audience for whom it is intended: Freshman–senior undergraduate.
    Prerequisites: None.
    Method of instruction: Lecture/discussion.
Texts: Numerous and varied reading from the biological, psychological, anthropologi-
    cal, and feminist literature bibliography which follows:
    Bem, S.L. "Gender Schema Theory: A Cognitive Account of Sex Typing." *Psycho-
    logical Review*, 1981.
    Bleier R. *Science and Gender*. New York: Pergamon Press, 1984.
    Brack, D.C. "Displaced – The Midwife by the Male Physician." In *Women Look at
    Biology*, 1979.
    Campbell, B. *Sexual Selection and the Descent of Man*. Chicago: Aldine, 1972.
    Clutton-Brock, T.H., and P.H. Harvey. *Readings on Sociobiology*. San Francisco:
    W.H. Freeman, 1978.
    Culpepper, E. "Exploring Menstrual Attitudes." In *Women Look at Biology*, 1979.
    Dawkins, R. *The Selfish Gene*. New York: Oxford University Press, 1976.
    Engels, F. *The Origin of the Family, Private Property, and the State*. New York:
    International Publishers, 1972.
    Fairweather, H. "Sex Differences in Cognition." *Cognition*, 4, 1976.
    Fee, E. "Is Feminism a Threat to Scientific Objectivity?" *International Journal of
    Women's Studies*, 1980.
    Fein, R.A. "Research on Fathering: Social Policy and an Emergent Perspective.
    Journal of Social Issues, 1978.

Friedman, R.C., et al. "Review Essay: Behavior and the Menstrual Cycle." *Signs*, 1980.

Gamble, E.B. *Evolution of Woman: An Inquiry into the Dogma of Her Inferiority to Man.* London, 1849.

Gould, S.J. "Women's Brains." *Natural History*, 1978.

Grossman, M., and P.B. Bart. "Taking the Men Out of Menopause." In R. Hubbard, M.S. Henifen, and B. Fried, eds., *Women Look at Biology Looking at Women.* Cambridge, Mass.: Schenkman Publishing Co., 1979.

Hrdy, S.B. *The Woman That Never Evolved.* Cambridge, Mass.: Harvard University Press, 1981.

Irons, W. "Human Female Reproductive Strategies." In S. Hrdy and G.C. Williams, eds., *Social Behavior of Female Vertebrates.* New York: Academic Press, 1983.

Jacklin, C.N., and E.E. Maccoby. "Issues of Gender Differentiation." In M.D. Levine, W.B. Carey, A.C. Crocker, and R.T. Cross, eds., *Developmental Behavioral Pediatrics.* Philadelphia: Saunders, 1983.

Jagger, A.M., and P.R. Struhl. *Feminist Frameworks.* New York: McGraw-Hill, 1978.

Kaplan, A.G. and J.P. Bean, eds. *Beyond Sex-Role Stereotypes: Readings Toward a Psychology of Androgyny.* Boston: Little, Brown and Co., 1976.

Keller, E.F. "Feminism and Science." *Signs*, 1983.

Kiltie, R.A. "On the Significance of Menstrual Synchrony in Closely Associated Women." *American Naturalist*, 1982.

Kitcher, P. *Abusing Science.* Cambridge, Mass.: MIT Press, 1982.

Leibowitz, L. *Females, Males, Families: A Biosocial Approach.* West Scituate, Mass.: Duxbury Press, 1978.

Lockard, J.S., P.C. Daley, and V.M. Gunderson. "Maternal and Paternal Differences in Infant Carry: U.S. and African Data." *American Naturalist*, 1979.

Longino, H. "Scientific Objectivity and Feminist Theorizing." *Liberal Education*, Fall 1981.

McMillan, C. *Women, Reason and Nature: Some Philosophical Problems with Feminism.* Princeton, N.J.: Princeton University Press, 1982.

Mead, M. *Male and Female: A Study of the Sexes in a Changing World.* New York: Dell Publishing Co., 1949.

Money, J., and A. Ehrhardt. *Man and Woman, Boy and Girl.* Baltimore: Johns Hopkins University Press, 1972.

Morgan, E. *The Descent of Woman.* New York: Stein and Day, 1972.

Notman, M. "Adult Life Cycles: Changing Roles and Changing Hormones." In J.E. Parsons, ed., *The Psychobiology of Sex Differences and Sex Roles.* New York: Hemisphere Publishing Co., 1980.

Parlee, M.B. "The Premenstrual Syndrome." *Psychological Bulletin*, 1973.

Reed, E. *Sexism and Science.* New York: Pathfinder Press, 1978.

Reed, E. *Woman's Evolution: From Matriarchal Clan to Patriarchal Family.* New York: Pathfinder Press, 1975.

Rich, A. *Of Woman Born: Motherhood as Experience and Institution.* New York: Norton, 1976.

Rothschild, J. *Machina Ex dea: Feminist Perspectives on Technology.* New York: Pergamon Press, 1983.

Ruble, D. "Premenstrual Symptoms: A Reinterpretation." *Science*, 1977.

Sayers, J. *Biological Politics.* New York: Tavistock, 1982.

Sherfey, M.J. *The Nature and Evolution of Female Sexuality.* New York: Random House, 1966.

Sherfey, M.J. "A Theory on Female Sexuality." In R. Morgan, ed., *Sisterhood Is Powerful.* New York: Vintage Books, 1970.

Springer, S.P., and G. Deutsch. *Left Brain, Right Brain.* San Francisco: W.H. Freeman, 1981.

Star, S.L. "The Politics of Right and Left: Sex Differences in Hemispheric Brain Asymmetry." In R. Hubbard, M.S. Henifin, and B. Fried, eds., *Women Look at Biology Looking at Women.* Cambridge, Mass.: Schenkman Publishing Co., 1979.

Symons, D. *The Evolution of Human Sexuality.* New York: Oxford University Press, 1979.

Tanner, N.M. *On Becoming Human.* New York: Cambridge University Press, 1981.

Tavris, C., and C. Offir. *The Longest War: Sex Differences in Perspective.* New York: Harcourt Brace Jovanovich, 1977.

Tiger, L. *Men in Groups.* New York: Random House, 1969.

Williams, G.C. *Sex and Evolution.* Princeton, N.J.: Princeton University Press, 1975.

Wilson, E.O. *Sociobiology: The New Synthesis.* Cambridge, Mass.: Harvard University Press, 1975.

Wilson, E.O. *On Human Nature.* New York: Bantam Books, 1978.

Methods of evaluation: Exams, projects, papers, class participation.

Brief course description: This course explores the contributions and limitations of biology in furthering our understanding of gender, and in shaping our attitudes and prejudices about gender-related issues. Topics include the scientific method and societal influences on the development of biological models; "traditional" and feminist conceptions of science; evolutionary and cultural models of sexuality, bonding patterns, sex roles, and parental behavior; human evolution (critical analyses of selected data); sex role stereotypes and gender identification during childhood; sex differences in hormones, cognitive development, athletic abilities, aggression, mortality; and gender-related conditions and illnesses—data, myths, and misconceptions.

Goals of the Course:

1. To teach specific information about the biology of gender using a scientifically accurate but relatively nontechnical approach, to make such material accessible to nonscience students, as well as to those concentrating on biology.

2. To analyze the strengths and weaknesses of the scientific method and the influences of society on the generation of biological models and methodology. Also, to explore the role of misinterpreted or poorly evaluated biological findings in shaping popular attitudes and prejudices about gender-related issues.

3. To critically examine both biological and feminist literature on complex gender-related topics, with the aim of fostering clear thinking and receptivity to new ideas.

4. To augment the Women's Studies course offerings at Colgate by providing a course that evaluates biological perspectives on feminist issues.

Syllabus

Week No.	Date		Topic	Required Readings; Assignments Due
1	*Sept.*	6	Introduction to course	
		7	How science works: introduction to the scientific method; theories and models; strengths and limitations of science and scientists	

(continued)

Week No.	Date	Topic	Required Readings; Assignments Due
2	10	Interplay between science and society: Darwin's theory of evolution, and Social Darwinism	Tanner, Chapter 1
	12, 14	Darwinism updated: brief over-view of modern evolutionary theory	Research Paper topic due (Sept. 12) Symons, Introduction
3	17	Continuing conflicts: Feminism, Sociobiology, and models of human behavior	Hrdy, Ch. 1 and pp. 189–191 Symons, Chapters 1 and 2 Keller, "Feminism and Science" Tanner, Chapter 2 Essay #1 due Parsons, "Psychosexual Neutrality: Is Anatomy Destiny?"
	19	Origins of sexuality: evolutionary models of anisogamy, sexual dimorphism, and reproductive stragtegies in animals	Hrdy, Chapter 2
	21	Promiscuity, polygamy, monogamy; evolutionary models of mating systems in animals	TBA (to be announced)
4	24	Parental investment patterns in animals	TBA
	26, 28	Bonding, mating systems, parental investment, and general social organization in non-human primates: over-view and selected topics	Hrdy, Chapters 3–6 Tanner, Chapters 3–6 (Skim details and focus on major themes in both of these texts) Preliminary bibliography for Review Paper due (Sept. 28)
5	*Oct.* 1 3, 5	Bonding, mating systems, and evolution of the family and sex roles in humans: models and problems	Hrdy, Chapters 7 and 8 Tanner, Chapters 7–11 (Skim details, focus on major themes) Symons, Chapters 4 and 7
6	8, 10	Continued	Irons, "Human Female Reproductive Strategies" Morris, "Origins" Tiger, "The Male Bond and Human Evolution" and "Work and Play" Reed, "Lionel Tiger's 'Men in Groups': Self-

(continued)

Week No.	Date	Topic	Required Readings; Assignments Due
			Portrait of a Women Hater" Morgan, "The Ape Remolded"
6	12	*Guest Lecture:* Ms. MaryAnne Sydlik, Department of Biology, Syracuse University. Informal coffee meeting with speaker follows; students welcome.	
7	15	Male and female biology: genetics of sex determination; embryology of anatomical sex differences	
	17	Physiology of human reproduction	Symons, Chapter 3 Hrdy, Chapter 8 (review) Ledwitz-Rigby, "Biochemical and Neuro-physiological Influences on Human Sexual Behavior"
	19	Menstruation: myths, facts, and theories	Culpepper, "Exploring Menstrual Attitudes" Kiltie, "On the Significance of Menstrual Synchrony in Closely Associated Women"
8	22	Childbirth: some biological and historical aspects	Rich, "Alienated Labor" Griffin, "Cows"
	24	MID-TERM EXAM	
	26	*MID-TERM RECESS*	
9	29	Sex-related changes in later life: menopause, aging, mortality	Notman, "Adult Life Cycles: Changing Roles and Changing Hormones
9	31	Sex-role stereotypes and gender identification during childhood: scientific and feminist perspectives; models and problems (Includes NOVA film, "The Pinks and the Blues," on Nov. 7)	Jacklin and Maccoby, "Issues of Gender Identification" Petersen, "Bio-psychosocial Processes in the Development of Sex-related Differences"
	Nov. 2	Continued	Bem, "Gender Schema Theory: A Cognitive Account of Sex Typing"
10	5, 7, 9	Continued (with NOVA film on Nov. 7)	

(continued)

Week No.	Date	Topic	Required Readings; Assignments Due
11	12	Functional significance of sex differences in the brain—*Guest Lecture:* Dr. Scott Kraly, Department of Psychology, Colgate	Springer and Deutsch, "Sex and Asymmetry" Essay #2 due
	14	Sex differences in the brain, continued	Gould, "Women's Brains"
	16	Aggression and gender	Symons, Chapter 5 Hrdy, Chapter 4 (review)
12	19	Rape—evolutionary, sociological, and feminist viewpoints	Symons, Chapter 8
	21, 25	*THANKSGIVING RECESS*	
13	26	Sex differences in size, strength, and athletic ability: data and misconceptions	Gould, "The Oddball Human Male"
	28, 30	Sex differences in parenting: are women predestined to be better parents than men?—and other questions	Review material on gender identification (influences of parents) Lockard et al., "Maternal and Paternal Influences in Infant Carry..."
14	Dec. 3	Homosexuality	TBA
	5	Women's health: gender-related illnesses	TBA
	7	FILM: Women's Health: A Question of Survival	Essay #3 due
15	10	Biology and Gender: Summary and Over-view	Review Paper due

*   *   *   *   *

Course Title: Biology and Health of Women, Biology Workshop (630-490)

Institution name: University of Wisconsin at Whitewater.
Name(s) and departmental affiliation(s) of individual(s) teaching this course: Jeanne A. Griffith, M.D., M.P.H., Director, Student Health Service.
Specific information regarding the course:
   Department(s) in which the course is listed: Biology.
   Course level and audience for whom it is intended: Open to graduate and undergraduate men and women. Graduate credit in Biology with approval of advisor. Credit toward minor in women's studies.

Prerequisites: None.
Method of instruction: Lecture/discussion.
Texts:
   Sloane, Ethel. *Biology of Women.* New York: John Wiley & Sons, 1980.
Methods of evaluation: Examination based upon written objectives given for each
   week of the course; required paper.
Brief course description: This course has been offered twice as a once-a-week workshop to make it more available to part-time or returning students, thus one-
   2½-hour session per week. The backgrounds of the individuals vary but, overall,
   most have had little biology.
      We review briefly the definitions of biology and the basic structure of cells and
   the major organs of the body. From that background, we then cover the normal
   stages of growth and development of the female through the life stages with pertinent, related health/illness topics.
      Students are introduced to broad health-planning issues and the topics to be
   understood by the informed consumer.
      In summary, this course could be defined as a survey of topics involved in the
   biology and health of women.
Other features of the course: We make generous use of "resource" people: a midwife,
   the teacher of Lamaze method, a Laleche League person, professionals with particular expertise such as an eating disorders counselor or a recovering female alco-
   holic. These individuals provide depth and a look at "the real world" of women's
   health issues.

Syllabus

January 23   Introduction and goals
             Requirements: Text
                           Immunization history
                           Research paper
                           Quizzes and final exam
                           Objectives for each session
                           Use of 3 × 5 cards for each class period
                              (Questions, need for clarification, evaluation)
             Overview of health
             Gross anatomy of female organs of reproduction and external genitals
             Film strip: *The Cell* (10 min.)

January 30   Read: Chapters 2 and 3
             "Build a body" — basic body parts
                (Bring scissors, paste or glue, crayons or colored pens/pencils)
             The menstrual cycle
             Film: *Achieving Sexual Maturity* (21 minutes)

Feburary 6   Read Chapter 5
             Subject for research paper must be submitted and approved by this date
                (submit topic on 8 × 11 paper)
             Embryology
             Adolescent development, Tanner staging
             What is growth and development?
             Film strip: *Meiosis and mitosis* (11 minutes)
                         DNA and RNA and a look into the future (15 minutes)

February 13 Quiz — 30 minutes
             Read Chapters 6, 8, and 9 to p. 222
             Sexuality in women

The gynecological examination
Common gynecological problems
Film strip: *Blueprint for Life* (14 minutes)
            Biography of the Unborn (17 minutes)

February 20   Read Chapter 10 to p. 323
              Diagnosis of pregnancy, body changes, complications
              Preparation for childbirth
              High risk pregnancies
              Resource person: Kathy Haven, Lamaze method teacher
              Film: teaching film used for Lamaze classes

February 27   Birth
              Midwifery
              Significance of child spacing, number of children
              Resource person: Midwife, to be arranged

March 5   Read Chapters 4, 7, and 10 (pp. 323-327)
              The mammary glands
              Menopause and aging
              Toxic shock syndrome
              Resource person: Mrs. Barbara Krahn from Laleche League

March 12   30 minute quiz
              Read Chapter 12
              Control of fertility
              Film: *Choice Is Yours (The Sex Quiz)* (32 minutes)

March 19   Read Chapters 9 (pp. 237–251) and 11
              Fertility
              Infertility
              Cancer: smoking, DES, BSE, risk factors
              Resource person: Chong Merz, Lab. technologist

April 2   Read Chapter 9 (pp. 222–237)
              Immunization records due
              Sexually transmitted diseases
              Urinary tract infections
              Film: *VD: Old Bugs, New Problems* (20 min)

April 9   Eating Disorders
              Obesity
              Resource persion: Ruth Swisher, R.N.

April 16   30 minute quiz
              Read Chapter 1
              Research papers due
              Self-care
              Is an annual exam necessary? What are women's health screening
                  needs?
              Selecting a physician. Getting into a system of health care.
              Prevention of diseases of mid and late life

April 30   Read Chapter 13
              Common surgical procedures
              Hysterectomy and the second opinion
              Women and medications
              Women and alcohol
              Resource person: Jean Sable will present "Please Remember Me" (a
                  dramatization)

May 7   Read Chapter 14
            Is war a women's health issue? Effects of radiation on reproduction.
            Is violence a women's health issue? Rape and sexual assault.
            Film: "If You Love This Planet."

May 14   Final exam, 6–8 pm

*   *   *   *   *

Course Title: Biology of Women

Institution name: Mankato State University.
Name(s) and departmental affiliation(s) of individual(s) teaching this course: Dr. Verona D. Burton, Biology.
Specific information regarding the course:
  Department(s) in which the course is listed: Biology.
  Course level and audience for whom it is intended: Freshmen.
  Prerequisites: None.
  Method of instruction: Lecture/discussion.
Texts:
  Sloane, Ethel. *Biology of Women*, New York: John Wiley and Sons, 1980.
Methods of evaluation (e.g. exams, journals, projects, papers): Exams.
Brief course description: This course is designed to introduce students to the biological basis of women's development. The subjects surveyed include reproductive anatomy, menstrual cycle, hormones, menopause, basis of biological differences between women and men, female sexuality, mammary glands, gynecology, pregnancy, labor, and delivery, problems of infertility and fertility, and cancer.

Syllabus

January 4   Introduction
January 11   Reproductive Anatomy, Chapter 2
January 18   Menstrual Cycle, Hormones, and Menopause, Chapters 3 and 4
January 25   The Basis of Biological Differences, Chapter 5
February 1   Female Sexuality; Mammary Glands, Chapters 6 and 7
February 8   Gynecology, Chapters 8 and 9
February 15   Pregnancy, Labor and Delivery, Chapter 10
February 22   Problems of Infertility and Fertility, Chapters 11 and 12
March 1   Women as Consumers, Chapters 13 and 14
March 8   Final Exam

*   *   *   *   *

Course Title: Biology of Women, Bio 318, WS 318

Institution name: Eastern Washington University.
Name(s) and departmental affiliation(s) of individual(s) teaching this course: Gertrude L. (Lee) Swedberg, Assistant Professor of Biology and Director of Women's Programs.

Specific information regarding the course:
  Department(s) in which the course is listed: Biology Department and Women's
    Studies Program.
  Course level and audience for whom it is intended: 300 level, but for the non-major
    (Biology).
  Prerequisites: English facility.
  Method of instruction: Lecture/discussion.
Texts:
  Sloane, Ethel. *Biology of Women.* Other reading will be on reserve at the library.
Methods of evaluation: Exams, papers, family research exercise.
Brief course description: In this course we will examine biological principles as they
    apply specifically to the human female. The functions of menstruation, meno-
    pause, pregnancy, contraception, postpartum, and lactation — unique to women
    though rarely discussed in elementary biology courses — are part of essential
    knowledge for women.
      The course is not limited to biological principle. Female body functions have
    traditionally and historically been intertwined with social and psychological fac-
    tors. Genetic and reproductive engineering may alter the human biological future
    by affecting women's reproductive limits and possibilities. These topics and the
    controversies surrounding them will also be discussed.

Syllabus

Date	Lecture-Discussion	Reading
Week 1	Historical Tradition	Text, Chap. 1
	Biological Control Systems	Chap. 3, pp. 54–57
	Reproductive Anatomy	Chap. 2
Week 2	Puberty and the Menarche	Chap. 3
	The Menstrual Taboo	Paula Weideger, *Menstruation and Menopause*
	Hormonal Relationships	Chap. 4
Week 3	The Menstrual Cycle	Text, Chap. 2
	Menopause	Chap. 4
Week 4	Chromosomes and Sex Determination	Chap. 5
	Sexual Dimorphism	
	Female Sexuality	Chap. 6
Week 5	Disease of Women — Gynecological	Chap. 9
	Disease of women — Cancer	
Week 6	Pregnancy and Birth	Chap. 10
	Postpartum and Lactation	
Week 7	Midterm or Paper Due	
	Hormones and Behavior	Chap. 7
	Fertility and Infertility	Chap. 11
Week 8	Contraception	Chap. 12
	Abortion	
Week 9	Reproductive Engineering	Steinbacher, "Preselection of
	Implications of Reproductive	Sex." Nelkin, "Tempest in
	Engineering	a Test Tube"

(continued)

Date	Lecture-Discussion	Reading
Week 10	Diet	Chap. 13
	Exercise	Chap. 14
Week 11	Social and Emotional Passages	Weideger, Chap. 8; Sheehy, *Passages*
	(Papers Due)	

*   *   *   *   *

Course Title: Biology of Women, Zoology 206

Institution name: University of Wisconsin, Milwaukee.
Name(s) and departmental affiliation(s) of individual(s) teaching this course: Ethel Sloane, Assoc. Prof., Dept. of Biological Sciences.
Specific information regarding the course:
   Department(s) in which the course is listed: Department of Biological Sciences.
   Course level and audience for whom it is intended: Sophomore and above.
   Prerequisites: Basic course in Biology.
   Method of instruction: Lecture.
Texts:
   Sloane, Ethel. *Biology of Women*, 2nd ed. New York: John Wiley & Sons, 1985.
Methods of evaluation: Exams.
Brief course description: Course Objectives:
1. To question the traditional assumptions about women's anatomy and physiology and evaluate the basis for current knowledge.
2. To present and analyze recent research findings and to stimulate new ideas about research on women.
3. To demystify medicine, dispel myths, and objectively separate fact from fiction on all aspects of biology of women.
4. To enable students to (a) recognize quality and competence in health care; (b) make informed choices about their own health; and (c) become better informed health care consumers.

Syllabus

Date	Topic	Assignment
Aug. 29	Issues of Women's Health	Chapter 1
Sept. 5	Reproductive Anatomy	Chapter 2
12	Endocrine System; Ovarian and Uterine Cycles	Chapter 3 (54–72)
19	Menstrual Disorders, Dysmenorrhea, Amenorrhea, Toxic Shock, Endometriosis, PMS	Chapter 3 (72–87)

(continued)

Date	Topic	Assignment
26	Menopause, ERT, Risks and Benefits	Chapter 4
Oct. 3	EXAM I Cells and Cell Division	Chapter 5
10	Genetic Defects Sex Differentiation Sex Differences	Chapter 5
17	Female Sexuality	Chapter 6
24	Mammary Glands Breast Cancer, Diagnosis and Treatment	Chapter 7
31	Pelvic Exam/Vaginitis, Gynecological Difficulties	Chapters 8, 9
Nov. 7	STD's	
14	EXAM II Pregnancy	Chapter 10
21	Teratology; Childbirth Alternatives	Chapter 10
28	Infertility; New Technologies of Treatment Contraception	Chapters 11, 12
Dec. 5	Health and the Working Woman	
	FINAL EXAM, Wednesday, December 12, 5:30 p.m.	

*   *   *   *   *

Course Title: Childbirth in the United States, WS 431

Institution name: University of Wisconsin – Madison.
Name(s) and departmental affiliation(s) of individual(s) teaching this course: Judith
    W. Leavitt.
Specific information regarding the course:
    Department(s) in which the course is listed: Women's Studies; History of Medicine;
        History of Science.
    Course level and audience for whom it is intended: Intermediate/advanced.
    Prerequisites: Junior–senior standing.
    Method of instruction: Lecture/discussion/seminar.
Texts:
    Rich, Adrienne. *Of Woman Born* (For graduate students only).
    Leavitt, Judith. *Women and Health in America.*
    Wertz, Richard and Dorothy. *Lying-In: A History of Childbirth in America.*
    Buss, Fran. *La Partera.*
    Romalis, Shelly. *Childbirth: Alternatives to Medical Control.*

Methods of evaluation: Exams, class participation, document analyses.

Brief course description: The course examines women's childbirth experiences through American history, analyzing the processes through which change occurred in birth attendants, interventions used, and birth location. It provides historical perspective on women's options in the late twentieth century and concentrates on understanding the complex interactions of factors that led to where we find ourselves today. Students will be expected to develop their own analyses of the processes of change through analyzing historical documents and fitting them into a broad sociohistoric context.

Syllabus

January 22   Introduction
No required readings

January 24   The Childbirth Experience
Film: "A Baby is Born"
Reading: Bromberg, "Having a Baby" in Romalis, pp. 31–62
431 Reader, "Manual of Obstetrics," Chapter 25

January 29   The Decision/Birth Control and Abortion
Film: "Do I Really Want a Child?"
Reading: Gordon, "Voluntary Motherhood" in Leavitt, pp. 104–116
Mohr, "Patterns of Abortion" in Leavitt, pp. 117–123

January 31   Childbirth and Women's Health
Reading: 431 Reader, Robert Wells, "Women's Lives Transformed"
Franklin Newell, "Effect of Overcivilization"

February 5   Analyzing the Childbirth Experience
Reading: 431 Reader, "Letters to Mamie Goodwater"
"Letter from Rose Williams to Lettie Mosher"
WRITTEN ASSIGNMENT DUE: FIRST DOCUMENT ANALYSIS

February 7   Pregnancy
Film: "When Life Begins"
Reading: 431 Reader, Theobald, "Normal Midwifery"

February 12   Anticipation
Reading: Leavitt & Walton, "Down to Death's Door" in Leavitt, pp. 155–165
431 Reader, "Elizabeth Gordon Correspondence"

February 14   Social Childbirth
Reading: Wertz and Wertz, Chapter 1, pp. 1–28
431 Reader, "Martha Ballard Diary"

February 19   Midwives
Reading: Donegan, "Safe Delivered" in Leavitt, pp. 302–317
Kobrin, "American Midwife Controversy" in Leavitt, pp. 318–326

February 21   Midwives
Film: "All My Babies"
Reading: Dye, "Mary Breckinridge" in Leavitt, pp. 327–344

February 26   Midwives
Reading: *La Partera*
WRITTEN ASSIGNMENT DUE: SECOND DOCUMENT ANALYSIS

February 28   Physicians
Film: "Semmelweis"

Reading: Sholten "Importance of Obstetric Art" in Leavitt, pp. 142–154
   Wertz & Wertz, Chapter 2, pp. 29–76

March 5   Physicians
   Reading: Drachman, "Loomis Trial" in Leavitt, pp. 166–174
   431 Reader, "H.B. Willard Obstetrical Journal"

March 7   Gender in the Birthing Room
   Reading: Smith-Rosenberg, "Female World" in Leavitt, pp. 70-89
   Morantz and Zschoche, "Professionalism, Feminism, and Gender
   Roles," in Leavitt, pp. 406–421

March 12   Analyzing the Change in Attendant
   Reading: Wertz & Wertz, Chapter 3, pp. 77–108
   431 Reader, Williams, "Medical Education and the Midwife Problem"
   DeLee, "Progress toward Ideal Obstetrics"

March 14   *EXAM IN CLASS*

March 19–21   Spring Recess

March 26   Drugs and Instruments of Birth
   Reading: Wertz & Wertz, Chapter 4, pp. 109–131
   431 Reader, Harris, "A Pair of Obstetrical Forceps"
   Ford, "Use of Drugs in Labor"

March 28   Anesthesia
   Reading: Leavitt, "Birthing and Anesthesia" in Leavitt, pp. 175–184
   431 Reader, Meigs and Simpson, "On Chloroform"
   Longfellow, Diary excerpts

April 2   Interventions and Safety
   Reading: 431 Reader: Mendenhall, "Prenatal and Natal Conditions in Wisconsin"

April 4   Location of Birth
   Reading: 431 Reader, Williams, "A Criticism of Certain Tendencies"
   Zinke, "Mortality and Morbidity"

April 9   Birth Moves to the Hospital
   Film: "Giving Birth" or "Not Me Alone"
   Reading: Wertz & Wertz, Chapter 5, pp. 132–177

April 11   Analyzing the Changes in Interventions and Location
   Reading: 431 Reader, McCormick Letters
   Davis, "The Need of Hospitals"

April 16   Complications
   Film: "Four Births"
   Reading: 431 Reader, Reynolds, "Major Obstetrical Operations"

April 18   Postpartum
   Film: "Are You Ready for the Postpartum Experience?"
   Reading: 431 Reader, "Bessie Rudd Letters"
   Longo, "Rise and Fall" in Leavitt, pp. 270–284
   WRITTEN ASSIGNMENT DUE: THIRD DOCUMENT ANALYSIS

April 23   Natural Childbirth
   Reading: Wertz & Wertz, Chapter 6, pp. 178–200
   Romalis, pp. 63–91

April 25   Childbirth and Public Policy
   Reading: Wertz & Wertz, Chapter 7, pp. 201–233
   Lubic, "Alternative Maternity Care" in Romalis, pp. 217–249

April 30   Women and Birth at the End of the Century
    Reading: Wertz & Wertz, pp. 234–248
              Barbara Rothman, "Awake and Aware" in Romalis, pp. 150–180

May 2   Analyzing the Process of Change, the Role of Gender, the State of Scholarship
    Reading: Jordan, "Studying Childbirth" in Romalis, pp. 181–216
              Morantz, "Perils of Feminist History" in Leavitt, pp. 239–245

May 7   Graduate Students

May 9   Final

Questions for Document Analysis

1. Who wrote the document?
2. Why was the document written?
3. To or for whom was the document written?
4. When was the document written?
5. What is the subject matter of the document?
6. How close was the writer to the events described?
7. What is the document's point of view?, i.e., What does the document say about the events described?
8. What are the biases or interests of the writer?
9. What are the biases or interests of the person or persons to whom the document is addressed?
10. How closely does the document correspond to what really happened?
11. In what ways does the document enlighten our understanding of what happened?
12. In what ways does it obscure what happened?
13. What was the effect of this document having been written?
14. Into what social, political, economic, or cultural context does the document fit?
15. What is the historiographic context into which this document fits?
16. What do you think is the significance of this document?
17. How does this document fit with other documents?
18. What information or other documents would we need to place this document in its historic context and establish its historiographic importance?

    Films also can be documents. Use similar questions to those above to think about and analyze the films we will see in class.
    The three written assignments comprising document analyses will be organized the following way:

1. The first will be based on a document or documents in the 431 Reader and will be specifically assigned in class.
2. The second can be based on a document or documents the student locates herself, or possibly one the student creates through oral histories.
3. The third will be an integrative analysis of five or more documents, some of which may be from the 431 Reader, but at least three of which must be student located.

    In all cases, an important part of the assignment will be to precisely identify the source and full citation for the documents under analysis and to xerox and append to the paper the complete documents.

For discussion

    There are certain questions and themes that will be important for us all semester. Thinking about these when you read and when you plan for class discussion will help move us along.

1. What were women concerned about before their births? How did they prepare for their confinements?

2. How did women feel about their birth experiences? How did age, sexual preference, socioeconomic class, ethnic or racial background, or marital status affect their experiences? Did women get what they wanted? Analyze their choices and their control.
3. How much did women decide about the kind of birth to have? How much did they want to decide? Who or what influenced their choices? How did this influence their control during their confinements? How much choice did women have?
4. What was the role of the birth attendant in the decision-making process? In the confinement itself?
5. What supports did the women have, or not have, or want?
6. What birth interventions were used by the birth attendant? Who decided what would be used?
7. Did the location of the birth affect the above issues? How and why? Who decided on the location and how did it fit with other parts of the experience?
8. Identify the strictly medical parts of the birth experience. Identify the strictly social parts. Mixed?
9. How much power do women have to determine their own labors and deliveries? How has this changed over time?

What is the meaning and function of history?

Which of the statements quoted below do you think best represents history's function and why?

1. History is the witness of the times
   The light of truth
   The life of memory
   The teacher of life
   The messenger of antiquity
                          Cicero

2. History is the record of what one age finds worthy of note in another.
                          Jakob Burkhardt

3. History is indeed little more than the register of the crimes, follies, and misfortunes of mankind.
                          Edward Gibbon

4. History is made out of the failures and heroism of each insignificant moment.
                          Franz Kafka

5. History is just one damn thing after another.
                          Anon.

6. The subject of history is the life of peoples and of humanity.
                          Leo Tolstoy

7. Human history is in essence a history of ideas.
                          H. G. Wells

8. The history of the world is the record of man in quest of his daily bread and butter.
                          Hendrik Van Loon

9. The function of history is to promote our understanding of the past in light of the present, and of the present in light of the past.
                          E. H. Carr

10. Those who cannot remember the past are condemned to repeat it.
                          George Santayana

11. Throughout his long existence, man has been not only a problem-maker, but also a problem-solver. This is the most important lesson of world history. Problems will

appear; they will be resolved; others will take their place; they in turn will be solved. The process is inevitable and without end. It is the way of human progress and civilization.

T. Walter Wallbank

12. The history of the world is but the biography of great men.

Thomas Carlyle

*   *   *   *   *

Course Title: Contemporary Issues in Women's Health & Health Care, HSCA 620

Institution name: University of Kansas.
Name(s) and departmental affiliation(s) of individual(s) teaching this course: Dr. Mary Zimmerman, History and Health Services.
Specific information regarding the course:
   Department(s) in which the course is listed: History; Health Services; Women's Studies.
   Prerequisites: None.
   Method of instruction: Lecture/discussion.
*Texts:*The following books will be supplemented by journal articles and chapters as indicated in the course outline. Additional supplementary material will be drawn from the Vital and Health Statistics Series of the National Center for Health Statistics (USDHHS).
   Marieskind, Helen. *Women in the Health Care System.* St. Louis: Mosby, 1980.
   Fee, Elizabeth, ed. *Women and Health: The Politics of Sex in Medicine.* Baywood, 1983.
   Lorde, Audre. *The Cancer Journals.* Spinsters Ink, 1980.
Methods of evaluation: Exams, class participation, class project.
Brief course description: In this course, we will develop and critically analyze a profile of the current health status and health needs of women in the U.S. We will also focus on historical trends in health and health care in relation to changing patterns in the social position and roles of women. A major analytic concern will be to explore the way that lay, medical, and research assumptions about women have developed and have influenced the existing clinical and scientific literature about women's health and the structure of health services as they relate to women's health care needs. The course also will examine the Women's Health Movement in terms of its origins, its theoretical perspectives, its organization, its programmatic aims, etc. Topical areas which will be covered in the course include chronic illnesses such as heart disease, hypertension, and cancer; reproductive health and childbirth; occupational health hazards; mental health; physical and sexual abuse; and eating disorders, as well as the position and roles of women as health care providers.
Syllabus

| Week 1 | Aug. 23/25 | A feminist approach to women's health: origins and significance. |
| Week 2 | Aug. 30/Sept. 1 | An overview of women's health status. Sex differences in morbidity and mortality. |

(1) Marieskind, Chapter 1.
(2) Constance Nathanson, "Illness and the Feminine Role," *Social Science and Medicine*, Vol. 9 (1975)
(3) Ingrid Waldron, "Why Do Women Live Longer Than Men?" *Social Science and Medicine*, Vol. 10 (1976).
(4) Lois M. Verbrugge, "Recent Trends in Sex Mortality Differentials in the U.S.," *Women and Health*, Vol. 5 (Fall, 1980).

Week 3   Sept. 6/8   Issues in the measurement of illness and the use of health services. Poverty and women's health.
(1) Marieskind, Chapter 2.
(2) Diane Pearce, "The Feminization of Poverty: Women, Work and Welfare," *The Urban and Social Change Review*, Vol. 11, Nos. 1 & 2 (1978).
(3) Lois Verbrugge, "Female Illness Rates and Illness Behavior: Testing Hypotheses About Sex Differences in Health," *Women and Health*, Vol. 4 (Spring, 1979).
(4) Stephen Cole and Robert Lejeune, "Illness and the Legitimation of Failure," *American Sociological Review*, Vol. 37 (June, 1972).

Week 4   Sept. 13/15   Theoretical perspectives on women's health and health care.
(1) Fee, Chapter 1 ("Women and Health Care: A Comparison of Theories").
(2) Marieskind, Chapter 8 ("Women's Health Activism").
(3) Helen Bequaert Holmes and Susan Rae Peterson, "Rights Over One's Own Body: A Women-Affirming Health Care Policy," *Human Rights Quarterly*, Vol. 3, No. 2 (Spring, 1981).

Week 5   Sept. 20/22   Medical education, the doctor-patient relationship, and women.
(1) Jeanne C. Quint, "Institutionalized Practices of Information Control," *Psychiatry*, Vol. 28 (1965).
(2) Diana Scully and Pauline Bart, "A Funny Thing Happened on the Way to the Orifice: Women in Gynecology Textbooks," *American Journal of Sociology*, Vol. 28, No. 4 (January, 1973).
(3) Sandra Danziger, "The Uses of Expertise in Doctor-Patient Encounters During Pregnancy," *Social Science and Medicine*, Vol. 12 (1978).
(4) Selections from Margaret Campbell, *Why Would a Girl Go Into Medicine?* The Feminist Press, 1973.

Week 6   Sept. 27/29   Control of reproduction: political history of birth control and abortion. Contemporary trends and services.
(1) Marieskind, pp. 235-247; 103-106.
(2) Fee, Chapter 8 ("The Politics of Birth Control...").
(3) "The Physicians' Crusade Against Abortion, 1857-1880," in James C. Mohr, *Abortion in America*, Oxford University Press, 1978.

(4) pp. 151–198 in Mary Zimmerman, *Passage Through Abortion: The Personal and Social Reality of Women's Experiences*, Praeger, 1977.

(5) Pauline Bart, "Seizing the Means of Reproduction: An Illegal Feminist Abortion Collective—How and Why It Worked," in Helen Roberts (ed.), *Women, Health and Reproduction*, Routledge and Kegan Paul, 1981.

Week 7   Oct. 4/6

Women's health movement. Women's clinics, self care.

(1) Selections from *How to Stay Out of the Gynecologist's Office*, Federation of Feminist Women's Health Centers, 1981.

(2) Chapter 3 ("The Rise of the Women's Health Movement") and Chapter 6 ("Strategies for Change") in Sheryl Ruzek, *The Women's Health Movement*, Praeger, 1978.

FILM: "Healthcaring: From Our End of the Speculum."

Week 8   Oct. 11/13

Rape and physical abuse.

(1) Lynda Lytle Holmstrom and Ann Wolbert Burgess, "Rape and Everyday Life," *Society*, July/August, 1983.

(2) Diana E. H. Russell and Nancy Howell, "The Prevalence of Rape in the United States Revisited," *Signs: Journal of Women in Culture and Society*, Vol. 8, No. 41 (1983).

(3) Fee, Chapter 9 ("Medicine and Patriarchal Violence: The Social Construction of a 'Private' Event").

(4) Kathleen Ferraro and John M. Johnson, "How Women Experience Battering: The Process of Victimization," *Social Problems*, Vol. 30, No. 3 (February, 1983).

(5) Ann Douglas, "Soft-Porn Culture," *New Republic*, Vol. 183 (Aug. 30, 1980).

(6) Susan Brownmiller, "Women Fight Back," in *Against Our Will: Men, Women and Rape*, Simon and Schuster, 1975.

Week 9   Oct. 18/20

Pregnancy and childbirth: socio-historical perspectives on ownership (definition and treatment). Current childbirth alternatives.

(1) Marieskind, Chapter 7 and pp. 117–127.

(2) Fee, Chapter 2 ("The Convenience and Occurrence of Births...").

(3) Richard Wertz and Dorothy Wertz, "Notes on the Decline of Midwives and the Rise of Medical Obstetricians," in P. Conrad and R. Kern (eds.) *The Sociology of Health and Illness*, St. Martins, 1981.

(4) Barbara Katz Rothman, "Midwives in Transition: The Structure of Clinical Revolution," *Social Problems*, Vol. 30, No. 3 (February, 1983).

		(5) Chapter VI ("Negotiating to Do Surgery") in Diana Scully, *Men Who Control Women's Health*, Houghton Mifflin, 1980.
Week 10	Oct. 25/27	Cancer: epidemiology, personal realities, and health care services.

Week 10   Oct. 25/27

Cancer: epidemiology, personal realities, and health care services.
(1) Audre Lorde, *The Cancer Journals*.
(2) Fee, Chapter 3 ("Vaginal Cancer: An Iatrogenic Disease?").

Week 11   Nov. 1/3

Cardiovascular disease and women. Employed women and the stress hypothesis.
(1) Fee, Chapter 6 ("Employment and Women's Health: Analysis of Causal Relationships").
(2) Mary Ann Haw, "Women, Work and Stress: A Review and Agenda for the Future," *Journal of Health and Social Behavior*, Vol. 23, No. 2 (June, 1982).
(3) Suzanne Haynes and Manning Feinleib, "Women, Work and Coronary Heart Disease," *American Journal of Public Health*, Vol. 70, No. 2 (February, 1980).
(4) Mary Zimmerman and Wynona Hartley, "High Blood Pressure Among Employed Women...," *Journal of Health and Social Behavior*, Vol. 24, No. 1 (March, 1983).
(5) Lois Verbrugge, "Multiple Roles and Physical Health," *Journal of Health and Social Behavior*, Vol. 24, No. 1 (March, 1983).
(6) Ingrid Waldron, *et al.*, "Reciprocal Effects of Health and Labor Force Participation Among Women: Evidence from Two Longitudinal Studies," *Journal of Occupational Medicine*, Vol. 24, No. 2 (February, 1982).

Week 12   Nov. 8/10

Occupational health hazards and politics.
(1) Fee, Chapters 5 and 7.
(2) Maraieskind, Chapter 5.

Week 13   Nov. 15/17

Mental health.
(1) Dorothy E. Smith, "Women and Psychiatry," in Dorothy Smith and Sara David (eds.), *Women Look at Psychiatry*, Vancouver: Press Gang, 1975.
(2) Walter R. Gove and Jeannette F. Tudor, "Adult Sex Roles and Mental Illness," *American Journal of Sociology*, Vol. 78 (January, 1973).
(3) Sarah Rosenfield, "Sex Differences in Depression: Do Women Always Have Higher Rates?" *Journal of Health and Social Behavior*, Vol. 21, No. 1 (March, 1980).
(4) Nancy M. Henley, "Assertiveness Training: Making the Political Personal," 1979 (mimeo).

Week 14   Nov. 22/24

Eating disorders.
(1) Chapters 3 and 4 in Kim Chernin, *The Obsession: Reflections on the Tyranny of Slenderness*, Harper and Row, 1981.

(2) Chapters 5 and 10 and Appendix III in Marchia Millman, *Such a Pretty Face: Being Fat in America*, Norton, 1980.
(3) Stanley M. Garn and Patricia Cole, "Do the Obese Remain Obese and the Lean Remain Lean?" *American Journal of Public Health*, Vol. 70, No. 4 (April, 1980).
(4) Selected Tables from National Centre for Health Statistics, "Obese and Overweight Adults in the U.S.," *Vital and Health Statistics*, Series 11, No. 230 (February, 1983).

Week 15   Nov. 29/Dec. 1   Student presentations.

*   *   *   *   *

Course Title: Discovering Women in Science

Credits: 1.
Institution name: Eastern Washington University.
Name(s) and departmental affiliation(s) of individual(s) teaching this course: Gertrude L. (Lee) Swedberg, Assistant Professor of Biology and Director of Women's Programs.
Specific information regarding the course:
 Department(s) in which the course is listed: Women's Studies Program; Biology; Chemistry; Physics; Geology; Education; History; Psychology.
 Course level and audience for whom it is intended: 300 level.
 Prerequisites: None.
 Method of instruction: Lecture/discussion, slides, and a panel of women scientists from the local area.
Texts: No assigned reading, but students are asked to prepare a written project.
Methods of evaluation: One credit course. The class meets on one day a week and turns in a paper at the end of the quarter.
Brief course description: Most of us, even those with good science backgrounds, would be hard pressed to name more than a few women contributors to science beyond Madame Curie. Both women and men, therefore, tend to think of science as an exclusively male area. The neglect of women in science texts and histories of science is unfortunate, not only because it may be an indirect reason for fewer women entering the field than would otherwise, but also because it is not justified. Numerous women can be mentioned whose contributions have advanced all the major fields of science.

 This workshop course will develop six twentieth century themes of science through the women whose work and discoveries contributed to them. You will see their faces and discuss their work. Each scientist is presented with a slide of her and her work, if appropriate, and her work is followed into the contributions of another woman until the theme has been completed. You will also meet a number of women scientists from the Spokane area with whom you can discuss the ramifications of careers in science for women.
Other features of the course: The instructor tells the class at the beginning that the class is not a "fair" course, since she does not mention the names of the men in the field. That is her intention because she is trying to make the point about the neglected contributions of women.

Syllabus

I. **Historical Western Overview**
    Mesopotamian midwife, Egyptian physician, Greek thought (Aspasia), Early
    Christian physician, Alexandria as center of scientific thought (Hypatia), The
    Middle Ages (Trotulla and Saint Hildegard, Abbess of Bingen), The Renaissance,
    The Enlightenment (Maria Agnesi, Emilie d'Breteiul, Sophie Germain, Mary
    Fairfax Somerville, Sonya Krukovsky Kovalevsky).

II. **Fragmenting the Atom**
    Radioactivity and atomic theory (Marie Curie), artificial radioisotopes (Irene
    Joliot Curie), splitting the atom (Lise Meitner), the atomic nucleus – shell model
    theory (Maria Mayer), the atomic nucleus – parity (Chien Shiung Wu), radio-
    isotope application – radioimmunoassay (Roslyn Yalow).

III. **Exploring the Infinitely Vast**
    Mapping and naming stars and comets (Caroline Herschel), comets and sunspots
    (Maria Mitchell), standard comparison stars (Williamina Fleming), periodicity
    and distances (Henrietta Leavitt), spectral analysis (Annie Cannon), the first pul-
    sar (Jocelyn Bell), quasars and stellar elements (Margaret Burbidge).

IV. **Medicine, the Greatest Battle**
    First American crusader (Hariot Hunt), early Americans to open medical schools
    (Elizabeth Blackwell, Marie Zakrzewska, Mary Jacobi, Mary Walker), early
    English pioneers (Elizabeth Garret Anderson, Sophia Jex-Blake), lymphocytes
    and blood vessels (Florence Sabin), heredity and cancer (Maud Slye), carbohy-
    drate metabolism (Gerti Core), structure of penicillin (Dorothy Hodgkin), the
    first good fungicide (Elizabeth Hazen and Rachel Brown), prostaglandin inhibi-
    tors for dysmennorhea (Penny Wise Budoff).

V. **Rescuing the Public Health**
    Modern nursing (Florence Nightingale, Marie Zakrzewska), public health nursing
    (Lillian Wald), water purification (Ellen Richards), industrial medicine (Alice
    Hamilton), refrigeration and milk inspection techniques (Mary Pennington), vita-
    min D and U.S. nutritional standards (Hazel Stiebeling), purification of tubercu-
    lin (Florence Seibert), FDA standards (Barbara Moulton, Frances Kelsey and
    Helen Taussig), DPT vaccine (Pearl Kendrick and Grace Eldering).

VI. **The Microstructure of Life**
    Sex chromosomes (Nettie Stevens), X-ray crystallography technique (Dorothy
    Hodgkin), crystallography of DNA (Rosalind Franklin), cytoplasmic inheritance
    (Ruth Sager), cellular evolution (Lynn Margulis), T & B lymphocytes (Lois
    Epstein), genetic engineering (Beatrice Mintz).

VII. **The World Around Us**
    First American naturalist (Jane Colden), collecting in the world's outback (Ynes
    Mexia, Mary Brandegee, Elizabeth Britton, Alice Eastwood), invertebrates
    (Cornelia Clapp), first anthropogeographer (Ellen Churchill Semple), limnoria
    (Dixy Lee Ray), lichens (Beatrix Potter), early humans (Mary Leakey), primate
    behavior (Jane Goodall), the environmental movement (Rachel Carson), bringing
    ecology to industry (Ruth Patrick).

*   *   *   *   *

Course Title: Female Sexuality

Institution name: University of Wisconsin, Platteville.
Name(s) and departmental affiliation(s) of individual(s) teaching this course: Elaine
  Wheeler, Women's Studies.
Specific information regarding the course:
  Department(s) in which the course is listed: Women's Studies.
  Course level and audience for whom it is intended: 300 level, but all levels of under-
    graduate students are admitted and occasional graduate students.
  Prerequisites: None.
  Method of instruction: Lecture, discussion, guest panels.
Texts:
  A Woman's Experience of Sex.
  The New Our Bodies, Ourselves. 1984 ed.
  Seizing Our Bodies (optional).
Methods of evaluation: Exams and one 8–10-page paper.
Brief course description: An inquiry into the nature of sexuality for women, including
  the sexuality of pregnancy and childbirth with the objective of increasing students'
  tolerance for a wide range of sexual behavior and enhancing the sexuality aspects
  of students' lives now and throughout their life span. Additionally, students are
  introduced to the process of feminist inquiry.
Other features of the course: An emphasis is put on the range of sexual lifestyles present in women's lives. A panel of women talk about their lives, which includes sex
  for money, monogamy (heterosexual), violence and its consequences, living
  together without desire for marriage, sex and love between women, celibacy. This
  is always very well received and students indicate that their attitudes change in the
  direction of increased tolerance and even appreciation for differences.

Syllabus

Topics Included: Origins of Attitudes Toward Sex, Sexism
                   Sexual Fantasy as Enhancer
                   Range of Adult Sexual Expression
                     a. Self-pleasuring
                     b. Same-sex interactions
                     c. Opposite sex interactions
                   Physiology of Sexual Response
                   Deciding About Sex
                   Communicating About Sex
                   Health Risks Associated with Heterosexuality
                     a. Birth control, abortion, pregnancy
                     b. Sexually transmitted diseases
                   Sexuality of Pregnancy, Birthing, and Breastfeeding
                   Sex, Power, and Violence
                   Sexual Lifestyles

Attendance: Regular attendance in class is expected since material will be pre-
                   sented in class on topics not included entirely in assigned reading.

*   *   *   *   *

Course Title: Feminist Perspectives on Women's Health, WOMS 325

Institution name: Sonoma State University.
Name(s) and departmental affiliation(s) of individual(s) teaching this course: Adele Clarke and Ruth Mahoney, Women's Studies Program.
Specific information regarding the course:
  Department(s) in which the course is listed: Women's Studies Program.
  Course level and audience for whom it is intended: Upper division—anyone may take this course (i.e., nurses from the Nursing Department or Women's Studies minors).
  Prerequisites: None.
  Method of instruction: Lecture/discussion.
Texts:
  Boston Women's Health Book Collective. *The New Our Bodies, Ourselves*, 3rd ed. New York: Simon and Schuster, 1984.
  Claudia Dreifus (ed.). *Seizing Our Bodies: The Politics of Women's Health*. New York: Vintage, 1978.
Methods of evaluation: Exams, class participation, special projects (research paper, critical review of books, student's own idea).
Brief course description: This is an introductory course on contemporary issues in women's health from feminist and women's health movement perspectives of "enhancing control of our bodies ourselves." This is intended as a survey course; adequate theory and research exist on most of the topics for an entire course to be devoted to them. Our basic approach is to provide on each topic both basic information on its physical and psychosocial dimensions and an analysis of related historical and current issues through feminist perspectives on health care politics. As in many areas of health today, there is considerable controversy about many of the topics; we attempt to present these debates clearly. Our overall goal is to improve our capacity to act as health care consumers and to forge feminist understanding of women's health concerns.

Syllabus

1/31   *INTRODUCTION: WOMEN, HEALTH AND MEDICINE*
        Provides an introduction and overview of the course.
        What is a femininist perspective on women's health?
        Brief overview of the women's health movements, women as providers and patients in health systems; origins and development of the issues addressed here.
        SLIDE SHOW: "Women Health Workers" by Phila Wmn's Hlth Coll.
        REQUIRED READING:
          HANDOUTS: B. Ehrenreich: "Our Bodies—Their Sales"
          D. Ruscavage: "How to be Your Own Second Opinion"
          Gena Corea: THE HIDDEN MALPRACTICE [CH. 4—The Patient/ Doctor Relationship]
          NWHN: Occupational Health History Form
          DREIFUS: Fee: "Women and Health Care: A Comparison of Theories" pp. 279–297. VERY IMPORTANT
          Weiss: "What Med. Students Learn About Women" pp. 212–222
          Brown: "Women Workers in Health Serv. Ind." pp. 235–250.

2/7   *SELFHOOD AND THE POLITICS OF APPEARANCE*
        The notion of selfhood includes the implicit right of self-definition and determination both independently and through relationships with others.

It encompasses physical, social and psychological dimensions. Appearance is one dimension which has been and continues to be especially important about women and to women ourselves. Class includes personal aspects of appearance ("standardized beauty" and its implications for self-concept and identity development); the beauty and fashion industries; the meanings of appearance to all women, especially women who do not "fit": big women, women of color, physically disabled women.

FILM: "Killing Us Softly" on women and advertising.

BEGIN HEALTH HERSTORIES: Each class member does an outline of her personal health history from birth to now. Ruth & Adele will go first. 10 min max. Do written outline to hand in.

REQUIRED READINGS:
    HANDOUTS: Alta: "Pretty"
        Disabled Women's Coal.: "Taking Our Bodies Back"
    OBOS: Changing Sense of Self pages TBA
    READER: Judy Chicago: "Waiting"
        K. Ryce: "Loving My Fat Body"
        K. Chernin: "In Praise of Large Women: The Body Holds Meaning" from THE OBSESSION
        Rodriguez-Rasor: "Sterilization of the Self"
        J. Randal: "Bigger Breasts NOT Necessarily Better"
        J. James: "...Black Women in Media Advertisements"
        R. Decker: "The Not So Pretty Risks of Cosmetics"
        Cheryl Clarke: "Hair"

2/14   *FEMALE CYCLE FROM BIRTH THROUGH MENSTRUATION*
POTLUCK Anatomy and physiology of females from birth through menstruation: development of reproductive system, hormonal cycles, problems of menstruation (PreMenstrual Syndrome [PMS], amenorrhea, dysmenorrhea). Recent research and treatment alternatives. Experiential aspects of menstruation; cultural myths & stereotypes.

CONTINUE HEALTH HERSTORIES.

REQUIRED READINGS:
    OBOS: on menstrual and hormone cycles: pp. TBA
    READER: G. Steinem: "If Men Could Menstruate"
        Birke & Best: "Changing Minds: Women, Biology & the Menstrual Cycle"
        A. Eagan: "The Selling of PreMenstrual Syndr."
        Second Opinion: Premenstrual Syndrome Issue
        L. Pogrebin: "Parenting: Talking About Menstruation"
        K. Wanda: "Tampons Can Be Harmful to Health"
        J. Beck and C. Oram: "Tampons: Beyond TSS"
        BWHBC: "Dear Women" letter for action on tampons
        Seaman & Seaman: "Home Cures for Those Days"
    RECOMMENDED READING: The journal WOMEN AND HEALTH Vol. 8, #2/3, Summer/Fall 1983 is a Special Double Issue on Lifting the Curse of Menstruation: A Feminist Appraisal of the Influence of Menstruation on Women's Lives. Excellent: in Library.

2/21   *RACE, CLASS AND WOMEN'S HEALTH ISSUES*
Race, class and gender are the three factors most determinant of health status (degree of well-being). In this session we examine the relations of class and race to feelings about our bodies, kinds of anticipated illnesses and health problems, available medical, prenatal and gynecological care, modes of care delivery and problems in the doctor/patient relationship.

REQUIRED READINGS:
OBOS: Ch. on American Health Care System, pp. TBA
DREIFUS: Baker: "The Class Factor: Mountain Women"
   Ehrenreich & English: "Complaints and Disorders: Sexual Politics of Sickness" pp. 43-56.
READER: H.D. Schwartz & C. Kart: "General Characteristics of Health & Health Care in America"
   V. Navarro: "The Underdevelopment of Health of Working America"
   A. Sablosky & R. Studley: "A Perspective on Health Care and Women in the Mississippi Delta"
   R. Dunbar: "Poor White Women"
   J. Malveaux: "Three Views of Black Women"
   Richmond: "The Silent Killer: High Blood Pressure"
   E. Maslow: "Storybook Lives: Growing Up Middle Class"
   D. D'Amico: "To My White Working Class Sisters"
   Second Opinion: Special Issue on Women of Color and Health Care
   R. McKnight: "Organizing for Community Health"
   R. Toneye: "Institutional Racism in the Med. Profn"
RECOMMENDED READINGS: see bib/ask instructors.

2/28   *THE PRACTICE AND POLITICS OF BIRTH CONTROL*
Session focused on history of the birth control movement and current methods of birth control. Anatomy and physiology of the major methods: barriers (foam, condom, jellies, diaphragms, cervical caps, sponge), pills, IUDs, sterilization (various methods), injectables (Depo Provera), abortion (aspiration, dilatation and curettage, labor induction). Why did/do we need a birth control movement? Why do we have the methods of birth control we do? Why are there few male contraceptives?
REQUIRED READINGS:
OBOS: pages TBA
READER: L. Gordon: "Birth Control: Historical Study"
   Kash: "Birth Control Survey: Steriliz. Tops"
   Berkeley Women's Health Coll.: "Birth Control Methods and Effectiveness Rates"
   Korenbrot: "Value Conflicts in Biomedical Research into Future Contraceptives"
   Blake: "Contraceptive Industry: Who Calls Shots?"
   Eagan: "The Contraceptive Sponge: Safe?"
   Amirrezvani: "The Today Sponge"
   Culverwell: "Is There a Cervical Cap in Your Future?"
   Wolfson: "The Reselling of the Pill"
   CARASA: "Methods of Sterilization"
   Kasindorf: "The Case Against IUD's"
   Shainwald: "Suing for Dalcon Shield Injuries"
   Rakusen: "Depo Provera: Extent of the Problem"
   CDRR: "[California] Cuts in Contraceptive Services"
DREIFUS: Sharpe: "Birth Controllers" pp. 57-74
   Dowie & Johnson: "A Case of Corporate Malpractice & the Dalcon Shield" pp. 86-104
   R. Arditti: "Have You Wondered Re Male Pill" pp. 121-130
   B. Seaman: "Dangers of Oral Contraceptives" pp. 75-84
RECOMMENDED READING: See Holmes et al: BIRTH CONTROL AND CONTROLLING BIRTH. Humana Press, 1980.

3/6   *REPRODUCTIVE RIGHTS: ACCESS/COERCION/POPULATION CONTROL*

This session is focused on the *politics and economics* of contraception and reproduction. We will distinguish among six major approaches including population control, anti-abortion and emphasizing the feminist movement for reproductive rights for all people. Focus on abortion, sterilization abuse and Depo Provera qua contraceptive imperialism.

REQUIRED READINGS:

READER: Clarke: "What ARE Reproductive Rights: A Comparison of Major Perspectives on Reproduction"

E. Frankfurt and Kisling: "Investigation of a Wrongful Death: Rosie Jimenez"

D. English: "The War Against Choice"

R2N2: "Cook County: Back to Coathangers"

Copelon: "Abortion Rights: Where Do We Go Next?"

CDRR: "Resolution on Disability & Repro. Rights"

CDRR: "Medicaid Funding Facts"

CARASA: "Abortion Cutbacks and Ster. Abuse"

Akwesasne Notes: "Killing Our Future"

CARASA: "Ster. NOT as Simple as Tying Your Tubes"

Wagman: "US Goal: Sterilize Millions of World's Women"

Clarke: "Subtle Sterilization Abuse"

Finger: "Cut in Waiting Period to Increase Abuse"

B. Ehrenreich, M. Dowie & S. Minkin: "The Charge Gynocide/The Accused: U.S. Gov't."

DREIFUS: Dreifus: "Abortion: For Remembrance" pp. 131–145

Dreifus: "Sterilizing the Poor" pp. 105–121.

3/13   *PREGNANCY AND CHILDBIRTH*

Session provides an historical overview of the experience of and issues in childbirth, the medicalization of childbirth and illegalization of midwifery at the turn of the century, puerperal fever, hospitalization as physicians' strategy, and the identicality of maternal and infant safety issues raised in 1933 and today.

The anatomy and physiology of pregnancy and childbirth, normal and complicated births, Caesarian sections and labor induction and their inappropriate and overuse, drugs, "natural" and autonomous childbirth movement, breastfeeding, miscarriage and other issues.

REQUIRED READINGS:

DREIFUS: A. Rich: "The Theft of Childbirth"

Spake: "The Pushers" [on DES]

OBOS: Pregnancy and Childbirth: pages TBA

READER: Ruzek: "Ethical Issues in Childbirth Technology"

Hard Facts: Infant Mortality & Lack of Prenatal Care"

W. Reed: "Suffer the Children: Some Effects of Racism on the Health of Black Infants"

H. Graham & A. Oakley: "Competing Ideologies of Reproduction: Medical and Maternal Perspectives on Preg."

Welch & Herman: "Why Miscarriage Is So Misunderstood?"

The Pregnant Patient's Bill of Rights

Frate et al: "Behavioral Reactions PostPartum"

Reviews of 'Choices in Childbirth' & 'Experience of Breastfeeding' & 'To Love and Let Go'

Helen Marieskind: "Caesarian Section"

Dowie & Marshall: "The Bendectin Cover-Up"
Sipe: "The Wonder Drug to Worry About" DES
P. Wetherill: "DES Exposure: A Continuing Disaster"
Abramson: "Policy Decisions in Prenatal Diagnosis: Example of
  Fetal Alcohol Syndrome"
Lainson: "Breast-Feeding: Two New Views"
Sprague: "Birth Defects by the Cup"
RECOMMENDED READINGS: There is lots in bibliography & see
  esp. the Fall/Winter 1982 WOMEN AND HEALTH Vol. 7, #3–4
  Issue on "Obstetrical Intervention & Technology in the 1980s" and
  Holmes et al., BIRTH CONTROL AND CONTROLLING BIRTH.
  Humana Press, 1980.

3/20   *DISABLED WOMEN'S ISSUES/REPRODUCTIVE TECHNOLOGIES*
We link these issues together because of their immediate relation to one
another. The technologies are commonly related to disability issues – and
often promote negative views of disability.
First, we address the diversity of disabling conditions, myths and stereotypes of disabilities, sexuality, contraception and the special needs of disabled women, and the consequences of disability for obtaining adequate
medical care.
Reproductive technologies of all kinds are proliferating. Many aid people
in addressing infertility, so we cover this here, along with Pelvic Inflammatory Disease (PID) which often causes infertility. We then review the
major reproductive technologies (amniocentesis, artificial insemination,
"test tube" babies, embryo transfer, ultrasound) – what they do and don't
do – and discuss the politics of their use and misuse and their implications.
GUEST LECTURE: (Hopefully) Anne Finger
REQUIRED READINGS: DISABILITY
  OBOS: pages TBA
  READER: excerpt from TOWARD INTIMACY: Family Planning and
      Sexuality Concerns of Physically Disabled Women
    Daniels: "Critical Issues in Sexuality & Disability"
    Resources: Sex Education for Disabled People
    Sprague: "Disabled Women & the Health System"
    Fine & Asch: "The Question of Disability & Reproductive Rights"
    A. Finger: "Disability and Reproductive Rights"
    A. Finger: "Baby Doe: A Complex Issue"
    A. Finger: "Feds Try to Enforce Care of Disabled Infants"
REQUIRED READINGS: INFERTILITY & REPRO. TECHNOLOGIES
  OBOS: pages TAB
  READER: United Press: "Infertility of U.S. Women Rises"
    Cooke & Dworkin: "Take Male Infertility Seriously"
    Coman: "Trying and Trying to Get Pregnant"
    Population Reports: "Infertility and STDs"
    Fugh-Berman: "Fetal Surgery: A Woman's Choice"
    Rothman: "How Science Is Redefining Parenthood"
    Schmeck: "New Help for Infertile Women"
    Hubbard: "Human Embryo and Gene Manipulation"
    Hubbard: "The Case Against Test-Tube Babies"
  RECOMMENDED READINGS: See esp. Holmes, et al., THE
    CUSTOM-MADE CHILD? Humana Press, 1980.

| 3/27 | SELF-HELP, BREAST SELF-EXAM, VAGINAL AND BLADDER |

3/27   *SELF-HELP, BREAST SELF-EXAM, VAGINAL AND BLADDER*
CLASS   *INFECTIONS*
AT HOME   This optional session is devoted to learning how to do a basic gynecologi-
OF A   cal self-examination through visual exam and use of the speculum with the
STUDENT   assistance and supervision of a Registered Nurse. Basic vaginal health and
   common disorders are discussed. The value and methods of basic Breast
POTLUCK   Self-Exam in early cancer detection are discussed and demonstrated. Our
goals are to learn prevention and early detection.
REQUIRED READINGS: [even if you don't attend]
     OBOS: pages on vaginal infections, self-exam TBA
     DREIFUS: E. Frankfurt: "Vaginal Politics" pp. 263–270
     HANDOUTS: "Hormonal Cycle Self-Exam"
     READER: "All About Kegels"
       Hasselbring: "Every Woman's Guide to Vaginal Infections"
       Bell: "Reclaiming Reproduction Control: Natural Family Plan"
       Reviews of 'No Pill No Risk Birth Control' and 'When BC Fails:
         How to Abort Ourselves'
       Ritz & Simons: "Bladder Infections"
       Gillespie & Margolis: "Cystitis Can Be Cured" & resp.
     RECOMMENDED READINGS: NWHN Booklet on Self-Help

4/3   *LESBIAN LIFESTYLE AND HEALTH ISSUES*
Session examines lesbian lives, lifestyles and a wide variety of lesbian
health issues. Includes a bit of history, sexuality, alternative insemination
as it particularly relates to lesbians desiring children, mental health, special clinics which attend to lesbian health care in a supportive environment.
FILM–MAYBE: "In the Best Interests of the Children"
RECOMMENDED READINGS:
     OBOS: pages TBA
     READER: Second Opinion: "Lesbian Health in a Straight World" –
       whole issue.
     M. O'Donnell: "Lesbian Health Care"
     J. Grahn: "Lesbians as Bogeywomen"
     L. C. Pogrebin: "Raising Free Children"
     Lewis: "Rites of Passage" [excerpt from SUNDAY'S WOMEN: Les-
       bian Life Today.]
     Due: "Love and Dr. Kinsey"
     HANDOUT: Ginny Vida: "Coming Out As Process"

4/10   *SEXUALITY: ANATOMY, PHYSIOLOGY AND EXPERIENTIAL*
ASPECTS
Women's sexuality is only recently becoming well understood. Session
examines the anatomy and physiology of human sexual response through
recent research; social and cultural images and expectations of sexuality
(especially women's) both historically and contemporarily; the implications of the 1960s "sexual revolution" and the current "backlash" against
it; the sexual politics of developing a sexual identity and a self-defined
sexuality (including homoerotic, heterosexual and homosexual); the new
"tyranny" of orgasm; problems with "phallocentric" heterosexuality;
relations of love and intimacy to sex; and sexually transmitted diseases
(STDs) including Herpes.
SLIDE SHOW: "Women's Bodies: Diversity and Commonality"

REQUIRED READINGS:
   OBOS: pages TBA
   READER: Koedt: "Myth of the Vaginal Orgasm"
      McCord: "The G Spot"
      English and Ehrenreich: "Sexual Liberation: The Shortest Revolution"
      Rotkin: "The Phallacy of our [Hetero] Sexual Norm"
      Rubin: "The Marriage Bed" from WORLDS OF PAIN
      Piercy: "The Turn On of Intimacy"
      Vitale: "A Herstorical Look at Some Aspects of Black Sexuality"
      J. Snow: "All We Really Are Is Open"
      Orlando: "Bisexuality: A Choice Not an Echo"
      Bogle and Shaul: "Still a Woman—Still a Man"
      Morgan: "Sex After Hysterectomy"
      Gonzales: "La Chicana: Malinche or Virgin?"
      Ehrenreich et al: "Report on the Sex Crisis"
      Nelson: "Is There Lust After Feminism?"
      Watkins: "STDs and the Black Female"
      Second Opinion: "Herpes Issue"
   RECOMMENDED READINGS: There is quite a bit on this—see bibliography for refs and project ideas.

4/17   *SPRING BREAK—NO CLASS—ENJOY*

4/24   *VIOLENCE AGAINST WOMEN: PHYSICAL AND MENTAL ASPECTS*
          Among the most difficult, painful, stressful and unhealthy relations of women in the social environment are the various forms of violence directed particularly (though not exclusively) against women. This session provides a brief overview of the physical and mental health aspects of incest, porn, sexual harassment, rape, and woman battering. Sexual slavery and genital mutilation are covered as well. We focus on feminist institutional responses and interventions for women as "survivors" rather than only as victims.
          FILM: "Battered Wives"
          REQUIRED READINGS:
             OBOS: pages TBA
             HANDOUTS: J. Gingold: "POW Right in the Kisser"
                Weber: "Sexual Abuse Begins at Home"
                Griffin: "Politics" [Rape the All American Crime]
             READER: Anon: "Incest: Personal Testimony"
                L. Van Gelder: "Street Porn"
                A. Walker: "Porn at Home"
                Lindsay: "Sex Harassment on the Job"
                A. Davis: "Rape from a Black Woman's Perspective"
                R. Morgan & G. Steinem: "The International Crime of Female Genital Mutilation"
                Smith: "Alcoholism: Violence Against Lesbians"
             RECOMMENDED READINGS: There is a huge literature on each of these problems—not all of it good. If you want help, we can guide you to the best through the bibliography.

5/1   *THE WOMEN'S HEALTH MOVEMENTS*
          The theories, analyses and methods of the women's health movement are the roots of this course and have informed our perspectives throughout. This large, vital international movement is examined in this session.

Includes educational and publication efforts, modes of direct feminist service delivery and their larger implications for medicine, its relation to other health movements (holistic and community health), its various organizational forms and chosen tasks, and the newly emerging Black Women's Health Movement.

REQUIRED READINGS:

DREIFUS: Fee: "Women and Health Care: A Comparison of Theories"

READER: Ruzek: Contents & chap. "Social Movements and Social Change" from THE WOMEN'S HEALTH MOVEMENT

Clark: "Reaganomics and Women's Health"

Hinton-Hoytt: "Sick and Tired of Being Sick and Tired"

Eisen: "I'm Sick and Tired of Being Sick and Tired" and "Black Women Mobilize for Health"

Ruzek: "Medical Response to Women's Health Activities Conflict, Accommodation and Cooptation"

Marieskind and Ehrenreich: "Toward Socialist Medicine: The Women's Health Movement"

Pubs. List from National Women's Health Network

DREIFUS: Marieskind: "Women's Health Movement: Past Roots" pp. 3–12

Fruchter et al: "The Women's Health Movement" pp. 271–278

OBOS: pages, if any, TBA

5/8   ISSUES IN WOMEN'S HEALTH: OCCUPATIONAL HEALTH, CANCER, BREAST CANCER, CERVICAL DYSPLASIA, HYSTERECTOMY

On each issue, we present the anatomy and physiology of the condition/disease, range of current treatments, controversies surrounding treatments (usually the women's health community versus medical community). Goal is *both* increased capacity to cope when such problems beset us and our friends, and the capacity to wade through present and future treatment debates to fight for safer, less intrusive treatments.

REQUIRED READINGS:

OBOS: pages TBA

DREIFUS: Seaman: "The Dangers of Sex Hormones" pp. 167–177

Kushner: "The Politics of Breast Cancer" pp. 186–194

Larned: "Epidemic in Unnecessary Hysterectomy" pp. 195–209

READER: CRROW Fact Sheet: "Workplace Hazards to Reproduction"

Stellman and Henifin: "No Fertile Women Need Apply: Employment Discrimination and Reproduction Hazards"

McAllister: "Carcinogen Information Program: What Is Cancer?"

Horowitz: "Why There Is NO Cancer Prevention"

Mann: "Cystic Breasts — A Condition, Not a Disease"

Napoli: "Breast Cancer: Truth About Early Detection"

Napoli: "Breast Cancer: An Update"

Belson: "Breast Reconstruction" [after mastectomy]

Second Opinion: "PAP Smears: How Often Necessary?"

Clarke & Reaves: "Dysplasia: Ambiguous Condition"

Brown: "DES Daughters: Warning on Cryosurgery Continued"

Patterson: "Cervical Cancer: A Feminist Critique"

Goldberg: "Fighting Cancer and the Medical Establishment: Two Women's Experiences"

Davies: "A Consumer's Guide to Hysterectomy"

Review of Morgan: COPING WITH HYSTERECTOMY

5/15   *WOMEN AND AGING: MENOPAUSE, OSTEOPOROSIS, ETC.*
A variety of new health issues affect us as we age—from issues of decreased social worth and their consequences for our mental health, to economics to physical health. In this session, we examine these issues plus: menopause (anatomy/physiology/cultural myths and stereotypes) and symptomatic treatments (ERT, nutrition); osteoporosis (fragile bones) and its prevention or minimization; sexuality issues; the feminization of poverty and its impact on older women.
REQUIRED READINGS:
  OBOS: pages TBA
  DREIFUS: Seaman: "Dangers of Sex Hormones" pp. 172–176
    Reitz: "What Docs Won't Tell You Re Menopause" pp. 209–211
  READER: Moss: "It Hurts to Be Alive and Obsolete"
    Smith-Yokel: "A Five Minute Summary of 78 Years"
    Rule: "Grandmothers"
    P. Bart and M. Grossman: "Menopause"
    Offit: "Sexuality: The Facts of Later Life"
    Findlay & Leibman: "Brittle Bones" [Osteoporosis]
    Brody: "Scary Results of Calcium Deficiency"
    Cooke and Dworkin: "Last Rights"
    MacDonald: "Barbara's Afterwords" [excerpt from LOOK ME IN THE EYE]
    Ambrogi: "Feminization of Poverty Examined"
    Options: "Seniors and Prescription Drugs"
  RECOMMENDED READINGS: Seaman and Seaman: Women and the Crisis in Sex Hormones. See bib.

5/22   *MENTAL HEALTH, ALCOHOLISM AND DRUG PROBLEMS*
Physical and mental health are deeply intertwined as are aspects of women's lives which "drive us crazy." Session examines linkages between these, a quickie overview of psychological theories of women and feminist critiques, emerging feminist theories and therapies, patterns in the institutionalization of women. Linked to mental health is the overprescription of psychoactive drugs for women—prescribed drug abuse. We also address drug abuse and alcoholism as women's issues.
REQUIRED READINGS:
  OBOS: pages, if any, TBA
  READER: B. Walker: Psychology & Feminism"
    P. Chessler: "Women and Madness" [excerpt]
    S. Kaplow: "Getting Angry"
    J. Syfers: "Why I Want a Wife"
    S. Griffin: "The Sink"
    A. Kaplan: "Androgyny as a Model of Mental Health for Women: from Theory to Therapy"
    E. Johnson: "Reflections on Black Feminist Therapy"
    DeMonteflores: "Conflicting Issues: Therapy Issues with Hispanic Lesbians"
    Rubin: "Clinical Issues with Disabled Lesbians"
    Psychotherapy and the Asian-American Woman
    I. Wolcott: "Women and Psychoactive Drug Use"
    Options: "Fact Sheets on Women's Drug and Alcohol Abuse"
    Sandmeier: "The Scope of the Problem" [excerpt from THE INVISIBLE ALCOHOLICS]
    O'Donnell et al.: "Alcoholism and Co-Alcoholism: There Is a Solution [from LESBIAN HEALTH MATTERS]

Hochschild: "Smile Wars: Counting the Casualties of Emotional Labor"

5/29   *WRAP UP AND FINAL EXAMS DUE*
POTLUCK ALL CLASS REQUIREMENTS MUST BE MET BY CLASS TIME. We will have a potluck, some student presentations of special projects, do class evaluations and deal with any leftover issues.

*   *   *   *   *

Course Title: History of American Medicine, Hist 64

Institution name: Kenyon College.
Name(s) and departmental affiliation(s) of individual(s) teaching this course: Joan Cadden, History Department.
Specific information regarding the course:
  Department(s) in which the course is listed: History.
  Course level and audience for whom it is intended: Introductory level seminar.
  Prerequisites: None.
  Method of instruction: Seminar.
Texts:
  Brown, E. Richard. *Rockefeller Medicine Men: Medicine and Capitalism in America.* Berkeley and Los Angeles: University of California Press, 1979.
  Curtis, James L. *Blacks, Medical Schools, and Society.* Ann Arbor: University of Michigan Press, 1971.
  Ehrenreich, Barbara, and Deirdre English. *For Her Own Good: 150 Years of the Experts' Advice to Women.* Garden City, N.Y.: Anchor Press/Doubleday, 1978.
  Haller, John S. *Outcasts from Evolution: Scientific Attitudes of Racial Inferiority, 1859-1900.* Urbana, Chicago, London: University of Illinois Press, 1971.
  Haller, John S., and Robin M. Haller. *The Physician and Sexuality in Victorian America.* New York and London: W. W. Norton, 1977 (orig. ed. 1974).
  Ivie, Sylvia Drew. "Health Care Access: If You're Black* (*Brown, Native American, Asian...) Stay Back," *Health Law Project Library Bulletin*, III (1978); 1-9.
  Jones, James H. *Bad Blood: The Tuskegee Syphilis Experiment.* New York: The Free Press, 1981.
  Leavitt, Judith Walzer, and Ronald L. Numbers, eds. *Sickness and Health in America: Readings in the History of Medicine and Public Health.* Madison: University of Wisconsin Press, 1978.
  Reverby, Susan, and David Rosner, eds. *Health Care in America: Essays in Social History.* Philadelphia: Temple University Press, 1979.
  Rosenberg, Charles E. *The Cholera Years: The United States in 1832, 1849, and 1866.* Chicago and London: University of Chicago Press, 1962.
  Shryock, Richard H. *Medicine and Society in America.* New York: New York University Press, 1960.
  Vogel, Morris J., and Charles E. Rosenberg, eds. *The Therapeutic Revolution: Essays in the Social History of American Medicine.* Philadelphia: University of Pennsylvania Press, 1979.
In addition to the above books, each student should have access to one of the following:
  Blum, John M., et al. *The National Experience: A History of the United States*, 5th ed. New York: Harcourt Brace Jovanovich, 1981.

Bailyn, Bernard, et al. *The Great Republic: A History of the American People.* Boston and Toronto: Little, Brown, 1977.

Methods of evaluation: Idea papers, oral presentations, class discussion, exam.

Brief course description: The course will explore the way in which medical knowledge and the practice of medicine have interacted with the social fabric and political forces of the United States. Three major areas of concern will be: (1) *medicine and class*, e.g., public health as social management, medical responses to immigration and industrialization; (2) *medicine and race*, e.g., discriminatory health care delivery, medical eugenics, experimentation on human subjects; (3) *medicine and gender*, e.g., medical politics of birth control and abortion, treatment of female complaints. The course will be conducted in a seminar format, with considerable emphasis on class discussion of common readings and sharing results of independent work. No prerequisites.

Other features of the course: This is not, as is clear from the description and syllabus, a course on women and health. It does, however, persistently raise feminist issues.

Syllabus

Jan. 16   I. Introduction
            — The course and the materials
            — Baby Fae

Jan. 23   II. Beginning American Medicine
            — The early years
            — Approaches and methods
            Reading:
                Shryock, ch. I–III
                Reverby and Rosner, ch. 1 ("Beyond the Great Doctors")
                Leavitt and Numbers, ch. 17 (Blake, "Inoculation"); ch. 18 (Pernick, "Politics, Parties and Pestilence"); ch. 24 (Eberlein, "When Society First Took a Bath")
            Idea papers
            Introductions
            Background
            Student Leaders

Jan. 30   III. Changing Concepts and Practices
            — Physicians, institutions, and ideas
            Reading:
                Shryock, ch. IV
                Reverby and Rosner, ch. 9 (Rosenkrantz and Vinovskis, "Culpability for Death")
                Vogel and Rosenberg, ch. 1 (Rosenberg, "Therapeutic Revolution")
            Idea papers
            Introductions
            Background
            Student Leaders

Feb. 6   IV. America and Public Health Redefined
            Reading:
                Rosenberg, *Cholera Years*
            Idea papers
            Introductions
            Background
            Student Leaders

Feb. 13   V. Victorian America and the Progressive Era
           — Race, class, and gender in the late nineteenth and twentieth centuries
           — Levels of historical analysis: patient, public, practitioner, hospital, school, science, economy, government
           Reading:
               Haller, *Outcasts from Evolution*, ch. 2 ("The Physician vs. the Negro") (Reserve)
               Curtis, *Blacks, Medical Schools, and Society*, ch. 1 ("Historical Perspectives") (Reserve)
               Vogel and Rosenberg, ch. 3 (Geison, "Physiologists and Clinicians"); ch. 5 (Reed, "Birth Control")
               Leavitt and Numbers, ch. 12 (Rosenberg, "Dispensary"); ch. 29 (Leavitt, "Smallpox in Milwaukee") [The Leavitt article is also found as ch. 5 of Reverby and Rosner.]
               Reverby and Rosner, ch. 7 (Rosner, "Healthcare in Brooklyn"); ch. 11 (Reverby, "Nursing")
           Idea papers
           Student Leaders

Feb. 20   VI. Health, Fitness, and Morality
           Reading:
               Haller and Haller
           Idea papers
           Introductions
           Background
           Student Leaders

Feb. 27   VII. Race, Class, and Research
           Reading:
               Jones
           Idea papers
           Introductions
           Background
           Student Leaders

March 20   VIII. Wealth, Power, and the Construction of Modern Medicine
           Reading:
               Brown
           Idea papers
           Introductions
           Background
           Student Leaders
           FIELD TRIP: At a date to be determined soon the class will travel to a library to make a historical survey of selected health-related journals. The trip is likely to occur during this or the following week, and will take all day.

March 27   IX. "All My Babies," and Discussion

April 3   X. Discussion of Field Trip Results
           Submit outline and sources

April 10   XI. Medicine in the Network of Social Control
           Reading:
               Vogel and Rosenberg, ch. 10 (Pellegrino, "Twentieth Century Therapeutics"); ch. 8 (Numbers, "Health Insurance") [The Numbers article is also ch. 11 of Leavitt and Numbers]

Reverby and Rosner, ch. 13 (Crawford, "Health Politics in the 1970s")
Ivie, "Health Care Access" (Reserve)

April 17   XII. Medical Experts and Social Management
Reading:
Ehrenreich and English, *For Her Own Good.*

April 24   XIII. Film: "La operación," and Discussion

May 1   XIV. Conclusions
— Discussion of final papers
— Course themes

*   *   *   *   *

Course Title: Issues in Women's Health, Women's Studies 300

Credits: 5.

Institution name: Ohio State University.

Name(s) and departmental affiliation(s) of individual(s) teaching this course: Chris Smithies, Center for Women's Studies.

Specific information regarding the course:

Department(s) in which the course is listed: Women's Studies.

Course level and audience for whom it is intended: Open to undergrad students. Fulfills requirements for Women's Studies courses.

Prerequisites: None required. However, two-thirds of the students have completed one or more Women's Studies courses.

Method of instruction: Lecture, discussion, slides/films, guest speakers, class presentations.

Texts:

Fee, Elizabeth, ed. *Women and Health: The Politics of Sex in Medicine.*.

Arditti, Rita, Renate Duelli Klein, and Shelley Minden, eds. *Test-Tube Women.*

Lorde, Audre, *The Cancer Journals.*

Kinko's packet of photocopied materials.

Methods of evaluation: Midterm exam, class discussion, class presentation or position paper, final examination.

Brief course description: This course will present a feminist analysis of women's health issues. We will consider the impact of women's reproductive capabilities on the construction of women's lives, methods of institutional and social discrimination in the American health care system, the implications of new medical technologies for women's lives, and strategies for women who seek to gain more control over their bodies and their health.

Course Objectives:

1. Students will learn how to apply the terms and concepts of feminist analysis to issues of women's health.

2. Students will study the relationship between the female reproductive capacity and gender-defined roles.

3. Students will survey and analyze the effectiveness of strategies by feminists to change practices of overt and covert discrimination in women's health.

4. Students will improve their skills in locating and analyzing literature relevant to women's health.

5. Students will learn information that will enable them to participate more effectively in relationship to their own health concerns.

It is not a requirement of this course that the student subscribe to the feminist perspective. All points of view will be respected in class discussions. The student is expected to demonstrate understanding of the feminist perspective when analyzing issues in the examinations and written assignments.

Other features of the course: As a doctoral student in psychology, I have great respect for the scientific method. However, I believe that instruction in women's health from a feminist perspective must include critique of male-identified science and methodology as well as validation for women's "subjective" experiences.

Syllabus

April 3		INTRODUCTION ERECTING THE GYNECOLOGIST
April 10		THE WOMEN'S HEALTH MOVEMENT Lecture, Discussion, and Slides
	Readings:	A, K, & M: Downer Fee: Chapter 8 Kinko's: Bullough & Voght
April 17		THE HEALTHCARE INDUSTRY
	Readings:	Fee: Chapters 3, 4, 5 A, K, & M: Kaufmann, Bunkle Kinko's: Melosh, Hine
April 24 and May 1		TAKING CARE, TAKING CHARGE

Through lecture, discussion, and the contributions of guest speakers, we will consider all or most of the following topics:
   1) the "well-woman" gynecological examination
   2) male/female physiology
   3) menstrual extraction and abortion
   4) eating disorders
   5) alcoholism
   6) breast cancer
   7) sickle cell anemia
   8) aging
   9) pre-menstrual syndrome
   10) lesbian health

Assignment: Read and analyze an article from any source (e.g., medical journal, popular literature, feminist publication, etc.) on one of the topics above, and come to class prepared to share your findings.

Readings: Kinko's: "A Well-Woman Exam"
"A Self-Help Approach to Premenstrual Syndrome"
"Ladies Don't Get Drunk"
"The Hazards of Treatment"
"America's Abortion Dilemma"
"Lesbian Health Matters!"
"The Best Little Girl..."
"Feminist Health Fund"
Lorde: *The Cancer Journals*

May 8   MIDTERM EXAMINATION (6:00–7:30)
Film: "The Price of Change"

May 15		(1) RESEARCH ISSUES AND FEMINIST METHOD-OLOGIES
		(2) BIRTHING
		Lecture, Discussion, Guest Speaker and Slides
	Readings:	"Experimental Pregnancy" (Handout)
		Fee: Chapter 2
		Kinko's: Sandmaier ("Introduction")
May 22		REPRODUCTIVE TECHNOLOGIES
		Class presentation
	Reading:	A, K, & M: *Test-Tube Women*
May 29		(1) REPRODUCTIVE TECHNOLOGIES (contd.)
PAPERS DUE		(2) THEORIES FOR CHANGE
	Reading:	Fee: Chapter 1
June 5		COMING TOGETHER
		Discussion, Guest Speaker
	Reading:	A, K, & M: Neely

*   *   *   *   *

Course Title: Perspectives on Women's Health

Credits: 3.
Institution name: State University College of Arts and Sciences, Plattsburgh, N.Y.
Name(s) and departmental affiliation(s) of individual(s) teaching this course: Janet T. Alexander, R.N., M.S.N., Associate Professor, Department of Nursing.
Specific information regarding the course:
   Department(s) in which the course is listed: Nursing; Women's Studies.
   Course level and audience for whom it is intended: Any college student; class is usually and preferably a mix of freshmen through seniors.
   Prerequisites: None.
   Method of instruction: Lecture, discussion.
Texts:
   Women's Health Book Collective. *The New Our Bodies, Ourselves*, 3d ed. New York: Simon and Schuster, 1984.
Methods of evaluation: Exams, group seminar presentation, classroom preparation/participation, submission of bibliographies (minimum of 10) on reading other than the text.
Brief course description: Explores the health concepts specific to women. Emphasis will be placed on self-management of health care. Focuses on growth and development throughout the life cycle and competency required for healthy adaptation to stressors.
Course Objectives: The student will
   1. Identify interrelationship of past and current attitudes, values, and practices related to a woman's health and health care.
   2. Identify responsibilities to self and others related to self-directed health care.
   3. Demonstrate knowledge of the biological, psychological, sociological, and cultural responses of the female through the life cycle.
   4. Analyze the female adaptive processes to minor and major stresses.
   5. Evaluate effect of current trends in women's health care on individual, family, and community.

Course Content:
   I. Comparison of past and present
      A. Morbidity and mortality statistics of women
      B. Relationship of women's role to health status
      C. Health care delivery systems
      D. Folklore and women's health
  II. Sense of self: Implications
      A. Significance of self-knowledge
      B. Relationship of self to others
      C. Self-motivation
      D. The responsible self
 III. Anatomy and physiology of the female body
      A. Maturation of the body systems
      B. Developmental milestones
      C. Self assessment during the life cycle
      D. Physiological and psychological relationships
  IV. Stress and adaptation
      A. Problem solving
      B. Common health problems
      C. 1. With changes in role or lifestyle
         2. With changes in health
   V. Life cycle decisions: Alternatives, responsibilities, implications
      A. Gender identity and sex roles
      B. Equality: paths and obstacles
      C. Preparing for future responsibilities

Syllabus

Date	Topic	Reading
Jan. 17	Orientation to Course	Prefaces, Introduction
Jan. 22	Basics of Mental & Physical Health	Chap. 1 and 2
Jan. 24	Women and the Health Care System	Chap. 24, 25
Jan. 29	Anatomy & Physiology The Pelvic Exam	Chap. 12 pp. 476–478
Jan. 31	The Menstrual Cycle Menarche — Menopause	pp. 211–219 Chap. 22
Feb. 5	Contraception	Chap. 13
Feb. 7	Rape L. Moeske, A. Cameron	Chap. 8
Feb. 12	Abortion	Chap. 16
Feb. 14	Sterilization: Male & Female G. Felix, L. Coffin, N. Leiker, L. Taillefer	pp. 256–259 pp. 511–517
Feb. 19	Exam 1	
Feb. 21	Pregnancy	Chap. 15, 18
Feb. 26	Labor	Chap. 19
Feb. 28	Delivery, Post-Partum	Chap. 20
Mar. 5	Alternatives to Hospital Births N. Levandowski, J. Hoeflin, E. Williams	
Mar. 7	Infertility	Chap. 17, 21
Mar. 26	Normal sexual physiology	Chap. 9, 11

(continued)

Date	Topic	Reading
Mar. 28	Homosexuality: Male and Female M. Sheridan, L. Courtney ***BIBLIOGRAPHIES DUE***	Chap. 10
Apr. 2	Breast self-exam	pp. 488–496, 523–539
Apr. 4	Exam 2	
Apr. 9	Common gyn problems Sexually transmitted diseases	Chap. 14, 23
Apr. 11	Eating disorders A. Pomilla, T. Soothcage, V. LaDuke	
Apr. 16	Sports and Women L. Reese, K. Dubay, K. Wilday	Chap. 4
Apr. 18	Depression and Suicide L. Tetrault, N. Sawyer, C. Leslie, B. Brown	Chap. 6
Apr. 23	Alcohol & Drug Abuse	Chap. 3
Apr. 25	Alcohol & Drug Abuse	
Apr. 30	Battered Women L. Teta, T. David	Chap. 8
May 2	Careers with and without Marriage A. Herne	
May 7	Cohabitation, Dating, Marriage E. Ruland, A. Spalding	
May 9	Assertiveness, Consumerism, Optimum Health	Chap. 5, 6, 7
Week of May 13 – Exam 3		

*   *   *   *   *

Course Title: Reproductive Health and Population Issues, HEP 406G

Institution name: University of Oregon.
Name(s) and departmental affiliation(s) of individual(s) teaching this course: Sandy Marie Harvey, Department of School and Community Health.
Specific information regarding the course:
  Department(s) in which the course is listed: Department of School and Community Health; Women's Studies.
  Course level and audience for whom it is intended: Upper division/graduate level.
  Prerequisites: Upper division or graduate standing. Basic knowledge in anatomy and physiology in the reproductive health area.
  Method of instruction: Seminar format. Lecture, discussion, guest speakers, student presentations.
  Texts: One week prior to each seminar a reading packet containing articles pertinent to the seminar topic will be available. The student presenter and discussion leader will participate in the selection of reading materials. Readings will be chosen from the following list:

Arras, J., and R. Hunt. *Ethical Issues in Modern Medicine*. Palo Alto, Calif.: Mayfield Publishing Company, 1983.

Barnes, F.E.F., ed. *Ambulatory Maternal Health Care and Family Services: Policies, Principles, Practices*. Washington, D.C.: American Psychological Association, 1978.

Berelson, B. *The Great Debate on Population Policy*. New York: The Population Council, 1975.

Eckholm, E., and K. Newland. *Health: The Family Planning Factor*. Worldwatch Paper #10, 1977.

Fawcett, J., ed. *Psychological Aspects of Population*. New York: Basic Books, 1973.

Gordon, L. *Woman's Body, Woman's Right*. New York: Grossman Publishers, 1976.

Hatcher, R.A. *Contraceptive Technology 1982-1983*. New York: Irvington Publishers, 1982.

Isaacs, S.L. *Population Law and Policy*. New York: Human Sciences Press, 1981.

Jelliffe, D.B., and P. Jelliffee. *Human Milk in the Modern World*. New York: Oxford University Press, 1978.

Klaus, M.H., and J.H. Kennell. *Maternal-Infant Bonding*. St. Louis: C.V. Mosby Company, 1976.

Luker, K. *Taking Chances: Abortion and the Decision Not to Contracept*. Berkeley: University of California Press, 1975.

Marshall, J.F., and S. Polgor. *Culture, Natality, and Family Planning*. Chapel Hill, N.C.: Carolina Population Center, 1976.

Moore, E.C. *Women and Health: United States, 1980*. Public Health reports (Supplement), 1980.

Newland, K. *Women and Population Growth: Choice Beyond Childbearing*. Worldwatch Paper #16, 1977.

Pohlman, E., ed. *Population: A Clash of Prophets*. New York: The New American Library, Inc., 1973.

Seaman, B. *The Doctors' Case Against the Pill*. New York: Doubleday and Company, 1980.

Seaman, B., and G. Seaman. *Women and the Crisis in Sex Hormones*. New York: Rawson Associates Publishers, 1977.

Sloane, E. *Biology of Women*. New York: John Wiley and Sons, 1980.

The Alan Guttmacher Institute. *Teenage Pregnancy: The Problem That Hasn't Gone Away*. 1981.

Journals:

American Journal of Obstetrics and Gynecology
American Journal of Public Health
Family Planning Perspectives
Fertility and Sterility
Journal of Health and Social Behavior
Journal of Health Politics, Policy and Law
Journal of Public Health Policy
Journal of Reproductive Medicine
Journal of the American Medical Association (JAMA)
Lancet
Medical Care
New England Journal of Medicine
Population Bulletin
Population Reports
Population Studies
Social Science and Medicine
Studies in Family Planning
Women and Health

Methods of evaluation: Issue paper and seminar presentation, discussion leadership, class participation.

Brief course description: This course will present a critical review of current public health and sociopolitical issues in reproductive health and population policy. Both national and international topics will be discussed. Students participate in selection of the issue to be discussed and apply reproductive health knowledge in identifying and seeking solutions to the issues, which concern health care providers, consumers, and policy makers.

The objectives of this course, therefore, are to introduce the student to important issues pertaining to reproductive health and population policy; to expose the student to the major positions and arguments of each issue; to increase the ability to critically analyze such issues and questions; and to encourage the student to examine, define, and understand values and opinions.

Syllabus

Date	Topic
Jan. 10	Introduction to course/seminar topics
Jan. 17	The Abortion Controversy
Jan. 24	Alternative Approaches to Childbirth *Speaker:* Kathryn Carr, Nurse-Midwife *Discussion Leader:* Kelly Jackson-Holmquist
Jan. 31	Cross-Cultural Approaches to Fertility *Speaker:* Carol Silverman, Assistant Professor, Department of Anthropology
Feb. 7	The Depo-Provera Debate—National and International *Speaker:* Sandy Harvey *Discussion Leader:* Leslie Keller
Feb. 14	Teenage Pregnancies *Speaker:* David Hascall *Discussion Leader:* Bee Bee Rubio
	Unnecessary Surgeries: Hysterectomy, Caesarean Section, Mastectomy *Speaker:* SeAnne Safaii *Discussion Leader:* Annette Guidry
Feb. 21	Reproductive Technologies: The Custom-Made Child *Speaker:* Leslie Keller *Discussion Leader:* Debbie Landforce
Feb. 28	Contraceptive and Sterilization Issues *Speaker:* Bee Bee Rubio *Discussion Leader:* David Hascall
	Women in Transition: Reproductive Issues *Speaker:* Debbie Landforce
March 7	Breastfeeding: National and International Issues *Speaker:* Kelly Jackson-Holmquist *Discussion Leader:* SeAnne Safaii
	Factors Influencing Population Growth in Third World Countries *Speaker:* Annette Guidry

(continued)

Date	Topic
March 14	Recommendations for Health Policy: Presentations and Adoptions of Resolutions *Moderator:* Sandy Harvey

*   *   *   *   *

Course Title: The Second X: The Biological Women, WS 33

Institution name: Dartmouth College.

Name(s) and departmental affiliation(s) of individual(s) teaching this course: Hilda Weyl, Department of Physiology.

Specific information regarding the course:

Department(s) in which the course is listed: Women's Studies Program.

Course level and audience for whom it is intended: Intermediate level; open to all students, fulfills the Science Distribution Requirement.

Prerequisites: None.

Method of instruction: Both lecture/discussion and discussion/lab.

Texts:

Sloane, Ethel. *Biology of Women.* New York: John Wiley and Sons, 1980.

Hunter College Women's Study Collective. *Women's Realities, Women's Choices: An Introduction to Women's Studies.* New York: Oxford University Press, 1983.

Brighton Women and Science Group. *Alice Through the Microscope: The Power of Science over Women's Lives.* New York: Vintage, 1980.

Other references on reserve in library.

Methods of evaluation: Exams and papers. There is also a required evaluation form of the course.

Brief course description: This course will trace the development of a human being into the female or male form. We will assess the importance of the rate of maturation, the timing of syntheses and titre of circulating hormones, and the effect of external environment on basic biological processes. We shall analyze the evidence for earlier as well as lesser specialization of the female brain that has been used to explain women's lesser achievement in mathematics relative to men. Lateralization of brain function and other genetically determined traits associated with it will also be explored. Recent women's athletic accomplishments will serve as a paradigm to demonstrate the effects of culture and environment on biological potential. The effects of technology (e.g., the contraceptive pill) on women's biology; women's interest in regaining control over their bodies; and the conflicting expectations regarding their sexuality will be analyzed. In a series of laboratory exercises and demonstrations animals illustrating abnormal sexual development will be studied.

Syllabus

Jan. 3   1. *Introduction: Female, Feminine, Feminist; Videotape, "The Brain"*
      Sloane   Preface v-vii; 1:1-14, Women and Their Health

Hunter   Preface ix–xii; Introduction pp. 3–17
Brighton Introduction pp. 3–21

Jan. 8   2. *The "Nature" of Women*
         Hunter   1:23–58, Imagery and Symbolism in the Definition of
                   Women
                   2:59–92, Ideas About Women's "Nature"
         Brighton 3:62–86, Sociobiology: So What?

Jan. 10 3. *The Evolution of Sexual Reproduction*
         Austin, C.R. & Short, R.V. eds., REPRODUCTION IN MAMMALS,
         Book 6, THE EVOLUTION OF REPRODUCTION, 1976, p. 1–31
         Lowe, M. "Sociobiology and Sex Differences," in SIGNS, 4.1:118–125,
         1978

Jan. 15 4. *Anatomy of the Reproductive System*
         Sloane   2:15–53, Reproductive Anatomy

Jan. 16 5. *Sex Determination and Differentiation*
         Sloane   5:97–138, The Basis of Biological Differences
         Austin, C.R. & Short, R.V. eds., REPRODUCTION IN MAMMALS,
         Book 2, EMBRYONIC AND FETAL DEVELOPMENT, 1972, pp. 43–71

Jan. 17 6. *Physiology of Reproduction: The Endocrine System*
         Hunter   3:93–131, Women's Bodies
         Sloane   3:54–67, The Menstrual Cycle and Its Hormonal
                   Interrelationships

Jan. 22 7. *LABORATORY I: Human Reproductive Anatomy*

Jan. 24 8. *Physiology of Reproduction: Maturation; The Menstrual Cycle*
         Sloane   3:67–87, The Menstrual Cycle and Its Hormonal
                   Interrelationships

Jan. 24 9. *Physiology of Reproduction: The Breasts*
         Sloane   7:162–200, The Mammary Glands

Jan. 29 10. *LABORATORY II: Rat and Mouse Reproductive Systems and Sexual
         Behavior*

Jan. 30 MIDTERM EXAMINATION

Jan. 31 11. *Physiology of Reproduction: Sexual Intercourse*
         Sloane   6:139–161, Female Sexuality
         Brighton 7:139–162, The Obsessive Orgasm: Science and Sex, and
                   Female Sexuality
                   5:108–123, From Zero to Infinity: Scientific Views of
                   Lesbians
         Austin & Short, REPRODUCTION IN MAMMALS, Book 8, Human
         Sexuality, 1980, pp. 1–68

Feb. 5   12. *Physiology of Reproduction: Pregnancy*
         Sloane   10:252–327, Pregnancy, Labor and Delivery
         Hunter   8:282–315, Motherhood

Feb. 6   13. *Menopause; Infertility*
         Sloane   4:88–96, Menopause
                   11:329–345, Problems of Infertility
         Brighton 4:89–107, The Tyrannical Womb: Menstruation and
                   Menopause
                   Appendix: 241–250, Some Biological Information

Feb. 7   14. *Control of Fertility*
         Sloane   12:346–416, Problems of Fertility-Contraception
         Brighton   9:182–207, Contraception: The Growth of a Technology

Feb. 12   15. *LABORATORY III: Abnormal Sexual Development*

Feb. 13   16. *Women's Health and the Medical Profession*
         Sloane   8:201–212, The Gynecological Exam
                     9:213–251, Gynecological Difficulties
         Hunter   12:438–478, Women and Health
         Brighton   6:124–138, 'Sickness Is a Woman's Business?': Reflections
                     on the Attribution of Illness
                     8:165–181, Technology in the Lying-In Room

Feb. 14   17. *Sexual Dimorphism: Biological*
         Hoyenga, K.L. and Hoyenga, K., THE QUESTION OF SEX DIFFER-
         ENCES, 1979, chapter 3.
         Sloane   14:467–516, Our Health in Our Own Hands

Feb. 19   18. *Women and Sports*
         Borm, J., Hebbelinck, H., Venerando, eds., "Woman and Sport. An
         Historical, Biological, Physiological and Sports Medicine Approach," in
         MEDICINE AND SPORTS, vol. 14, 1981.
         "The Female Athlete. A Sociopsychological and Kinanthropometric
         Approach," in MEDICINE AND SPORTS, vol. 15, 1981

Feb. 20   19. *Sexual Dimorphism: Intellectual; Psychosociological*
         Hunter   4:132–172, Women's Personalities
                     5:173–209, Social Roles
         Brighton   2:42–61, Psychological Sex Differences
         Shields, S.A., "The Variability Hypothesis: The History of a Biological
         Model of Sex Differences in Intelligence" in SIGNS, 7.4, pp. 769–797,
         1982

Feb. 21   20. *LABORATORY IV: Experimental Alteration of Sexual Development*

Feb. 26   21. *Sexual Dimorphism: Morbidity and Mortality*
         Hoyenga & Hoyenga, THE QUESTION OF SEX DIFFERENCES,
         Chapter 12 and Appendix B

Feb. 28   22. *Women in Science (A Different Approach to Seeking the Truth?)*
         Brighton   11:228–240, The Masculine Face of Science
         Keller, E.F., A FEELING FOR THE ORGANISM: THE LIFE AND
         WORK OF BARBARA McCLINTOCK, Freeman, 1983, pp. ix–vii,
         96–105, 114–119, 124–138, 139–151, 197–207

Mar. 1   TERM PAPER DUE

Mar. 5   23. *The Status of Women of the Future*
         Hunter   15:574–609, Changing the Present: A Look to the Future

Mar. 6   24. Summary and Conclusions

LABORATORY EXERCISES

Four 2-hour sessions are planned for the course. The X-hour will be used for lectures
in those weeks when a laboratory assignment is scheduled, as well as for examinations.
Directions for the laboratory exercises will be distributed on the day of the lab.

LABORATORY I: *NORMAL HUMAN REPRODUCTIVE ANATOMY*
            Use of plastic models, photographs, and microscopic slides of
            reproductive organs.

LABORATORY II: *MOUSE AND RAT REPRODUCTIVE SYSTEMS
AND SEXUAL BEHAVIOR*
1. Observations will be made of male-female interactions when
previously isolated sexes are put together.
2. Demonstration dissections of adult male and female reproductive systems of rats and mice. Students will also perform their
own dissections.

LABORATORY III: *INHERITED ABNORMALITIES OF SEXUAL
DEVELOPMENT*
Two different animal models will be examined. The reproductive
anatomy and sexual behavior of (1) the hypogonadal mouse
(which is deficient in gonadotropin releasing hormone, GnRH, a
brain hormone), and (2) the mouse and/or rat with testicular
feminization in which an individual with a male genotype (XY) is
a phenotypic female because of an insensitivity to androgens.

LABORATORY IV: *EXPERIMENTAL MANIPULATION OF SEXUAL
DEVELOPMENT*
Newborn rats which have been (1) castrated or (2) given single
injections of sex steroid hormones 2 months earlier will be
observed with regard to their sexual behavior and anatomy.

*   *   *   *   *

Course Title: Women and Health, WS 365

Institution name: San Diego State University.
Name(s) and departmental affiliation(s) of individual(s) teaching this course: Ashley E.
Phillips, Department of Women's Studies.
Specific information regarding the course:
Department(s) in which the course is listed: Women's Studies.
Course level and audience for whom it is intended: Upper division; Women's Studies
minors, nursing students, general education students.
Prerequisites: Upper division, junior or senior class standing.
Method of instruction: Lecture and some discussion.
Texts:
Dreifus, Claudia. *Seizing Our Bodies.*
Leavitt, Judith Walzer. *Women and Health in America.*
Sloane, Ethel. *The Biology of Women.*
Public Health Reports. *Women and Health, 1984–85.*
Students are encouraged to supplement the required readings with ancillary mate-
rials. In order to facilitate access to additional texts, several relevant books have
been ordered and are available in the campus bookstore. Numerous other readings
and journal articles are available in the library here on campus, and in the Bio-
Medical library at UCSD. *Ancillary readings are required for the term paper.*
Arms, S. *I'm Dancing as Fast as I Can.*
Cohen, N. and Ester, L. *Silent Knife.*
Demetrakopoulos, S. *Listening to Our Bodies.*
Ehrenreich, B., and English, D. *Complaints and Disorders.*
Ehrenreich, B., and English, D. *Witches, Midwives and Nurses.*

Harrison, M. *A Woman in Residence.*
Luker, K. *Taking Chances.*
Sandelowski, M. *Women, Health, and Choice.*
Sandmaier, M. *The Invisible Alcoholics.*
Scully, D. *Men Who Control Women's Health.*
Wertz, R. and Wertz, D. *Lying In.*
Journals of Interest:
  American Journal of Nursing
  American Journal of Obstetrics and Gynecology
  American Journal of Public Health
  American Journal of Sociology
  Contraceptive Technology
  Family Planning Perspectives
  Feminist Studies
  HealthPac
  HealthRight
  Journal of Health and Human Behavior
  Journal of Social Issues
  New England Journal of Medicine
  Signs
  Social Policy
  Social Problems
  Women and Health
Methods of evaluation: Three exams; two papers.
Brief course description: This course is designed to introduce the student to theory and research about women in their roles as both providers and consumers of medical care. The relationship between women and the institution of medicine will be examined as the history of the women healers is investigated. The status of female health-care workers in contemporary society will be discussed and analyzed. Specific health concerns of women, and their political, social, and economic facets, will be discussed in detail.

The student should be prepared to read, summarize, analyze, and articulate the concepts that will be presented in the course. Students should expect rigorous reading and writing assignments. Grading will be based on an evaluation of both content and style of the student's work. Class participation, based on information gleaned from required reading assignments and lecture materials, is required. Regular attendance is required. The completion of all assignments is required.

Other features of the course: This is the oldest department of Women's Studies in the U.S. The course is well attended and gets a lot of positive response. Women say "it changed my life."

Syllabus

LECTURES		READING ASSIGNMENTS
Week		*Read*
I	Administrative Details Introduction to Women and Health	Intro to *all* books; Sloane, Ch. 1 Leavitt, Ch. 28,30,31
II	Herstory: Past Roots of Women's Health Complaints and Disorders	Leavitt, Ch. 15,16,18,19,20
III	Biological Differences	Sloane, Ch. 5

IV	Reproductive Anatomy	Sloane, Ch. 2
	The Gynecological Examination	Sloane, Ch. 8
	Sexual Preference	
V	The Menstrual Cycle	Sloane, Ch. 3
		Leavitt, Ch. 1,2
VI	Contraception: Reproductive Freedom	Sloane, Ch. 12; (skip
VII	vs. Health Hazard	pp. 403–411); SOB III:2;
		Sloane, pp. 412–414
		Leavitt, Ch. 7,9
VIII	Abortion and Infertility	Sloane, 403–411;136;396
		Sloane, Ch. 10
		Leavitt, Ch. 8
IX	Pregnancy: Immaculate Deception?	Sloane, Ch. 10
		Leavitt, Ch. 10,11,12,13,
		21,22,23
X	Childbirth	
	Film: *Five Women, Five Births*	
XI	Aging and Menopause	Sloane, Ch. 10
		Sloane, Ch. 4
XII	Breast Health and Disease	Sloane, Ch. 7
	The Politics of Breast Cancer	
XIII	Other Concerns:	
	Women & Work; Disability	
XIV	The Politics of Medical Practice	
XV	Why Would a Girl Want to Go Into	Leavitt, Ch. 32,33,34,35,27
	Medicine?	Sloane, Ch. 14
	Towards the Future of Health and	
	Medical Care	

*   *   *   *   *

Course Title: Women and Health, WOST 320

Institution name: Wellesley College.
Name(s) and departmental affiliation(s) of individual(s) teaching this course: Susan
    Reverby, Women and Health, Women's Studies.
Specific information regarding the course:
    Department(s) in which the course is listed: Women's Studies and History.
    Course level and audience for whom it is intended: Women's Studies majors and
        science students (300 level).
    Prerequisites: Some other history or social science.
    Method of instruction: Seminar, with a great deal of student reporting, lecture and
        discussion.
Texts:
    Leavitt, Judith Walzer, ed. *Women and Health in America.*
    Lorde, Audre. *The Cancer Journals.*

Mann, Thomas. *The Black Swan* (to be purchased in October).
Sanger, Margaret. *Autobiography.*
Walsh, Mary Roth. *"Doctors Wanted: No Women Need Apply."*
Methods of evaluation: Regular attendance and participation; writing assignments (health diary, reading critique, group research projects).
Brief course description: The Women and Health course will examine various elements in the relationship between women and the health care system as it has evolved over the last 150 years in the United States. Physicians, in particular, have played a crucial role in providing "scientific" legitimation for women's sphere and in determining normalcy for women's emotional, sexual, and physical development. Women, in turn, have been both the majority of the patients in the health care system, and (with the notable exception of physicians) the majority of the practitioners of the healing arts. The tensions that arise between women and healers are created in the context of changes in cultural expectations, therapeutic relationships, and power balances. The course will explore these factors as we evaluate differing critiques of medicine that have been voiced since the 1830s.

The goals of the course are (1) to provide an historical perspective on the structural, ideological, and cultural factors that shape the relationship between women and the health care system; (2) to consider some of the criticisms of contemporary health care by exploring women's health issues; and (3) to explore the effect of gender on American women through an in-depth examination of one arena of social existence that has shaped our lives.
Other features of the course: The instructor considers the group reports as *very* important to the course.

Syllabus

September 5   Introduction
Susan Reverby, "Women and Health — 1982," in *The Women's Almanac — 1982*, ed. Barbara Haber, typescript copy.
John Ehrenreich, "Introduction," in *The Cultural Crisis of Modern Medicine*, ed. John Ehrenreich, pp. 1–35.

September 12   Great Expectations: The Relationship Between Health and Medical Care
John B. McKinlay and Sonja M. McKinlay, "The Questionable Effect of Medical Measures on the Decline of Mortality in the U.S. in the 20th Century," *Health and Society* (Summer 1977): 405–428.
John Knowles, "The Responsibility of the Individual," *Daedalus: Doing Better and Feeling Worse: Health in the U.S.* 106 (Winter 1977): 57–80.
E.G. Mishler, "Critical Perspectives on the Biomedical Model," in *Social Contexts of Health, Illness and Patient Care*, ed. Mishler et al., pp. 1–19.
Ingrid Waldron, "Why Do Women Live Longer than Men?" in *The Sociology of Health and Illness*, eds. Peter Conrad and Rochelle Kern, pp. 45–66.

September 19   Therapeutic Relationship or Social Control? Women and Medical Care in the 19th Century: An Introduction
Carroll Smith-Rosenberg and Charles Rosenberg, "The Female Animal: Medical and Biological Views of Woman and Her 19th Century America," in Leavitt, pp. 12–27.
Ann Douglas Wood, "'The Fashionable Diseases': Women's Complaints and Their Treatment in 19th Century America," in Leavitt, pp. 222–238.
Regina Mackell Morantz, "The Perils of Feminist History," in Leavitt, pp. 239–245.
Kathryn Kish Sklar, "All Hail to Pure Cold Water," in Leavitt, pp. 246–254.
Ronald L. Numbers and Rennie B. Schoepflin, "Ministries of Healing: Mary Baker Eddy, Ellen G. White, and the Religion of Health," in Leavitt, pp. 376–390.

September 26   Women as Infectors: The Case of Venereal Disease
Prince Morrow, *Social Diseases and Marriage* (1904), selected pages.
Charlotte Perkins Gilman, *The Crux* (1911), selected pages.
Claudia Wallis, "Herpes: Today's Scarlet Letter," *Time* 120 (August 2, 1982): 62–69.
Jack McClintock, "Love's Labor's Cost: You Wake from the Sweetest Night Imaginable. You Think Your Troubles Are Over. Then She Tells You About the Herpes." *Esquire* (November 1982): 145–156.
    Film: *End of the Road*, a 1919 silent film on venereal disease and women.

October 3   Reproductive Rights: Birth Control
Sanger, *Autobiography*, pp. 68–152, 163–279, 292–315, 358–375, 393–412, 493–496.
Linda Gordon, "Voluntary Motherhood: The Beginnings of Feminist Birth Control Ideas in the United States," in Leavitt, pp. 104–116.
Rosalind Pollack Petchesky, "Reproductive Freedom: Beyond a Woman's Right to Choose," *Signs* 5 (Summer 1980): 661–685. Also reprinted in Ethel Person and Catherine Stimpson, eds. *Women — Sex and Sexuality*.

October 10   Fall Break, Monday schedule

October 17   Reproductive Rights: Abortion and Sterilization Abuse
James Mohr, "Patterns of Abortion and the Response of American Physicians, 1790–1930," in Leavitt, pp. 117–123.
Kristin Luker, *Abortion and the Politics of Motherhood*, pp. 158–215.
Adele Clarke, "Subtle Forms of Sterilization Abuse: A Reproductive Rights Analysis," in *Test-Tube Women: What Future for Motherhood?*, pp. 188–212.

October 24   Pregnancy and Childbirth
Catherine M. Scholten, "On the Importance of the Obstetrick Art," in Leavitt, pp. 141–154.
Judith Walzer Leavitt and Whitney Walton, "Down to Death's Door: Women's Perceptions of Childbirth in America," in Leavitt, pp. 155–165.
Frances C. Kobrin, "The American Midwife Controversy," in Leavitt, pp. 318–326.
Ruth Hubbard, "Personal Courage Is Not Enough: Some Hazards of Childbearing in the 1980s," in *Test-Tube Women*, pp. 331–355.
Francie Hornstein, "Children by Donor Insemination: A New Choice for Lesbians," in *Test-Tube Women*, pp. 373–381.

October 31   DES: Why Do We Wonder about a Wonder Drug?
    Health Diary due
Sally Nash, et al., "Identifying and Tracing a Population-at-Risk: The DESAD Project Experience," *American Journal of Public Health* 73 (March 1983): 253–259.
Patricia Sipe, "The Wonder Drug We Should Wonder About," *Science for the People* (November–December 1982): 9–16, 30–33.
Susan E. Bell , "A New Model of Medical Technology Development: A Case Study of DES," *Research in the Sociology of Health Care*, eds. Julius Roth and Sheryl Ruzek (forthcoming), typescript copy.
    Film: *DES — The Time Bomb Drug*

November 7   Cancer: The Perspective
Audre Lorde, *The Cancer Journals*.
Thomas Mann, *The Black Swan*.

November 14   Nursing: Women's Work
Susan Reverby, "Neither for the Drawing Room Nor for the Kitchen," in Leavitt, pp. 454–466.
Nancy Tomes, "Little World of Our Own," in Leavitt, pp. 467–481.
Barbara Melosh, "More than 'the Physician's Hand,'" in Leavitt, pp. 481–496.

Darlene Clark Hine, "Mabel K. Staupers and the Integration of Black Nurses into the Armed Forces," in Leavitt, pp. 497–508.

Barbara Katz Rothman, "Midwives in Transition: The Structure of a Clinical Revolution," *Social Problems* 30 (1983): 262–271.

November 21   Medicine: Women's Work?
Walsh, *"Doctors Wanted: No Women Need Apply."*

November 28   Student Presentations

December 5   Student Presentations
   All Research Papers Due

*   *   *   *   *

Course Title: Women & Health Care, Wo St 297

Institution name: University of Massachusetts, Amherst.

Name(s) and departmental affiliation(s) of individual(s) teaching this course: Janice Raymond, Associate Professor, Women's Studies & Medical Ethics.

Specific information regarding the course:
   Department(s) in which the course is listed: Women's Studies; Continuing Education.
   Course level and audience for whom it is intended: Wo St 297; Beginning students interested in an overview of women and health issues.
   Prerequisites: Introduction to Women's Studies helpful, but not required.
   Method of instruction: Lecture-discussion.

Methods of evaluation: Exams, journals, class participation.

Texts:
   Ehrenreich & English. *For Her Own Good*
   Daly, Mary. *Gyn/Ecolcogy*
   Dreifus, Claudia (ed.), *Seizing Our Bodies*
   Holmes, Helen et al. (Eds.), *Birth Control and Controlling Birth*
   Gilman, Charlotte Perkins. *The Yellow Wallpaper.*

Brief course description: This course will examine three areas under the general heading of "Women & Health Care:" the history of women and healing, and the professionalization of medicine; gynecology, obstetrics, and sexual surgery; and feminist philosophies of health and alternatives to established health care. This is not only a course about women and health issues. It is an attempt to place such issues into a larger context of, for example, violence against women, as well as the more positive history of women's healing traditions. The emphasis of the course is philosophical and ethical; i.e. the course constantly asks 'why'. What values produced, and continue to produce, the current wave of unnecessary hysterectomies? What is the true nature of medical reality in women's lives — political, economic, or ideational? Or, how do these combine to structure medicine as an institution? Finally, from a feminist perspective(s), what ought to be?

Syllabus

I — *The History of Women and Healing and the Professionalization*
   of Regular Medicine

January 29–31 Introductory class: general introduction to the syllabus and class requirements; first lecture on the history of women and medicine

February 5–7   Lecture and discussion on the history of women and healing, also on
                the witch movement in western Europe and its relationship to women's
                healing traditions
                Readings for next week:
                1) Ehrenreich & English, *For Her Own Good*, Chaps. 1, 2 & 3
                2) Mary Daly, *Gyn/Ecology*, preface to p. 222

February 12   Discussion of above readings; come prepared with journal notes to dis-
                cuss these assignments

February 14   Lecture on the professions, professionalism and the professionaliza-
                tion of medicine
                Readings for next week:
                1) *Seizing Our Bodies*, pp. 3–12
                2) Everett Hughes, "Professions," from *Daedalus*, Fall, 1963, pp.
                   655–668 (On Reserve)
                Supplementary Reading (Not required but some is encouraged)
                1) Mary Roth Walsh, *Doctors Wanted, No Women Need Apply*
                2) Michelle Harrison, M.D., *A Woman in Residence*
                3) Burton Bledstein, *The Culture of Professionalism*
                4) Rosemary Stevens, *American Medicine & The Public Interest*

February 19   No Classes; Monday schedule is followed

February 21   Discussion of above required readings; come prepared to discuss the
                advantages and disadvantages of being professional
                Readings for next week:
                1) Adrienne Rich, "The Theft of Childbirth," pp. 146–162 in *Seizing
                   Our Bodies*
                2) Holmes et al., *Birth Control and Controlling Birth*, pp. 143–264

February 26   Lectures on the American midwife's history; a crisis in professionaliza-
                tion and feminism; the Black midwife

February 28   Discussion of above readings
                Readings for next week:
                1) Kay Weiss, "What Medical Students Learn About Women," in
                   Seizing Our Bodies, pp. 212–222
                2) Ehrenreich & English, *For Her Own Good*, Chaps. 4 to end
                Supplementary Reading:
                Carroll Smith-Rosenberg, "The Hysterical Woman: Sex Roles and
                Role Conflict in 19th Century America," in *Social Research*, Vol. 39,
                No. 4, Winter, 1972

March 5   Lecture on childbirth technologies and the castration of women; alter-
                natives to hospital-based deliveries

March 7   Discussion of above required readings

March 12   Review for Mid-term

March 14   In-class Mid-term exam

March 19–21   Spring Vacation
                Readings for next week:
                1) Charlotte Perkins Gilman, *The Yellow Wallpaper*

II — *Gynecology, Obstetrics, and Sexual Surgery*

March 26   Lecture on hysteria; the conservation of energy theory, and the history
                of sexual surgery

March 28	Discussion of *The Yellow Wallpaper* *Readings for next week:* 1) G. J. Barker-Benfield, "Sexual Surgery in Late Nineteenth Century America," in *Seizing Our Bodies*, pp. 13–41 2) Deborah Larned, "The Epidemic in Unnecessary Hysterectomy," in *Seizing Our Bodies*, pp. 195–208. 3) Mary Daly, *Gyn/Ecology.* pp. 223–312
April 2–4	Lectures on a general introduction to unnecessary surgery: hysterectomy as a case study
April 9	Discussions of above required readings
April 11	Lecture on menstruation and menopause *Readings for next week:* 1) Emily Culpepper, "Exploring Menstrual Attitudes," in *Women Look at Biology Looking at Women* 2) Marilyn Grossman and Pauline Bart, "Taking the Men Out of Menopause," pp. 163–185, in *Women Look at Biology Looking at Women* *Supplementary Reading:* 1) *Menstruation and Menopause* by Paula Weideger 2) Barbara Seaman, "The Dangers of Sex Hormones," in *Seizing Our Bodies*, pp. 167–176 3) Penny Budoff, M.D., *No More Menstrual Cramps and Other Good News*, pp. 1–75 4) "Toxic-Shock Syndrome in Menstruating Women," by Shands et al., *New England Journal of Medicine.* pp. 1436–1442
April 16	Discussion of above required readings
April 18	Lecture on Eugenics Theories as basis for sterilization abuse *Readings for next class:* 1) C. Dreifus, "Sterilizing the Poor," in *Seizing Our Bodies* 2) Holmes et al., *Birth Control and Controlling Birth*, pp. 97–139 *Supplementary Reading:* 1) Linda Gordon, *Woman's Body, Woman's Right*
April 23	Discussion of above required reading

III — *Philosophies of Medicine and the Women's Health Movement*

April 25	Lecture on Medicine as Religion *Reading for next week:* 1) Ivan Illich, *Medical Nemesis*, pp. 3–154 (On Reserve) *Supplementary Readings:* 1) Vincente Navarro, Medicine Under Capitalism 2) Rick Carlson, *The End of Medicine* 3) Janice Raymond, "Medicine as Patriarchal Religion," *Journal of Medicine and Philosophy*, 7 (1982). pp. 197–216
April 30	Continuation of Lecture on Medicine as Religion
May 2	Discussion of Ivan Illich, *Medical Nemesis* *Reading for next week:* 1) Sheryl Ruzek, *The Women's Health Movement*, sections to be assigned (On Reserve)
May 7	Lecture on a Feminist Philosophy of Health

May 9   Discussion of Sheryl Ruzek, *The Women's Health Movement*

May 14   Summary and Evaluation Day; you will be asked to do an in-class self-evaluation; no one will complete the course without doing this evaluation; it is required!
             Final exam passed out (due May 20)

Class Requirements:
1) Mid-term exam in class
2) Final take-home exam
3) Oral participation in class
4) Journal on class lectures and readings

*   *   *   *   *

Course Title: Women and Health in American History, 531

Institution name: University of Wisconsin — Madison.
Name(s) and departmental affiliation(s) of individual(s) teaching this course: Judith W. Leavitt.
Specific information regarding the course:
   Department(s) in which the course is listed: Women's Studies; History of Medicine; History of Science.
   Course level and audience for whom it is intended: Intermediate/advanced.
   Prerequisites: Junior/Senior standing.
   Method of instruction: Lecture/discussion/seminar.
Texts (required):
   Betts, Helen. "Dress of Women in Its Relation to the Etiology and Treatment of Pelvic Disease." *Journal of the American Medical Association.*
   Clarke, Edward H. *Sex in Education; or, a Fair Chance for Girls.* 1873.
   Haller, John, and Robin Haller. *The Physician and Sexuality in Victorian America.* Norton paperback.
   Hartmann, Mary, and Lois Banner, eds. *Clio's Consciousness Raised.* New York: Harper Torchbook.
   Kennedy, Helen. "Effect of High School Work upon Girls During Adolescence." *The Pedagogical Seminary.* 1896.
   Melosh, Barbara. *The Physician's Hand: Nurses and Nursing in the Twentieth Century.* Temple University Press.
   Mitchell, S. Weir. *Fat and Blood.*
   Parsons, Ralph Wait. "The American Girl Versus Higher Education, Considered from a Medical Point of View." *New York Medical Journal* (1907).
   Sims, J. Marion. *The Story of My Life.*
   Toner, J. M. "Abortion in Its Medical and Moral Aspects." *Medical and Surgical Reporter.*
   Walsh, Mary Roth. *"Doctors Wanted, No Women Need Apply": Sexual Barriers to Women in Medicine.* New Haven, Conn.: Yale University Press.
   Wertz, Richard, and Dorothy Wertz. *Lying In: A History of Childbirth in America* (Schocken paperback).
Texts (supplemental):
   Barker-Benfield, G.J. *The Horrors of the Half-Known Life: Male Attitudes Toward Women and Sexuality in 19th Century America.* New York: Harper and Row, 1976.

Barker-Benfield, G.J. "A Historical Perspective on Women's Health Care—Female Circumcision." *Women and Health* (1976).

Beecher, Catherine. "Statistics of Female Health." In *Letters to the People on Health and Happiness.* 1855.

Brown, Elizabeth Stow. "The Working Women of New York: Their Health and Occupations." *Journal of Social Sciences,* 1889.

Blackwell, Elizabeth. "On Sexual Passion in Men and Women." Excerpted in Nancy Cott, *Root of Bitterness.*

Bullough, Vern, and Bonnie Bullough. "Lesbianism in the 1920s and 1930s: A Newfound Study." *Signs* 2 (1977).

Bullough, Vern, and Martha Voght. "Women, Menstruation and Nineteenth Century Medicine." *Bulletin of the History of Medicine,* 1973.

Clouston, T.S. "Female Education from a Medical Point of View." *The Popular Science Monthly* (1883).

Cook, Blanche Wiesen. "Female Support Networks and Political Activism: Lillian Wald, Crystal Eastman and Emma Goldman." *Chrysalis* no. 3 (1977).

Cook, Blanche Wiesen. "The Historical Denial of Lesbianism." *Radical History Review* 20 (1979).

Connally, Mark Thomas. "Prostitution, Venereal Disease, and American Medicine." In Connally, *The Response to Prostitution in the Progressive Era.*

Cott, Nancy. "Passionlessness: An Interpretation of Victorian Sexual Ideology 1790–1850." *Signs* (1978).

Cutright, Phillips, and Edward Shorter. "The Effects of Health on the Completed Fertility of Nonwhite and White U.S. Women Born Between 1867 and 1935." *Journal of Social History* (1979).

Davis, Katharine Bement. *Factors in the Sex Life of Twenty-Two Hundred Women.* New York: Harper and Brothers, 1929.

Degler, Carl. "What Ought to Be and What Was: Women's Sexuality in the 19th Century." *American Historical Review,* 1974.

Dewey, John. "Health and Sex in Higher Education." *Popular Science Monthly* (1886).

DuBois, Ellen, MariJo Buhle, Temma Kaplan, Gerda Lerner, and Carroll Smith-Rosenberg. "Politics and Culture in Women's History: A Symposium." *Feminist Studies.* 1980.

Duffy, John. "Masturbation and Clitoridectomy." *Journal of the American Medical Association* (1963).

Edgar, Clifton J. "Bathing During the Menstrual Period." *American Journal of Obstetrics* (1904).

Engelhardt, H. Tristram, Jr. "The Disease of Masturbation: Values and the Concept of Disease." *Bulletin of Historical Medicine* (1974).

Fee, Elizabeth. "Nineteenth Century Craniology: The Study of the Female Skull." *Bulletin of Historical Medicine* (1979).

Gilman, Charlotte Perkins. *The Yellow Wallpaper.*

Gordon, Linda. *Woman's Body, Woman's Right: A Social History of Birth Control in America.* 1976.

Himes, Norman E. *Medical History of Contraception.*

Hollander, Mark. "The Medical Profession and Sex in 1900." *American Journal of Obstetrics,* 1970.

Hollingworth, Leta Stetter. *Functional Periodicity: An Experimental Study of the Mental and Motor Abilities of Women During Menstruation,* Teachers College, Columbia University Contributions to Education, #69. New York: Columbia University Press, 1914.

Hudson, Robert. "The Biography of Disease: Lessons from Chlorosis." *Bulletin of Historical Medicine* (1977).

Jacobi, Mary Putnam. *The Question of Rest During Menstruation for Women.*

Kaiser, Irwin H. "Reappraisals of J. Marion Sims." *American Journal of Obstetrics and Gynecology* (1978).

Kennedy, David. *Birth Control in America: The Career of Margaret Sanger.*

Kern, Louis J. "Ideology and Reality: Sexuality and Woman's Status in the Oneida Community." *Radical History Review* (1979).

Kern, Stephen. *Anatomy and Destiny.* 1975.

Knopf, S. Adolphus. "Tuberculosis Among Young Women." *Journal of the American Medical Association* (1928).

Langer, William L. "Infanticide: A Historical Survey." *History of Childhood Quarterly* (1974).

LaSorte, Michael A. "Nineteenth Century Family Planning Practices." *Journal of Psychohistory* (1976).

Lewis, Dio. "The Health of American Women." *North American Review* (1882).

Longo, Lawrence. "The Rise and Fall of Battey's Operation: A Fashion in Surgery." *Bulletin of Historical Medicine* (1979).

Morgan, Edmund S. "The Puritans and Sex." *New England Quarterly* (1942).

Mosher, Clelia Duel. "Some of the Causal Factors in the Increased Height of College Women." *Journal of the American Medical Association* (1923).

Mosher, Clelia D., and Ernest G. Martin. "The Muscular Strength of College Women." *Journal of the American Medical Association* (1918).

Parsons, Gail Pat. "Equal Treatment for All: American Medical Remedies for Male Sexual Problems, 1850–1900." *Journal of the History of Medicine* (1977).

Perry, Lewis. "Progress, Not Pleasure, Is Our Aim: The Sexual Advice of an Antebellum Radical." *Journal of Social History* (1979).

Reed, James. "Doctors, Birth Control, and Social Values, 1830–1970." In *Therapeutic Revolution: Essays in the Social History of American Medicine*, eds. Morris J. Vogel and Charles E. Rosenberg.

Reed, James. *From Private Vice to Public Virtue.*

Rosenberg, Charles E. "Sexuality, Class and Role in 19th Century America." *American Quarterly* (1973).

Rudofsky, Bernard. *The Unfashionable Human Body.* 1974.

Rupp, Leila J. "Imagine My Surprise: Women's Relationships in Historical Perspective." *Frontiers* (1980).

Ryan, Mary P. "The Power of Women's Networks: A Case Study of Female Moral Reform in Antebellum America." *Feminist Studies* (1979).

Sahli, Nancy. "Sexuality in 19th and 20th Century America: The Sources and Their Problems." *Radical History Review* (1979).

Sanger, Margaret. *What Every Girl Should Know* (reprint edition paperback available).

Sauer, R. "Attitudes to Abortion in America 1800–1973." *Population Studies* (1974).

Schroeder, Fred E.H. "Feminine Hygiene, Fashion and the Emancipation of American Women." *American Studies* (1976).

Scully, D., and P. Bart. "A Funny Thing Happened on the Way to the Orifice: Women in Gynecology Textbooks." *American Journal of Sociology*, 1973.

Scully, Diana. *Men Who Control Women's Health: The Miseducation of Obstetricians and Gynecologists.* 1980.

Showalter, Elaine, and English Schowalter. "Victorian Women and Menstruation." *Victorian Studies* (1970).

Sicherman, Barbara. "The Uses of a Diagnosis: Doctors, Patients and Neurasthenia." *Journal of the History of Medicine and Allied Sciences* (1977).

Sklar, Katherine. "All Hail to Pure Cold Water!" *American Heritage* (1974).

Smith-Rosenberg, Carroll. "The Female World of Love and Ritual: Relations Between Women in 19th Century America." *Signs* (1975).

Smith-Rosenberg, Carroll, and Charles E. Rosenberg. "The Female Animal: Medi-

cal and Biological Views of Woman and Her Role in 19th Century America."
Journal of American History (1973).

Stage, Sarah. *Female Complaints: Lydia Pinkham and the Business of Women's Medicine.* 1979.

Vecoli, Rudolph J. "Sterilization: Progressive Measure?" *Wisconsin Magazine of History* (1960).

Methods of evaluation: Exams, papers, class participation.

Syllabus

January	25	Introduction and Expectations	
	27	Female Invalidism	
February	1	Menstrual cycle	
	3	Menstrual cycle	
	8	Sexuality	
	10	Sexuality	
	15	Birth control	"Margaret Sanger"
	17	Birth control	
		EXAM OR PAPER TOPIC	
	22	Abortion	
	24	Abortion	
March	1	Gynec Surgery and Treatment	
	3	Gynec Surgery and Treatment	
	8	Childbirth	"Semmelweis"
	10	Childbirth	
	15	Childbirth	"Fight for Life"
	17	Childbirth	
	22	Midwives	"All My Babies"
	24	Midwives	
		PAPER OUTLINES AND BIBLIOGRAPHIES OR EXAM	
	29	SPRING RECESS	
	31	SPRING RECESS	
April	5	Physicians	
	7	Physicians	
	12	Physicians	"Kate Pelham Newcomb"
	14	Physicians	
		PAPERS	
	19	Nurses	
	21	Nurses	
	26	Health Reformers	
	28	Conclusions	
May	3	Student Reports	
	5	Student Reports	
	10	Student Reports	
	12	Evaluations	

FINAL EXAM: May 17, 1983 – 9:30–11:30 a.m.

Discussion Questions:
 1. Were women sickly in the 19th century? What evidence do we need to answer this question?
 2. What is neurasthenia? How and why did it affect women?
 3. What role did the medical profession play in defining "female complaints"?
 4. Why do women get sick?
 5. Are women today sickly? How do we know?
 6. Is biology destiny?
 7. Were 19th century women's capabilities different from men's?
 8. What were the 19th century medical theories about the significance of puberty?
 9. Did physicians really believe in cyclic control?
10. Where did their beliefs come from?
11. What did feminist physicians believe? How do you account for differing beliefs about women's physiology?
12. What should a 19th century woman have done to maintain her health?
13. How did 19th century women's menstrual experiences compare with today's? How do you account for the differences?
14. What did physicians believe in the 19th century about women's sexuality?
15. What do we know about actual sexual behavior in 19th century women?
16. What was the significance of sex for women's health?
17. How do disease concepts and states of health get defined historically? today?
18. What is birth control?
19. What were the options for limiting the number of children available to 19th century women? Who used these methods?
20. How did the birth control movement get started? Was it a radical or a conservative movement? Who opposed it? supported it?
21. Why did Margaret Sanger believe the pill was the final and best solution to the birth control problem?
22. Assess Margaret Sanger's importance to the birth control movement.
23. Whose responsibility was family limitation? How did abortion fit with other options?
24. Who tried to abort in the 19th century? What reasons prompted this decision?
25. By what methods did women abort in the 19th century?
26. How did 19th century physicians feel about abortion? What did they do about it?
27. What role did the Church play in the anti-abortion movement?
28. How did the law change in relation to abortion? Why?
29. What was the quickening doctrine and how did it affect abortion policy?
30. When and how has infanticide been used to limit family size?
31. What have been the effects of dress on women's health? Why did women wear corsets?
32. What did physicians believe about women's clothing? What did feminists believe?
33. Why did (and do) women continue to wear clothing that was uncomfortable and unhealthy?
34. How have physicians treated women's diseases? Why?
35. Assess Marion Sims. Was his contribution positive or negative? What criteria do you use? What about S. Weir Mitchell?
36. Were 19th century men's treatments different from women's treatments? How? Why?
37. What techniques have been available to women for childbirth? For alleviation of pain during childbirth?
38. How and why have these changed over time?
39. Was childbirth a dangerous procedure in 19th century America?
40. How did doctors view childbirth? What was their role?
41. How did women experience childbirth?

42. What were typical positions for labor and delivery? How and why did they change over time?
43. What role did the midwife play? What happened to the midwife?
44. Who makes decisions about childbirth procedure? location? attendants?
45. How did women's role and "sphere" change during 19th century and how did these changes affect motherhood?
46. What was scientific motherhood?
47. What choices did women have over their lives? Were they different for women who chose motherhood and those who did not? Was motherhood a choice? or a destiny?
48. Why were midwives traditionally women? What was their role in childbirth? How did this change over time?
49. Why were midwives replaced as childbirth attendants? When? How? Whose decision was it largely? How do we know?
50. How did or does a midwife-attended birth differ from a physician-attended birth?
51. How were midwives trained? How did their training differ from physicians? What differences did this make?
52. What women chose midwives? What women chose not to have midwives? Why? When and how did this change?
53. Who were the first generation of medical women in America? Why did they choose medicine?
54. What was medical education like for 19th century women? Did it differ from men's medical education?
55. What were the experiences of early women doctors? What problems did they encounter? Successes? Who supported them?
56. What kinds of problems did women face in setting up medical practices? Why? Who were their patients? What specialties did they enter?
57. Why did numbers of women in medicine decline in the 20th century? Will history repeat itself?
58. In what ways were women physicians special?
59. Why and how did professional nursing develop in this country? How did it differ from what came before?
60. Who chose nursing as a career? Why? How did nurses differ from women doctors as to class, residence, age, etc.?
61. What is the role of the nurse? How did this evolve? What is the legacy of Florence Nightingale?
62. How do nurses relate to other members of the health team? How does modern nursing differ from turn-of-the-century nursing?
63. What role did women play in health reform? Why were they so important to the movement?
64. In what ways did municipal housekeeping and health reform in general fit women's traditional roles? conflict with?
65. What were the limitations on women's health reform work?

* * * * *

Course Title: Women and Medicine WS 220

Institution name: Goucher College.
Name(s) and departmental affiliation(s) of individual(s) teaching this course: Judith Beris-Markowitz, Women's Studies.

Specific information regarding the course:
  Department(s) in which the course is listed: Women's Studies.
  Course level and audience for whom it is intended: Taught at 200 level; general
    audience.
  Prerequisites: Sophomore standing or Women's Studies 100 (introductory Women's
    Studies course).
  Method of instruction: Lecture/discussion.
Texts:
  Ehrenreich, J., and English, D. *For Her Own Good: 150 Years of Experts' Advice*
    to Women.
  Fee, Elizabeth, ed. *Women and Health: The Politics of Sex in Medicine.*
  Hubbard, Ruth, et al., eds. *Biological Woman — The Convenient Myth.*
  Melosh, Barbara. *"The Physician's Hand": Work Culture and Conflict in American*
    Nursing.
  Walsh, Mary Roth. *"Doctors Wanted — No Women Need Apply": Sexual Barriers*
    to Women in Medicine, 1835-1975.
  Plus articles on reserve in the library.
Methods of evaluation: Exams, papers, and class participation.
Brief course description: An interdisciplinary study of disease theory, treatment, and
    medical professionalism as they relate to cultural assumptions about women's
    social role, women's nature and women's reproductive capacity; and to women's
    actual role and status (historically and at present) as practitioners and patients.

Syllabus

Jan. 30	Introduction
Feb. 1	Current Issues and Problems for Women
Feb. 3	In Hubbard, pp. 1-16
	In Walsh: Preface, pp. ix-xix
	On Reserve: Levinson, "Sexism in Medicine"
Feb. 6	Medicine and Society
	In Fee: Fee, pp. 17-34
Feb. 8	Science and Women: Women in Science
	In Hubbard: Hubbard, pp. 17-46
	In Fee: Lewonton, pp. 243-260
Feb. 10	In Hubbard: Lowe, pp. 91-116
	Weisstein, pp. 265-282
	On Reserve: Wilson, "Dancing Dogs..."
Feb. 13	The Woman Question
	Ehrenreich/English: pp. 1-29
Feb. 15	Medicine Before the 19th Century
Feb. 17	Women in Medicine Before the 19th Century
Feb. 20	Midwives and Obstetrics
	Ehrenreich/English, pp. 33-48
Feb. 22	Medicine in the 19th Century: Theory, Practice and Challenge
Feb. 24	Ehrenreich/English, pp. 48-58
Feb. 27	Gynecology: Medicine Treats and Defines Women
Feb. 29	Ehrenreich/English, pp. 101-140
	On Reserve: Action, "The Perfect Ideal..."
	Brown, "Curing Insanity..."
Mar. 2	Medicine Limits Women
Mar. 5	Walsh, Chapter 1
	On Reserve: Maudsley, "Sex and Mind in Education"
	Anderson, "...A Reply"
	Maurice, "Women's Education..."

Mar. 7   Medicine and Social Issues: Abortion
Mar. 9   Medicine and Social Issues: Prostitution
             On Reserve: Action, "The Need for Legislation..."
                            "The Examination"
                    Butler, "The Ladies; Appeal..."
                            "Men, Men, Only Men"
                            "Abuses..."
Mar. 12   EXAM
Mar. 14   Birthing: Theories and Practices
Mar. 16   Ehrenreich/English, pp. 93–98
             In Hubbard: Brack, pp. 207–226
Mar. 19   On Reserve: Bragdan, "Care or Cure..."
                    Layton, "A Midwife's Career"
                    Englishwoman's Review, "The Need..."
Mar. 21   Hospitals
Mar. 23   Beginnings of Nursing
             Melosh, Chapter 1, pp. 15–35
             On Reserve: Nightingale, "Advice to..."
                    The Lancet, "Woman as Doctor – or Nurse?"
Apr. 2   Women as Physicians
             Walsh, Chapters 2, 3, and 4
             On Reserve: Jex Blake, "Speech for Admission..."
             Ehrenreich/English, pp. 58–68
Apr. 4   Walsh, Chapters 5, 6 and 7
Apr. 6   Professionalization and Reform in Medicine
             Ehrenreich/English, pp. 69–93
Apr. 9   Cultural Changes in the Early 20th Century
Apr. 11   Ehrenreich/English, pp. 183–210
Apr. 13   Nursing: Profession or Craft?
             Melosh, Chapters 2 and 3
Apr. 16   Melosh, Chapters 4 and 5
Apr. 18   Birth Control
             In Fee: Gordon, pp. 151–176
Apr. 20   Motherhood: New Definitions
             Ehrenreich/English, pp. 211–235
Apr. 23   Ehrenreich/English, pp. 235–265
Apr. 25   Sexuality and Reproductive Processes
             Ehrenreich/English, pp. 269–297
Apr. 27   In Hubbard: Birke, pp. 71–90
             Ehrenreich/English, pp. 297–311
Apr. 30   In Hubbard: Birke and West, pp. 161–184
                        Grossman and Bart, pp. 185–206
May 2   Medical Intervention
             In Fee: Weiss, pp. 59–76
                      Stark, et al., pp. 177–210
             In Hubbard: Rodriguez-Trias, pp. 147–160
May 4   Employment Hazards and Discrimination for Women Health Workers
             In Fee: Waldron, pp. 119–138
                      Messing, pp. 139–148
May 7   In Hubbard: Stellman and Henefin, pp. 117–146
May 9   In Fee: Brown, pp. 105–116
                      Weaver and Garrett, pp. 79–104
May 11   Women as Health Professionals: As Physicians
             Walsh, Chapters 8 and 9

On Reserve: Howell, "Can We Be..."
                Angell, "Women in Medicine..."
May 14   As Nurses
                Melosh, Conclusion, pp. 207–219
                On Reserve: "Sex Discrimination..." Cleland
                Hull, "Dealing with Sexism..."
May 16   The Women's Health Movement — and Beyond
                Ehrenreich/English, pp. 314–324

*   *   *   *   *

Course Title: Women and Medicine in American History, History 615

Institution name: University of Kansas, Lawrence.
Name(s) and departmental affiliation(s) of individual(s) teaching this course: Dr. Gina Morantz.
Specific information regarding the course:
  Department(s) in which the course is listed: History.
  Prerequisites: None.
  Method of instruction: Lectures, reading, and discussion.
Texts:
  Beecher, Catherine. "Statistics on Female Health." In *Letters to the People on Health and Happiness*.
  Beecher, Catherine. "Circular to Mothers and Teachers: Health Reform Articles on Dress." *Water Cure Journal*.
  Betts, Helen R. "Dress of Women and its Relation to the Etiology and Treatment of Pelvic Disease." *Journal of the American Medical Association* 10 (1888): 509–513.
  Bigelow, Jacob. *A Discourse on Self-Limited Diseases*.
  Blackwell, Elizabeth. *Pioneer Work in Opening the Medical Profession to Women*.
  Buck, D.W., M.D. "A Raid on the Uterus." *New York Medical Journal* (1867).
  Cabot, Richard C. "Women in Medicine." *Journal of the American Medical Association* (1915).
  Clarke, E.H. *Sex in Education.* pp. 1–117.
  Cook, G.W., "Should Marriage Be Recommended As a Remedy for Disease in Women?" *American Journal of Obstetrics* (1893).
  Dewey, John. "Health and Sex in Higher Education." *Popular Science Monthly* (1886).
  Dickinson, Robert L. "Bicycling for Women from the Standpoint of the Gynecologist." *American Journal of Obstetrics* (1895).
  Gilman, Charlotte Perkins. "The Yellow Wallpaper" and passages from Gilman's autobiography describing her breakdown.
  Goffe, J.R. "The Physical, Mental and Social Hygiene of Growing Girl." *American Journal of Obstetrics* (1911).
  Haller, John S., and Robin Haller. *The Physician and Sexuality*.
  Hanaford, Dr. J.H. "Unity of Reforms."
  Hollender, Mark, M.D. "The Medical Profession and Sex in 1900." *American Journal of Obstetrics & Gynecology* 108 (Sept. 1, 1970): 139–148.
  "Lady Abettors of Quackery." *Boston Medical and Surgical Journal*.
  Lerner, Gerda. *The Female Experience*.

Mosher, Clelia, M.D. "Normal Menstruation and Some Factors Modifying It." *Johns Hopkins Hospital Bulletin* (1901).

Munroe, George J. "Cliteradectomy." *Medical Record* (1868).

Munroe, George J. "A Case in Practice." *Alabama Medical and Surgical Age* (1889/90).

Newell, Franklin S. "The Effects of Overcivilization on Maternity." *American Journal of Medical Sciences* (1908).

Nichols, Thomas L. *The Curse Removed, The Efficacy of Water Cure in the Treatment of Uterine Diseases and Pregnancy.*

Rohe, George H., M.D. "The Relation of Pelvic Disease and Psychical Disturbances in Women." *American Journal of Obstetrics* (1892).

Shryock, Richard. *Medicine and Society in America.*

Smith, Steven, M.D. "Woman Student in a Medical College." In *In Memory of Dr. Elizabeth Blackwell and Dr. Emily Blackwell.*

Wilson, H.P.C. "The Indiscriminate Use of Opiates in the Pelvic Diseases of Women." *Transactions of the Southern Surgical and Gynecological Association* (1890).

Yarnall, M. "Too Much Surgery." *Texas Health Journal* (1891).

Methods of evaluation: Exams, papers, class participation.

Brief course description: This course will deal with the development of medical practice in nineteenth century America, placing particular emphasis on the influence of women, as both patients and practitioners, on the course of nineteenth century medicine. The state of women's health, including female invalidism, hysteria, pregnancy, childbirth, birth control, and sexuality will be studied, as well as medical theories and therapies devised to cope with these problems. The nineteenth century health reform movement will also be investigated and women's contribution to the nineteenth century health revolution, as both physicians and lay reformers, will be explored. Finally, the lives of selected women doctors will be discussed and examined as representative examples.

Students are advised that the success of this course is partially dependent on preparation prior to class. Participation in class discussion is important. Class participation, attendance, and the familiarity of the student with the reading assignments will be taken into account by the instructor upon the determination of the student's grade.

Syllabus

January 19–31 I. Colonial Medicine and 19th Century Medical Therapeutics
Read: Richard Shryock, *Medicine & Society in America*
Jacob Bigelow, *A Discourse on Self-Limited Diseases*, (on reserve)

February 2–23 II. Changes in Women's Status and Their Effects on Concepts of Health, Disease and Reform
Read: Gerda Lerner, *The Female Experience*, 201–250
(Section II) and Essays #1, 4, 5, 6, 19, 20, 21, 22, 23, 30, 31, 32, 33, 35, 37, 47, 48
Catherine Beecher, "Statistics on Female Health" from *Letters to the People on Health & Happiness*
Catherine Beecher, "Circular to Mothers & Teachers: Health Reform Articles on Dress," *Water Cure Journal*
"Lady Abettors of Quackery," *Boston Medical & Surgical Journal*
Dr. J.H. Hanaford, "Unity of Reforms."
John S. and Robin Haller, *The Physician & Sexuality*, 1–87.

February 23   No class. Study of Midterm

February 28   MIDTERM

March 2–9   III. Women as Patients. Midwifery and Childbirth
                   Read: Haller, 191–303
                         Lerner, #12, 13, 14
                         Thomas L. Nichols, *The Curse Removed, The Efficacy of
                         Water Cure in the Treatment of Uterine Diseases &
                         Pregnancy* (on reserve)
                         Charlotte Perkins Gilman, "The Yellow Wallpaper" and
                         passages from Gilman's autobiography describing her
                         breakdown

March 14–20   VACATION

March 21–23   IV. Surgery and the Development of Gynecology
                   Read: D.W. Buck, M.D. "A Raid on the Uterus" *New York Med.
                         Jour.* (1867)
                         M. Yarnall, "Too Much Surgery" *Texas Health Jour.*
                         (1891)
                         George H. Rohe, M.D. "The Relation of Pelvic Disease
                         and Psychical Disturbances in Women," *American Jour.
                         of Obstetrics* (1892)

March 28–April 4   V. Women Enter the Medical Profession
                   Read: Elizabeth Blackwell, *Pioneer Work in Opening the Medical
                         Profession to Women*
                         Steven Smith, M.D. "Woman Student in a Medical Col-
                         ege" from *In Memory of Dr. Elizabeth Blackwell and
                         Dr. Emily Blackwell* (on reserve)
                         Lerner, #3, 36, 37, 72, 74

April 6   VI. Nineteenth Century Sexual Morality
                   Read: Haller, 89–138
                         Mark Hollender, M.D., "The Medical Profession and Sex
                         in 1900," in *Amer. Jour. of Obstetrics & Gyn.* 108,
                         (Sept. 1, 1970) 139–148
                         George J. Munroe, "A Case in Practice," *Alabama Med
                         and Surg. Age* 1889/90
                         "Cliteradectomy," *Medical Record* (1868)

April 11–13   Reading Period. Work on Paper

April 18–May 4   VII. The Development of Medical Institutions and the Debate
                        Over Higher Education for Women
                   Read: E.H. Clarke, *Sex in Education* 1–117 (on reserve)
                         Clelia Mosher, M.D., "Normal Menstruation & Some Fac-
                         tors Modifying It" *Johns Hopkins Hospital Bull.* (1901)
                         John Dewey, "Health & Sex in Higher Education" *Popular
                         Science Monthly*, 1886.
                         G.W. Cook, "Should Marriage Be Recommended As a
                         Remedy for Disease in Women?" *Am. J. of Obs.* 1893
                         Robert L. Dickinson, "Bicycling for Women from the
                         Standpoint of the Gynecologist" *Am. J. of Obs.* 1895
                         Franklin S. Newell, "The Effects of Overcivilization on
                         Maternity," *Am. J. of Med. Sciences*, 1908
                         J.R. Goffe, "The Physical, Mental and Social Hygiene of
                         Growing Girl" *Am. J. of Obs.* 1911

H.P.C. Wilson, "The Indiscriminate Use of Opiates in the Pelvic Diseases of Women," *Trans. of the South. Surg. & Gyn. Ass.* 1890

Richard C. Cabot, Women in Medicine," *JAMA* 1915

Helen R. Betts, "Dress of Women and Its Relation to the Etiology and Treatment of Pelvic Disease,"*JAMA* 10, (1888) 509–513

PAPERS DUE

May 9   Summary & Discussion

*   *   *   *   *

Course Title: Women and Science

Institution name: Hunter College.
Name(s) and departmental affiliation(s) of individual(s) teaching this course: Denise Frechet, Chemistry Department.
Specific information regarding the course:
  Department(s) in which the course is listed: Women's Studies.
  Course level and audience for whom it is intended: Undergraduate.
  Prerequisites: Introduction to Women's Studies plus one course in science.
  Method of instruction: Lectures, films, discussion.
Texts:

Beckwith, Jon, and John Durkin. "Girls, Boys, and Math." In *Biology as Destiny*, Science for the People, eds., pp. 37–42. 1984.

Briscoe, Anne. "Hormones and Gender." In *Genes and Gender I*, E. Tobach and B. Rosoff eds., pp. 31–50. New York: Gordian Press, 1978.

Calvin, William H. "Woman the Toolmaker?" In *The Throwing Madonna*, pp. 22–27, McGraw-Hill Paperbacks, 1983.

Crompton, Robin. "Old Bones Shatter Hunter Myths: Reexamining the Anthropological Records." In *Biology as Destiny*, Science for the People, eds., pp. 43–47. 1984.

Curran, Libby. "Science Education: Did She Drop Out or Was She Pushed?" In *Alice Through the Microscope*, pp. 22–41. London: Virago, 1980.

Fee, Elizabeth. "A Feminist Critique of Scientific Objectivity." *Science for the People* (1982).

Fox-Keller, Evelyn. "Feminism and Science." *Signs* (1982).

Hall, Paula Quick. *Problems and Solutions in the Education, Employment, and Personal Choices of Minority Women in Science.* AAAS, 1981.

Hartsock, Nancy. "The Feminist Standpoint: Developing the Ground for a Specifically Feminist Historical Materialism." In *Discovering Reality*, Sandra Harding and Merrill Hintikka, eds. Dordrecht: Reidel Publishing Co., 1983.

Longino, Helen, and Ruth Doell. "Body, Bias and Behavior: A Comparative Analysis of Reasoning in Two Areas of Biological Science." *Signs* (1983).

Merchant, Carolyn. "Nature as Female." In *The Death of Nature*, pp. 1–41. New York: Harper and Row, 1983.

Rose, Hilary. "Hand, Brain and Heart: A Feminist Epistemology for the Natural Sciences." *Signs* (1983).

Salzman, Freda. "Are Sex Roles Biologically Determined?" In *Biology as Destiny*, Science for the People, eds., pp. 30–36. 1984.

Sayers, Janet. "Sex Differences in the Brain." In *Biological Politics*. pp. 84–104. New York: Tavistock Publication, 1982.

Tobias, Sheila. "Mathematics and Sex." In *Overcoming Math Anxiety*, pp. 70–100. Boston: Houghton Mifflin Co., 1978.

Wallsgrive, Ruth. "The Masculine Face of Science." In *Alice Through the Microscope*, pp. 228–240. London: Virago.

Weisstein, Naomi. "How Can a Little Girl Like You Teach a Great Big Class of Men the Chairman Said, and Other Adventures of a Women in Science." In *Working It Out*, pp. 77–91. New York: Pantheon Books, 1977.

Methods of evaluation: Journals and oral presentations.

Brief course description: The aim of this course is to help students develop a critical attitude towards science, looking at topics such as: What is Science? What is Objectivity?, Science and Its Theories About Women, etc. Make students aware of the achievements of women scientists (History of women scientists, films about contemporary women scientists, etc.). Discuss the problems encountered by women scientists and solutions to these problems (panels with women scientists, presentation about the activities of feminist associations of women scientists).

Syllabus

Class I 2/4	Introduction Description of the Course Requirements Film: "Rosalyn Yalow" Discussion
Class II 2/11	What is Science? What is Objectivity? Where Do Scientific Theories Come From? The Feminist Critique of Science
Class III 2/25	Lecture by Nancy Leys-Stepan (Columbia U.) "Race, Class and Gender in Science"
Class IV 3/4	Lecture by Anne Briscoe (Columbia U.) "Women Scientists in History"
Class V 3/11	Is Science a Masculine Endeavour? Why are there so few women scientists? Views from Biology, Psychoanalysis and Sociology.
Class VI 3/18	Panel with Hunter College Women Scientists: How does a woman decide to become a scientist? What kind of difficulties does she encounter? What are the rewards?
Class VII 3/25	Lecture by Pam Surko (Bell Labs) "Feminist Associations of Women Scientists"
4/1 Spring recess	
Class VIII 4/8	Science and its theories about women: Examples from endocrinology, the theory of evolution and neurophysiology
Class IX 4/15	Lecture by Elizabeth Fee (Johns Hopkins University) "Caring and Curing: Towards a Gender Free Medical Care"

Class X   Films: "Science Women's Work"
4/22   "Shannon Lucid"
                   "Shirley Jackson"
             Discussion

Class XI   Women and Math:
4/29   Panel with Hunter College Women Scientists

Class XII   Lecture by Sandra Harding (University of Delaware)
5/6   "Feminism and Science: Epistemological Studies"

Class XIII   Presentation by students of a topic of their choice related to the course.
5/13

Evaluation: Students will be asked to keep a journal recording their impressions concerning the topics discussed in class and their readings.

There will also be one oral presentation (see class XII)

*   *   *   *   *

Course Title: Women in Sport and Physical Activity

Credits: 3.
Institution name: University of Wisconsin, Milwaukee.
Name(s) and departmental affiliation(s) of individual(s) teaching this course: Thelma Sternberg Horn, Ph.D., Assistant Professor, Department of Human Kinetics; School of Allied Health Professionals.
Specific information regarding the course:
  Department(s) in which the course is listed: Primarily listed with Department of Human Kinetics (School of Allied Health Professionals) and cross-listed with Women's Studies Program.
  Course level and audience for whom it is intended: Undergraduate and/or graduate students.
  Prerequisites: None.
  Method of instruction: Lecture/discussion.
Text:
  Boutilier, M., and SanGiovanni, L. *The Sporting Woman.* Champaign, Ill.: Human Kinetics Publishers, 1983.
Supporting Texts:
  Gerber, E., Felshin, J., Berlin, P. & Wyrick, W., eds. *The American Woman in Sport.* Reading, Mass.: Addison-Wesley, 1974.
  Hall, M.A. "Sport and Gender." *A Feminist Perspective on the Sociology of Sport.* Ottawa, Canada: CAHPER, 1978.
  Oglesby, C.A., ed. *Women and Sport: From Myth to Reality.* Philadelphia: Lea and Febiger, 1978.
  Additional readings from appropriate science journals will also be assigned.
Methods of evaluation: Regular attendance/participation, two written exams, course project (for graduate students only).
Brief course description: This course has been designed to provide the student with an introduction to the existing literature in regard to the female sport experience. Specifically, course content will reflect consideration of the historical, biophysi-

cal, psychosocial, and political factors that influence the behavior and performance of females in physical activity.

Course Rationale: Within the past decade, the advent of both the feminist movement and Title IX legislation has contributed to a significant increase in the number of females participating in physical activity. This increase is evident at all levels of participation: from the recreational and/or fitness-oriented programs to the competitive, elite Olympic/professional programs.

Although research pertaining to the performance and behavior of female athletes has not kept pace with the rapid increase in participatory rates, there is available a small but significant number of relevant research findings that contribute to an understanding of the female sport experience. However, because such information has not been adequately disseminated, integrated or implemented into existing curricula, the majority of courses in the human movement sciences, as well as the available textbooks for use in such classes, present facts, concepts, and theories concerning physical activity derived from research using male participants (Hall 1977). Generalizations made on the basis of such study are not necessarily applicable to females in sport and physical activity. Sports for American women has been a neglected phenomenon, both in terms of providing adequate opportunities for varied participation and in regard to the scholarly study of the sportswoman (Gerber et al. 1974).

It seems essential, then, to integrate the relevant but limited sport science research that has been conducted with females, along with the literature in such supporting fields as psychology, sociology, physiology, education, and history, for the purpose of obtaining a comprehensive perspective on women in sport and physical activity.

Therefore, this course was designed to (1) provide all students with an awareness of the various social and physical factors that influence female participation in sports and physical activity; (2) provide the practitioner (coach, teacher, athletic administrator, program director, parent) with some practical, applicable knowledge needed to provide quality sport experiences for female participants; (3) stimulate research interests among academicians in issues relating to the female in physical activity.

Syllabus

I. INTRODUCTION TO THE STUDY OF WOMEN IN PHYSICAL ACTIVITY
   A. Goals, philosophies, orientation to the study of sportswomen
   B. Important questions/issues
   C. Methodology and research design

II. SOCIOCULTURAL PERSPECTIVES
   A. Historical analysis
      1. Sociocultural history of the female role in society
      2. Society's perspective of the American woman in sport and physical activity
   B. Sociological analysis
      1. Influence of various social systems (e.g., family, educational institutions, mass media...) on the socialization of females into physical activity
      2. Role conflict and the female participant

III. PSYCHOLOGICAL ASPECTS
   A. Sex-role orientation
   B. Achievement orientation
   C. Attributional patterns
   D. Self-confidence
   E. Competence motivation
   F. Aggression/competitiveness

IV. BIOPHYSIOLOGICAL PERSPECTIVES
   A. Physiological capacities of females
      1. Genetic issues
      2. Developmental patterns
   B. Special topics in the physiology of sportswomen (e.g., pregnancy, amenor-rhea/dysmenorrhea, female children in sport, reproductive system)

READING ASSIGNMENTS

INTRODUCTION   Due Date—Jan. 30
1. Coackley, J. Females in sport: Liberation or equality with males? In *Sport and Society: Issues and Controversies.* St. Louis: C.V. Mosby Company, 1982.
2. Boutilier & SanGiovanni. Chapter 8, pp. 219-235 only.

SOCIOCULTURAL ASPECTS   Due Date—Feb. 20
3. Boutilier & SanGiovanni. Chapter 2, pp. 32-47 only.
4. Boutilier & SanGiovanni. Chapter 5.
5. Duquin, M. Differential sex role socialization toward amplitude appropriation. In A. Yiannakis, T.D. McIntyre, M.J. Melnick & D. Hard (Eds.) *Sport Sociology: Contemporary Themes.* Dubuque, Iowa: Kendall/Hunt, 1979.
6. Weitzman, L.J. *Sex Role Socialization.* Palo Alto, California: Mayfield Publishing Company, 1979 (pp. 48-80 only).
7. Viorst, J. Three Cheers for the Girls. In R. Martens (Ed.), *Joy and Sadness in Children's Sports.* Champaign, Ill.: Human Kinetics Press, 1976.
8. Rommel, E. Grade School Blues. *MS Magazine,* 1984, *12,* 32-35.
9. Kaplan, J. *Women and Sports.* New York: Avon Books, 1979. Chapter 4, pp. 73-103.

PSYCHOLOGICAL ASPECTS   Due Date—April 2
10. Duquin, M. The androgynous advantage. In C.A. Oglesby (Ed.) *Women and Sport: From Myth to Reality.* Philadelphia: Lea and Febiger, 1978, Chapter 5.
11. McHugh, J.C., Duquin, M.E. & Frieze, I.H. Beliefs about success and failure: Attribution and the female athlete. In C.A. Oglesby, Chapter 9.
12. Dweck, C.S. *Learned helplessness in sport.* Invited address at the International Congress of Physical Education, Trois-Rivieres, Canada, June, 1979.

PHYSIOLOGICAL ASPECTS   Due Date—May 7
13. Hudson, J. Physical parameters used for female exclusion from law enforcement and athletics. In C.A. Oglesby (Ed.), Chapter 2.
14. Wilmore, J.H. The application of science to sport: Physiological profiles of male and female athletes. *Canadian Journal of Applied Sport Sciences.*
15. Sasiene, G.H. Secondary amenorrhea among female athletes. *Journal of Physical Education, Recreation and Dance,* 1983, *54* (6), 61-63.
16. Kaplan, J. *Women and Sports.* Chapter 2.

*   *   *   *   *

Course Title: Women Leaders in Science

Credits: 3.
Institution name: University of Wisconsin, Green Bay.
Name(s) and departmental affiliation(s) of individual(s) teaching this course: Alice I. Goldsby, Ph.D., Environmental Sciences.

Specific information regarding the course:
  Department(s) in which the course is listed: Women's Studies and Environmental
  Studies.
  Course level and audience for whom it is intended: Juniors and Seniors.
  Prerequisites: None.
  Method of instruction: Lecture by instructor and guest lecturers. Discussion groups
  of young scientists out in the work force.
Texts: Readings will be assigned.
  Benedict, Ruth. *An Anthropologist at Work: Writings of Ruth Benedict*, Margaret
    Mead, ed. Calistoga, Calif.: Greenwood Press, 1977.
  Bettelheim, Bruno. *Women in the Scientific Profession.* Cambridge, Mass.: M.I.T.
    Press, 1965.
  Bowman, Kathleen. *New Women in Medicine.* Mankato, Minn.: Creative Ed., 1976.
  Bullivant, S. "U.S. Women Break into Engineering." *New Science* 95 (Sept. 30,
    1982): 918–921.
  Cherfas, J., and S. Connor. "How Restless DNA Was Tamed." *New Science* 100
    (Oct. 13, 1983): 78–79.
  Curie, Eve. *Madame Curie, A Biography.* Translated by Vincent Sheahan. New
    York: Doubleday, 1937.
  Donnison, Jean. *Midwives and Medical Men.* New York: Schocken Books, 1977.
  Eagles, Juanita, et al. *Mary Swartz Rose, 1874–1941: Pioneer in Nutrition.* New
    York: Teachers College Press, Columbia University.
  Ehrenreich, B., and English, D. *Witches, Midwives, and Nurses: A History of
    Women Healers.* Old Westbury: Feminist Press.
  Elder, E.S. "Women in Early Geology." *Journal of Geological Education* 30 (1982):
    287–293.
  Ferry, G. "Great Women Scientists on Display." *New Science* 102 (1984): 46.
  Fins, Alice. *Women in Science.* Lincolnwood, Ill.: National Textbook, 1983.
  Galkin, K. *The Training of Scientists in the Soviet Union.* Publishing House, 1959.
  Golde, P. *Women in Field-Anthropological Experiences.* Chicago: Aldine Publish-
    ing, 1970.
  Hellstedt, Leone. *Women Physicians of the World: Autobiographies of Medical
    Pioneers.* Wallingford, Conn.: McGraw-Hill, 1978.
  Hennings, M., and L. Barrett. "Women Physicists and Their Research: A Video
    Course." *American Journal of Physics* 51 (June 1983): 576.
  Hurd-Mead, Campbell. *A History of Women in Medicine from the Earliest Times to
    the Beginning of the 19th Century.* New York: American Medical Society, 1976.
  Jochnowitz, Carol. *Careers in Medicine for the New Women.* New York: Franklin
    Watts, 1978.
  Jones, G. "Second Chance for Women Engineers." *New Science* 94 (1982): 282–285.
  Julian, M.M. "Rosalind Franklin, From Coal to DNA to Plant Viruses." *Journal of
    Chemical Education* 60 (Aug. 1983): 660–662.
  Koshelva, I. *Women in Science.* USSR: Progress Publications. Chicago: Imported
    Publications, 1983.
  Lapote, C. *Women in Medicine.* Baltimore: Johns Hopkins University Press, 1968.
  Mark, Geoffrey, and W.K. Beatty. *Women in White.* New York: Scribners, 1972.
  Matthew, Scott. *The First Woman of Medicine: The Story of Elizabeth Blackwell.*
    Madison, Wisc.: Silver, 1978.
  McKelway. "Women in Oceanography." *Oceanus* 25 (Winter 1982–83): 75–79.
  Meyers, N. "Women in Science: No Home from Home in Israel." *Nature* 306 (Nov.
    10, 1983): 104.
  Miller, J.A. "Nobel Prize to McClintock and Her Mobile Elements." *Science News*
    124 (Oct. 15, 1983): 244.
  Moody, J.B. "Status of Women in the Earth Sciences." *Geology* 12 (1984): 191.

Mozans, H.J. *Women in Science.* New York: Appleton, 1918.

Ranahan, Demerris. *Contributions of Women: Medicine.* Dillon Press, 1981.

Rudolph, E.D. "Women in Nineteenth Century American Botany: A Generally Unrecognized Constituency." *American Journal of Botany* 69 (Sept. 1982): 1346–1355.

Tarbell, A.T., and D.S. Tarbell. "Helen Abbott Michael: Pioneer in Plant Chemistry." *Journal of Chemical Education* 59 (July 1982): 548–549.

Watkins, S.A. "Lise Meitner: The Making of a Physicist." *Physics Teacher* 22 (Jan. 1984): 12–15.

"Women in Science in the United Kingdom." *Nature* 302 (March 1983): 9.

"Women in the Age of Science and Technology, the Status and Job Opportunities for Women in Science in Finland, Hungary, Russia, England and the U.S. and the Developing Countries." *Impact of Science in Society* 20 (1970): 5–105.

Rather, J. "Programs Provide a History Lesson — Blacks and Women in Science." *Science* 220 (April 8, 1983): 186–187.

Zahn, J.A. *Women in Science.* Cambridge, Mass.: M.I.T. Press, 1974.

Methods of evaluation: Exams, discussions, papers.

Brief course description: The contributions of leading women scientists to science from early times to the present will be included in this course. Specific scientists, including outstanding temporary young scientists and the women Nobel Laureates will be discussed. The discussions will also include personal and educational backgrounds, as well as factors leading to success. Educational backgrounds of women of science in countries other than Western Europe and the U.S. will be included. There will be class periods in which a panel of women scientists or employees from the community will be invited to talk to the class.

Syllabus

Week 1: Early women scientists, midwives and witches.

Week 2: A discussion of women in the allied health area from early times to the present; this will include nurses, medical technicians, etc. A guest speaker will be invited for the last hour of class to discuss recent changes in the allied health area.

Week 3: A discussion of early physicians; the first American female physician, Elizabeth Blackwell and early scientists, including Eve Curie and others.

Week 4: The training of women scientists in the U.S., Russia, England, Finland and other countries and the status of job opportunities in these countries (Hour 1).

Hour 2: A panel of young beginning scientists (women) selected from the community and the campus, will discuss their background, education, and career.

Hour 3: A panel of foreign students, male and female, will discuss the education of women scientists in their countries.

Week 5: A discussion of prominent women in modern medicine, their background, education, accomplishments, the practices and factors leading to success.

Week 6: Test.

Women in anthropology, in the field and in the laboratory. A discussion of the background, education, accomplishments, and factors leading to the success of women anthropologists.

Week 7: Women in chemistry and physics, their education, background, accomplishments and factors leading to their success. Two video tapes will be shown dealing with women physicists and their research.

Week 8: Women in mathematics will be the topic of discussion, including their background, education, factors of success, and their accomplishments.

Week 9: A discussion of women engineers and inventors from early times to the present, including their background, education, accomplishments, and factors leading to their success.

Week 10: A discussion of the background, education, accomplishments and factors leading to the success of natural scientists, including botanists and zoologists.

Week 11: Women scientists in earth science and nutrition will be the topic of discussion, including their background, education, accomplishments, and factors leading to their success.

Week 12: The discussion will include the changing emphasis on the utilization of outstanding science-trained women in the job market (education, government, industry, and management). A panel of personnel directors selected from local industries will be invited for one hour to discuss these changes and how they choose outstanding women employees for science positions.

Week 13: The topic of discussion will be women environmentalists. Women the caliber of Rachel Carson & others will be discussed, including their education, background, accomplishments and factors contributing to their success.

Weeks 14 & 15: The women laureates will be the prime topic of discussion. We will center on their contribution to science, their background, education, accomplishments and factors leading to their success.

Marie Curie – physics and chemistry, 1903, 1911
Irene Joliet-Curie – chemistry, 1935
Gerty Cori – physiology and medicine, 1947
Marie Goephert-Mayer – physics, 1963
Dorothy Crowfoot Hodgkin – chemistry, 1964
Rosalyn Yalow – physiology and medicine, 1977
Barbara McClintock – botany, 1982.

A *final exam* and paper dealing with some feature of women in science will be assigned.

Readings will be assigned.

*   *   *   *   *

Course Title: Women's Health, HE 3560

Institution name: Eastern Illinois University.

Name(s) and departmental affiliation(s) of individual(s) teaching this course: Susan Woods, Department of Health Education.

Specific information regarding the course:

Department(s) in which the course is listed: Health Education.

Course level and audience for whom it is intended: Junior/Senior level course for all majors.

Prerequisites: Junior/Senior level standing.

Method of instruction: Lecture/discussion.

Texts:

Women's Health by Shephard & Shephard.

Our Bodies, Ourselves by Boston Women's Health Book Collective.

Selected journal readings.

Methods of evaluation: Exams, issue reaction papers, journal reviews.

Brief course description: The course is designed to assist students in understanding the normal conditions and special problems of women's physiology; developing an awareness of the problems women face when dealing with the health care system; examining cultural attitudes towards women, and analyzing the impact of cultural stereotyping on women's physical and emotional health; identifying agencies, groups, and organizations that are potential resources when investigating women's health concerns.

Syllabus

Date	Topic	Assigned Reading
1/11	Issues in Women's Health	Section 1, 2
1/16	Film: "A Question of Survival"	Section 1, 2
1/18	Film: "A Question of Survival"	Section 1, 2
1/21	Historical Perspectives	Section 1, 2
1/23	Female Anatomy	Section 3
1/25	Female Anatomy, Film: "Pelvic Exams"	Section 4, 36
1/28	Menstrual Cycle	Section 4
1/30	Dysmenorrhea, PMS, Endometriosis	Section 32, 34, 76–79, 82
2/1	Menopause	26, 27, 28, 68
2/4	Women & Aging	Class notes
2/6	Film on Aging	
2/8	Breast Health – Video Tape "Breast Exam"	3, 33, 55, 56, 57
2/11	Vaginitis	84, 85
2/13	Sexually Transmitted Diseases	24
2/15	Test I	
2/18	Hormonal Contraceptives	9
2/20	IUD, Barrier Methods	7, 8
2/22	Rhythm, Issues in Contraceptive Choices	5, 6
2/25	Sterilization	42
2/27	Abortion & Film: "Four Young Women"	43
3/1	Teenage Pregnancy & Film: "Mother May I"?	Class notes
3/4	Fertilization/1st Trimester of Pregnancy	16
3/6	Film: "Issues in Pre-Natal Diagnosis"	11–16
3/8	Pregnancy/2nd Trimester	14–21
3/11	Pregnancy/3rd Trimester	14–21
3/13	Childbirth Film	14–21
3/15	Film on Leboyer Method for Infant/Childbirth Alternatives	14–21
3/18	Film: "Bonding at Birth"	14–21
3/20	Film: "Midwives"	14–21
3/22	Film: "Fathers and Child Rearing"	14–21
4/1	Catch up day or Discussion on Birthing In America	14–21
4/3	Test II	
4/5	Sexual Harassment	Class notes
4/8	Sexual Assault	Notes and 25
4/10	Domestic Violence	Notes
4/12	*Images of Women in Advertising*	Guest Lecture
4/15	Body Image	Class notes
4/17	Nutrition Issues	Notes and 46, 87
4/19	Eating Disorders	Notes and 87
4/22	Women and Drugs/Alcohol	29, 30 and notes
4/24	Fitness for Women	47 and notes
4/26	Film: "Women and Sports"	
4/29	Emotional Health	60, 69, 79
5/1	Emotional Health	60, 69, 79
5/3	Evaluation, Final Review	

* * * * *

Course Title: Women's Health, H 43407 & WS 78420

Institution name: The University of Tennessee, Knoxville, Division of Health & Safety.
Name(s) and departmental affiliation(s) of individual(s) teaching this course: Dr. June
   Gorski, Ph.D., Professor; Dr. Velma Pressly, Ed.D., M.S., R.N., Assistant
   Professor.
Specific information regarding the course:
   Department(s) in which the course is listed: Health and Safety H 4430; Women's
   Studies WS 4430.
   Course level and audience for whom it is intended: Upper division and graduate;
   men and women elect to take the course.
   Prerequisites: None.
   Method of instruction: Lecture/discussion, films, filmstrips, discussions, student
   reports on research papers, guest lecturers, graduate students' presentations.
Texts:
   American Medical Association. *Straight Talk, No Nonsense Guide to Woman Care*,
   revised, updated version. 1984.
   Margareta Sandalowski. *Women, Health and Choice.*
   Women, Work and Health: Challenges to Corporate Policy.
Methods of evaluation: Class participation, exams, philosophical paper, health
   research paper, and oral report.
Brief course description: Women's Health: "A study of factors influencing women's
   health and of women as consumers of the nation's health service delivery
   systems."
      The assignments: lectures, discussions and classroom activities are planned to
   enable the student to describe and discuss the physical, emotional, and social
   aspects of being female; demonstrate strategies for self-expression; define and
   practice safety procedures for self-protection; describe the nature and consequences of diseases, illnesses, and surgeries peculiar to females; identify traditional and alternative forms of health services for women; list and describe
   adjunct resources that assist women in receiving adequate health care; elucidate
   upon the factors to be considered when opting for parenthood or nonparenthood.
Other features of the course: There is a high level of participation by students in class
   activities. Strong friendships often develop from the course. There is a large
   degree of awareness and knowledge acquisition of women's health issues to be
   obtained through this course.

Syllabus

March	27	Course Overview	
	29	Female Body	Chapter 1
April	1	Ground Rules for Health	Chapter 2
	3	Ground Rules for Health	Chapter 2
	5	HOLIDAY, No class	
	8	You and Your Doctor	Chapter 3
	10	How Do You Feel? What Should You Do?	Chapter 4
	12	Physical Fitness	
	15	Menstrual Cycle	Chapter 5, also Sandalowski, Chapter 5
	17	Infertility	Chapter 8
	19	Pregnancy Controls	Chapter 7
	22	Pregnancy & Child Birth	Chapter 6
	24	Pregnancy & Child Birth	Chapter 6

	26	Gyn. Infections	Chapter 9
	29	Gyn. Surgery	Chapter 10
May	1	Gyn. Symptoms	Chapter 11
	3	Exam I	
	6	Cancer	Chapter 14
	8	The Aging Woman	Chapter 12
	10	The Aging Woman	Chapter 13
	13	Women, Work, Health	Walsh & Egdahl, Chapter 2, 6, 7
	15	Women, Work, Health	12, 13, 15
	17	Women, Work, Health	
May 20–31		ORAL REPORTS OF HEALTH PROBLEM RESEARCH	
June	3	Study Day	
	5	Alternative Period — 10:00–11:40	

Exam II (1) Chapter 12, 13, 14, 15, Text, and 2, 6, 7, 12, 13, 15 Walsh, Egdahl, (2) Reports

*   *   *   *   *

Course Title: The Women's Health Care Movement, WS 133

Institution name: California State University, Sacramento.

Name(s) and departmental affiliation(s) of individual(s) teaching this course: Core course of program — different faculty members teach it.

Specific information regarding the course:

Department(s) in which the course is listed: Women's Studies.

Course level and audience for whom it is intended: Undergraduate students, juniors and seniors. It is a general education and advanced studies class for the university.

Prerequisites: Must pass writing proficiency exam.

Method of instruction: Lecture, discussion.

Texts:

Boston Women's Health Book Collective. *The New Our Bodies, Our Selves.* New York: Simon & Schuster, 1984. (OBOS).

Dreifus, Claudia, Ed. *Seizing Our Bodies: The Politics of Women's Health.* New York: Vintage, 1977.

Greenwood, Sadja. *Menopause Naturally.* San Francisco: Volcano Press, 1984.

A reader of photocopied articles will be available for purchase. It will also be in the Reserve Book Room at the Library.

Methods of evaluation: Papers and exams.

Brief course description: The Women's Health Care Movement discusses a number of major social issues confronting Americans. Using the general topic of the Women's Health Care Movement, this course carefully examines how poverty, race, unemployment, and age critically affect the development of health care policies, as well as the provision of health care services to women.

These issues will be studied in light of facts such as 85 percent of all employees in the health field are women; women are the majority consumers of health care, using the system twice as often as men do, not only for themselves but for their children, spouses, and aging parents; women account for more than 60 percent of all patient-physician encounters; twice as many women as men are regularly prescribed antianxiety drugs, and so on.

An important emphasis of the course will be on critically discussing issues such as the effort to once again criminalize abortion, the use and abuse of sterilization, bioethical questions of genetic engineering, the growing field of midwifery, the increasing use of medical technology during childbirth, artificial insemination, and embryo transfer, pre- and post-menopause, nutrition and diet, eating disorders, mental illness, and aging.

Each of these issues will be discussed from a variety of perspectives. For example, the history of abortion will be examined in terms of the actions of the women's movement in the 1960s to legalize abortion and the current efforts by the antichoice movement to recriminalize abortion. The controversy between physicians trained in obstetrics and the growing popularity of midwives will be another issue examined from a variety of perspectives.

The approach is to provide, on each topic, both basic information on its physical and psychosocial dimensions and an analysis of related historical and current issues through various perspectives on health care. As in many areas of health today, there is considerable controversy about many of the topics. The overall goal is to improve our capacity to act as health care consumers and to forge greater understanding of women's health concerns.

An important emphasis of the course is to assess the information currently available in this area and to examine the reasons for a general lack of information and study in areas important to women's health, for example, the general absence of a serious financial commitment by researchers and drug companies to developing a safe method of birth control for women or men.

Course Objectives:
1. Analyze how poverty, age, race, and class affect the development of health care services and policies for women.
2. Examine current domestic issues of abortion, sterilization, genetic engineering, bioethics, medical technology, aging, eating disorders, diet, mental illness, menopause in terms of how these issues affect women's lives as both recipients and practitioners of health care.
3. Analyze the political movement of women to influence and alter existing medical practices.
4. Analyze the various research techniques appropriate to studying health care practices and policies. These techniques include epidemiological, demographics, case-study, participant observation, sampling, intersubjectivity, and so on.

Syllabus

Week 1   *INTRODUCTION: WOMEN, HEALTH AND MEDICINE*
          Provides an introduction and overview of the course. What is a feminist perspective on women's health? Brief overview of the women's health movements, women as providers and patients in health systems; origins and development of the issues addressed here.

          SLIDE SHOW: "Women Health Workers" by Phila. Women's Health Collective.

          REQUIRED READING:
          Handouts:
          D. Ruscavage: "How to Be Your Own Second Opinion"
          Gena Corea: THE HIDDEN MALPRACTICE (Ch. 4: The Patient-Doctor Relationship)

National Women's Health Network: Occupational Health History Form
DREIFUS: Fee: "Women and Health Care: A Comparison of Theories,"
pp. 279–297. VERY IMPORTANT.
Optional: Marieskind: "The Women's Health Movement: Past Roots,"
pp. 3–12.
OBOS: Ch. 24; The Politics of Women and Medical Care, pp. 555–597.

Week 2   *IMAGES OF WOMEN IN HEALTH AND HEALING SYSTEMS*
A general discussion of the overall treatment of women by various components of the health care system.

REQUIRED READING:
READER: Scully and Bart, "A Funny Thing Happened on the Way to the Orifice"
Prather and Fidell, "Sex Differences in the Content and Style of Medical Advertising"
Lennane and Lennane, "Alleged Psychogenic Disorders in Women — A Possible Manifestation of Sexual Prejudice"
McCranie, et al., "Alleged Sex Role Stereotyping in the Assessment of Women's Physical Complaints: A Study of General Practitioners"
Bernstein and Kane, "Physicians' Attitudes Toward Female Patients"
Armstage, Schnerderman and Bass, "Response of Physicians to Medical Complaints in Men and Women"

FIRST PAPER DUE

Week 3   *RACE, CLASS AND WOMEN'S HEALTH ISSUES*
Race, class and gender are the three factors most determinant of health status (degree of well-being). In this session we examine the relations of class and race to illnesses and health problems, available medical, prenatal and gynecological care, modes of care delivery and problems in the doctor/patient relationship.

REQUIRED READINGS:
OBOS: Review Ch. 24, pp. 555–597.
DREIFUS: Baker: "The Class Factor: Mountain Women"
Ehrenreich & English: "Complaints and Disorders: Sexual Politics of Sickness," pp. 43–56.
READER: H.D. Schwartz & C. Kart: "General Characteristics of Health & Health Care in America"
V. Navarro: "The Underdevelopment of Health of Working America"
R. Dunbar: "Poor White Women"
J. Malveaux: "Three Views of Black Women"
Richmond: "The Silent Killer: High Blood Pressure"
E. Maslow: "Storybook Lives: Growing Up Middle Class"
D. D'Amico: "To My White Working Class Sisters"
Second Opinion: Special Issue on Women of Color and Health Care
R. McKnight: "Organizing for Community Health"
R. Toneye: "Institutional Racism in the Med. Profession"
Eisen: "I'm Sick & Tired of Being Sick & Tired"

Week 4   *WOMEN AS PROVIDERS OF HEALTH CARE*
Women are 85% of all employees in the health field. Most of these women are in the lowest paying and lowest status jobs.

REQUIRED READING:
READER: West: "When the Doctor Is a 'Lady': Power, Status and Gender in Physician-Patient Conversations"

Graham: "Providers, Negotiators and Mediators: Women as the Hidden Carers"
Brown: "Women Workers in the Health Service Industry"
Clelland: "Sex Discrimination: Nursing's Most Pervasive Problem"
Weaver and Garrett, "Sexism and Racism in the American Health Care Industry Providers"
Alvarado, "The Status of Hispanic Women in Nursing"

Week 5   *FEMALE CYCLE FROM BIRTH THROUGH MENSTRUATION*
Anatomy and physiology of females from birth through menstruation: development of reproductive system, hormonal cycles, problems of menstruation [PreMenstrual Syndrome (PMS), amenorrhea, dysmenorrhea]. Experiential aspects of menstruation; cultural myths and stereotypes.

REQUIRED READINGS:
OBOS: "Stages in the Reproductive Cycle," pp. 209–219.
READER: G. Steinem: "If Men Could Menstruate"
Birke & Best: "Changing Minds: Women, Biology & the Menstrual Cycle"
Eagan: "The Selling of Premenstrual Syndrome"
Second Opinion: Premenstrual Syndrome Issue
L. Pogrebin: "Parenting: Talking About Menstruation"
J. Beck and C. Oram: "Tampons: Beyond TSS"
Seaman & Seaman: "Home Cures for Those Days"
RECOMMENDED READING: The journal *WOMEN AND HEALTH*, Vol. 8, #2 & 3, Summer/Fall 1983 is a Special Double Issue on "Lifting the Curse of Menstruation: A Feminist Appraisal of the Influence of Menstruation on Women's Lives"

*Interview due.

Week 6   *THE PRACTICE AND POLITICS OF BIRTH CONTROL*
Session focused on history of the birth control movement and current methods of birth control. Anatomy and physiology of the major methods: barriers (foam, condom, jellies, diaphragms, cervical caps, sponge), pills, IUDs, sterilization (various methods), injectables (Depo Provera), abortion (aspiration, dilatation and curettage, labor induction). Why did/do we need a birth control movement? Why do we have the methods of birth control we do? Why are there few male contraceptives?

REQUIRED READINGS:
OBOS: Ch. 13: Birth Control, pp. 220–262.
Ch. 16: Abortion, Medical Techniques, pp. 293–308.
READER. L. Gordon: "Birth Control: Historical Study"
Kash: "Birth Control Survey: Sterilization Tops"
Berkeley Women's Health Collective: "Birth Control Methods and Effectiveness Rates"
Korenbrot: "Value Conflicts in Biomedical Research into Future Contraceptives"
Blake: "Contraceptive Industry: Who Calls Shots?"
Kasindorf: "The Case Against IUDs"
Shainwald: "Suing for Dalcon Shield Injuries"
CDRR: "California Cuts in Contraceptive Services"
DREIFUS: (optional) Sharpe: "Birth Controllers" pp. 57–74
Dowie & Johnson: "A Case of Corporate Malpractice & the Dalcon Shield," pp. 86–104.

R. Arditti: "Have You Wondered Re Male Pill," pp. 121–130.
B. Seaman: "Dangers of Oral Contraceptives," pp. 75–84.

Week 7   *REPRODUCTIVE RIGHTS: ACCESS/COERCION/POPULATION CONTROL*
This session is focused on the *politics and economics* of contraception and reproduction. We will distinguish among six major approaches including population control, anti-abortion and emphasizing the feminist movement for reproductive rights for all people. Focus on abortion, sterilization abuse and Depo Provera.

REQUIRED READINGS:
OBOS: "History & Politics of Abortion" pp. 308–316.
READER: Clarke: "What ARE Reproductive Rights: A Comparison of Major Perspectives on Reproduction"
D. English: "The War Against Choice"
R2N2: "Cook County: Back to Coathangers"
Copelon: "Abortion Rights: Where Do We Go Next"
CDRR: "Resolution on Disability & Reproduction Rights"
CDRR: "Medicaid Funding Facts"
Akwesasne Notes: "Killing Our Future"
Wagman: "US Goal: Sterilize Millions of World's Women"
Clarke: "Subtle Forms of Sterilization Abuse"
Finger: "Cut in Waiting Period to Increase Abuse"
B. Ehrenreich, M. Dowie & S. Minkin: "The Charge Gynocide/The Accused: U.S. Gov't."
Rakusen: "Depo Provera: Extent of the Problem"
DREIFUS: (optional) "Abortion: This piece is for Remembrance"

Week 8   IN CLASS EXAM

PREGNANCY AND CHILDBIRTH
This session provides an historical overview of the experience of and issues in childbirth, the medicalization of childbirth and illegalization of midwifery at the turn of the century, puerperal fever, hospitalization as physicians' strategy, and the identicality of maternal and infant safety issues raised in 1933 and today. The anatomy and physiology of pregnancy and childbirth, normal and complicated births, Caesarian sections and labor induction and their appropriate and overuse, drugs, "natural" and autonomous childbirth movement, breastfeeding, miscarriage and other issues.

REQUIRED READINGS:
DREIFUS: A. Rich: "The Theft of Childbirth"
Spake: "The Pushers" (on DES)
OBOS: Ch. 18: Pregnancy, pp. 329–360.
Ch. 19: Childbirth, pp. 361–395.
Ch. 20: Postpartum, pp. 396–418.
READER: Ruzek: "Ethical Issues in Childbirth Technology"
"Hard Facts: Infant Mortality & Lack of Prenatal Care"
W. Reed: "Suffer the Children: Some Effects of Racism on the Health of Black Infants"
H. Graham & A. Oakley: "Competing Ideologies of Reproduction: Medical and Maternal Perspectives on Pregnancy"
The Pregnant Patient's Bill of Rights
Helen Marieskind: "Caesarian Section"

Dowie & Marshall: "The Benedictin Cover-Up"
Sprague: "Birth Defects by the Cup"
Leiber: "Fetal Alcohol Syndrome"
Lainson: "Breast-Feeding: Two New Views"
RECOMMENDED READINGS: Fall/Winter 1982 *WOMEN AND HEALTH*, Vol. 7, #3-4 Issue on "Obstetrical Intervention & Technology in the 1980s"

Week 9   *DISABLED WOMEN'S ISSUES*
Address the diversity of disabling conditions, myths and stereotypes of disabilities, sexuality, contraception and the special needs of disabled women, and the consequences of disability for obtaining adequate medical care.

REQUIRED READINGS:
OBOS: Sex & Physical Disabilities, pp. 191-194
READER: excerpt from TOWARD INTIMACY: Family Planning & Sexuality Concerns of Physically Disabled Women
Daniels: "Critical Issues in Sexuality & Disability"
Resources: Sex Education for Disabled People
Sprague: "Disabled Women and the Health System"
Fine & Asch: "The Question of Disability and Reproduction Rights"
A. Finger: "Claiming All of Our Bodies"
A. Finger: "Baby Doe: A Complex Issue"
A. Finger: "Feds Try Again to Enforce Care of Disabled Infants"

Week 10   *REPRODUCTIVE TECHNOLOGIES*
Reproductive technologies of all kinds are proliferating. Many aid people in addressing infertility, so we cover this here, along with Pelvic Inflammatory Disease (PID) which often causes infertility. We then review the major reproductive technologies (amniocentesis, artificial insemination, "test tube" babies, embryo transfer, ultrasound)—what they do and don't do—and discuss the politics of their use and misuse and their implications.

REQUIRED READINGS:
OBOS: Ch. 21: Infertility & Pregnancy Loss, pp. 419-431.
Ch. 17: New Reproductive Technologies, pp. 317-324.
READER: United Press: "Infertility of U.S. Women Rises"
Cooke: "It's Time To Take Male Infertility Seriously"
Coman: "Trying and Trying to Get Pregnant"
Population Reports: "Infertility and STDs"
Fugh-Berman: "Fetal Surgery: A Woman's Choice"
Rothman: "How Science Is Redefining Parenthood"
Hubbard: "Human Embryo and Gene Manipulation"

Weeks 11 *WOMEN AND AGING: MENOPAUSE, OSTEOPOROSIS, ETC.*
and 12   A variety of new health issues affect us as we age—from issues of decreased social worth and their consequences for our mental health, to economics, to physical health. In this session, we examine those issues plus: menopause (anatomy/physiology/cultural myths and stereotypes) and symptomatic treatments (ERT, nutrition); osteoporosis (fragile bones) and its prevention or minimization; sexuality issues.

REQUIRED READINGS:
OBOS: Ch. 22: Women Growing Older, pp. 435-472
DREIFUS: Seaman: "Dangers of Sex Hormones," pp. 172-176

Reitz: "What Docs Won't Tell You Re Menopause," pp. 209–211
Greenwood: "Menopause Naturally"
READER: Smith-Yokel: "A Five Minute Summary of 78 Years"
Rule: "Grandmothers"
Brody: "Scary Results of Calcium Deficiency"
MacDonald: "Barbara's Afterwords"
Ambrogi: "Feminization of Poverty Examined"
Options: "Seniors and Prescription Drugs"

*REVIEW ESSAY DUE

Week 13   *ISSUES IN WOMEN'S HEALTH: OCCUPATIONAL HEALTH,
CANCER, BREAST CANCER, CERVICAL DYSPLASIA,
HYSTERECTOMY, EATING DISORDERS*
On each issue, we present the anatomy and physiology of the condition/disease, range of current treatments, controversies surrounding treatments (usually the women's health community versus medical community).

REQUIRED READINGS:
OBOS: Ch. 23: "Introduction to Cancer" et al., pp. 511–517
Ch. 7: Environmental and Occupational Health, pp. 77–98
DREIFUS:
Kushner: "The Politics of Breast Cancer," pp. 186–194
Larned: "Epidemic: Unnecessary Hysterectomy," pp. 195–209
READER: Horowitz: "Why There Is NO Cancer Prevention"
Belson: "Breast Reconstruction" (after mastectomy)
Second Opinion: "PAP Smears: How Often Necessary?"
Clarke & Reaves: "Cervical Dysplasia: Ambiguous Condition"
Brown: "DES Daughters: Warning on Cryosurgery Cont."
Patterson: "Cervical Cancer: A Feminist Critique"
Goldberg: "Fighting Cancer and the Medical Establishment: Two
    Women's Experiences"
Review of Morgan: COPING WITH HYSTERECTOMY

Week 14   *MENTAL HEALTH, ALCOHOLISM AND DRUG PROBLEMS*
Physical and mental health are deeply intertwined as are aspects of women's lives which "drive us crazy." Session examines linkages between these, a quick overview of psychological theories of women and feminist critiques, emerging feminist theories and therapies, patterns in the institutionalization of women. Linked to mental health is the overprescription of psychoactive drugs for women — prescribed drug abuse. We also address drug abuse and alcoholism as women's issues.

REQUIRED READINGS:
OBOS: Ch. 5: Health & Healing, pp. 54–72
Ch. 6: Psychotherapy, pp. 73–76
Ch. 3: Alcohol, Mood-Altering Drugs & Smoking, pp. 33–40
READER: B. Walker: "Psychology and Feminism"
S. Kaplow: "Getting Angry"
J. Syfers: "Why I Want a Wife"
S. Griffin: "The Sink"
A. Kaplan: "Androgyny as a Model of Mental Health for Women: from
    Theory to Therapy"
E. Johnson: "Reflections on Black Feminist Therapy"

Week 15   *WRAP UP*

*   *   *   *   *

Course Title: Women's Health: Choices & Decisions, PAC 412

Institution name: Sangamon State University.
Name(s) and departmental affiliation(s) of individual(s) teaching this course: Margie Schinneer, R.N., M.S.N., Assistant Professor, Nursing Program.
Specific information regarding the course:
  Department(s) in which the course is listed: PAC (Public Affairs Colloquia).
  Course level and audience for whom it is intended: Open to all upper level and graduate students.
  Prerequisites: None.
  Method of instruction: Lecture/discussion.
Texts and Bibliography:
  Ashley, J. *Hospitals, Paternalism and the Role of the Nurse.* New York: Teachers College Press, 1976.
  Bermosk, L.S., and Porter, S.E. *Women's Health and Human Wholeness.* New York: Appleton-Century-Crofts, 1979.
  Dreifus, C. ed. *Seizing Our Bodies.* New York: Vintage Books, 1978.
  Eckholm, E., and Newland, K. *Health: The Family Planning Factor,* World Watch Paper 10. World Watch Institute, January 1977.
  Ehrenreich, B., and English, D. *Witches, Midwives, and Nurses: A History of Women Healers.* Oyster Bay, N.Y.: Glass Mountain Pamphlets.
  Flora, R.R., and Lang, T.A. *Health Behaviors.* St. Paul, Minn.: West Publishing Co., 1982.
  Fogel, C.I, and Woods, N.F. *Health Care of Women.* St. Louis: C.V. Mosby, 1981.
  Grissum, M., and Spengler, W.T. *Core Concepts in Health,* 3rd ed., Palo Alto, Calif.: Mayfield, 1982.
  Hongladarom, G., R. McCorkle, and N.F. Woods. *The Complete Book of Women's Health.* Englewood Cliffs, N.J.: Prentice-Hall,, 1982.
  Kjerrik, D.K. *Women in Stress: A Nursing Perspective.* New York: Appleton-Century-Crofts, 1979.
  Lesnoff-Caravaglia, G. *Health Care of the Elderly: Strategies for Prevention and Intervention.* New York: Human Sciences Press, 1980.
  Levy, S.M. "The Adjustment of the Older Woman: Effects of Chronic Ill Health and Attitudes Toward Retirement." *International Journal of Aging and Human Development* 12, no. 2 (1980): 93–110.
  Marieskind, H.I. *Women in the Health System.* St. Louis: C.V. Mosby, 1980.
  Martin, L.L. *Health Care of Women.* New York: Lippincott, 1978.
  Maxwell, R. *The Booze Battle.* New York: Ballantine Books, 1977.
  McGrory, A. "Women and Mental Illness: A Sexist Trap?" *Journal of Psychiatric Nursing* 18, no. 9 (1980): 13–19.
  Mercer, R.T. *Perspectives on Adolescent Health Care.* Philadelphia: Lippincott, 1979.
  Notman, M.T., and Nadelson, C.C. *The Woman Patient: Medical and Psychological Interfaces.* New York: Plenum Press, 1978.
  Pearson, L. "Climacteric." *American Journal of Nursing* (July 1982): 1098–1102.
  Ruzek, S.B. *The Women's Health Movement: Feminist Alternatives to Medical Control.* New York: Praeger Publishers, 1978.
  Sandelowski, M. *Women, Health, and Choice.* Englewood Cliffs, N.J.: Prentice-Hall, 1981.

Sandmaier, M. *The Invisible Alcoholics.* New York: McGraw-Hill, 1980.
Sheehy, G. *Passages.* New York: Bantam Books, 1976.
Staines, G., C. Tavris, and T. Jyaratue. "The Queen Bee Syndrome." *Psychology Today* 7 (January 1974): 55–60.
Steinmetz, S.K. "Women and Violence: Victims and Perpetrators." *American Journal of Psychotherapy* 34, no. 3 (1980): 334–350.
Stellman, J.M. *Women's Work, Women's Health: Myths and Realities.* New York: Pantheon Books, 1977.

Methods of evaluation: Final exam; class discussion; class participation; research paper.

Brief course description: This course will focus on historical, sociological, professional, and legal issues that have shaped present day approaches to women's health care. A developmental approach will be utilized in discussing specific health problems, as well as behaviors and life styles conducive to promoting health, anatomy and physiology, problems related to reproduction, physical activity, nutrition, stress management, and social problems such as substance abuse, divorce, depression, suicide, chronic illness, widowhood, aging, death, and dying.

The main goal of this course is to provide a knowledge-base of information to stimulate an active and responsible participation in the health care process, and to give alternatives to the health care system via preventive health care, that is, self-help and self-health.

Upon completion of the course students will be able to discuss how socialization of women has influenced attitudes toward women's health/illness and the health care system; give an overview of the history of women as providers and consumers of health care; discuss issues related to contemporary women's health care; define health and wellness behaviors appropriate for each stage of the women's life cycle; describe normal anatomy and physiology of the female reproductive system; discuss issues and/or problems related to each stage of the life cycle; develop a personal approach to maximizing own level of wellness; develop strategies for responsible participation in the health care system.

Other features of the course: The course takes a developmental approach.

Syllabus

Date	Topic	Assignment
8/20	Introduction to course	
8/22	Socialization of Women Touch Film	Sandelowski, Ch. 6, 7
8/27	What is health?	Sandelowski, Ch. 1, 3
8/29	Wellness as well-being	Sheehy, Ch. 1
		Hongladarom, Ch. 1
9/5	Women in Health Care Professions	Sandelowski, Ch. 9
9/10	Sexism in Health	Sandelowski, Ch. 8
	Women and Health Care: Rise in the Women's Health Movement	Hongladarom, Ch. 3
9/12	Status of Women's Health	Sandelowski, Ch. 4
		Hongladarom, Ch. 2
9/17	Introduction: Issues in the Life Cycle V.T. — What you are is where you were when	Sheehy, Ch. 1, 2
9/19	Female adolescent: Developmental tasks	Sheehy, Ch. 3, 4, 5, 6
9/24	Female anatomy and physiology: menstrual cycle	Hongladarom, Ch. 4, 5
9/26	Adolescent nutrition & exercise	Hongladarom, p. 112
		Student selected readings
10/1	Sexuality, contraception, and pregnancy	Hongladarom, Ch. 7

10/3	Sexually Transmitted Diseases	SSR
10/8	Adolescent suicide	TBA
10/10	Young adulthood: develomental tasks	Sheehy, Ch. 7, 8, 9, 10
10/15	Reproductive rights and issues	Hongladarom, Ch. 17
10/17	Physiology of pregnancy and childbirth	Hongladarom, Ch. 16
10/22	Nutrition and exercise	Hongladarom, Ch. 9, 11 Self assessment
10/24	Stress and Stress Management Film: You pack your own chute	Hongladarom, Ch. 13 Sheehy, Ch. 11
10/29	Alcohol Abuse	Sandelowski, Ch. 12, pp. 240–251 Hongladarom, Ch. 12
10/31	Drug abuse	Sandelowski, Ch. 12, pp. 234–240
11/5	Menstrual problems	SSR
11/7	Women and abuse: rape and battering	Hongladarom, Ch. 19
11/12	Middle adulthood: tasks and issues	Sheehy, Ch. 12, 13, 14
11/14	Delayed childbearing; menopause	Hongladarom, Ch. 8 Sandelowski, pp. 55–61 Sheehy, Ch. 22
11/19	Issues in Mental Health, Depression	Sheehy, Ch. 15, 16, 17, 18, 19
11/21	Older adulthood: issues and tasks Film: Helping Older Adults – Peer Counseling in Rural America	Sheehy, Ch. 25
11/26	Physiological changes: Nutrition and exercise	TBA
11/28	Loss and grief Begin with Goodbye #3	Hongladarom, Ch. 18
12/3	Strategies for change	Sheehy, Ch. 15, 16, 17 Hongladarom, Ch. 23, 24, 28, 29, 30
12/5	Student Presentations	
12/12	FINAL EXAM DUE	

*   *   *   *   *

Course Title: Women's Health Issues, Hlth 3901

Credits: 3.
Institution name: University of Minnesota, Duluth.
Name(s) and departmental affiliation(s) of individual(s) teaching this course: Dr. Georgia Keeney.
Specific information regarding the course:
   Department(s) in which the course is listed: Department of Health, Physical Education & Recreation, taught as Health 3901, Special Topics in Health Education: Women's Health Issues, Dr. Georgia Keeney, Department of Health, Physical Education and Recreation, Spring 1985. Proposed as Health 3118. Women's Health Issues for Spring 1986 to be taught by faculty member in the Department of Health, Physical Education and Recreation during day school and other appropriate faculty member in evening school. Has been taught as WS 3500 (even-

ings), Special Topics in Women's Studies: Women's Health Issues, Charlotte MacLeod, Department of Physiology, Medical School, Fall 1984. Department of Physiology, Medical School.

Course level and audience for whom it is intended: 3000 level. All interested students. Can be used for credit toward a minor in Women's Studies.

Prerequisites: None, other than permission of the instructor.

Method of instruction: Discussion and lecture with much group participation. Many community leaders for agencies and programs related specifically to women have also been invited to class. A personal discovery type class.

Texts:

The Boston Women's Health Book Collective. *The New Our Bodies, Ourselves.* New York: Simon and Schuster, Inc., 1984.

Dreifus, Claudia, ed. *Seizing Our Bodies.* New York: Vintage Books, 1977.

Methods of evaluation: Participation in class, exams; individual project (presentation to class), research paper, periodical review, book review, a project of the student's own design.

Brief course description: "Survey of various health issues as they relate to American women. Analysis of the roles of women as patients and as health care providers. Language, politics, and economics of women's health care," UMD Catalogue description. Content will include the history of women's health care; the development of contraception and drug therapies; the economics of women's health; terminology; diseases of women; women's drug use; nutrition and fitness for women; self-responsibility and assertiveness; and decision making.

Other features of the course: The variety of guest speakers includes free clinic director, abortion clinic director, drug abuse counselor, birthing alternatives nurse, director of a battered women's shelter, a leader in women's health in our community. Tried to get a female physician and psychologist but couldn't work out schedules.

Syllabus

| Date | Topic | Chapters | |
		Dreifus	Boston
March 4	Introduction and requirements		
6	History/Herstory	Intro	
8	History/Herstory	Part I	
11	History/Herstory		
13	The idea of wellness		1, 2, 4
15	Outside assignment		
18	Drugs, alcohol and women		3
20	Drugs, alcohol and women		
22	Outside assignment		
25	The means of reproduction	Part 2	12, 13
27	Dating violence — guest speaker		
29	Contraception, abortion, etc.		15, 16
April 1	Contraception, abortion, etc.		17
3	Contraception, abortion, etc.		
5	Mid-term exam		
8	Classes excused		
10	Childbearing	pp. 146–166	18–21
12	Childbearing		
15	Childbearing		
17	Outside assignments		

(continued)

Date		Topic	Chapters	
			Dreifus	*Boston*
	19	Outside assignments		
	22	Women growing old	Part 3	22
	24	The Women's Health Movement	Part 5	24, 26
	26	The Women's Health Movement		
April	29 to May 10	Project presentations		
May	14	FINAL, 12:00–2:00 p.m. (Tuesday)		

*   *   *   *   *

Course Title: Women's Health Issues, H & S 490

Credits: 3.
Institution name: Portland State University.
Name(s) and departmental affiliation(s) of individual(s) teaching this course: Leslie B.
McBride, Assistant Professor, Department of Health Studies, School of Health
and Physical Education.
Specific information regarding the course:
Department(s) in which the course is listed: Women's Studies Program; Health
Studies.
Course level and audience for whom it is intended: Upper level and graduate.
Prerequisites: None.
Method of instruction: Depending upon size (which is variable), lecture-discussion/
seminar.
Texts and Bibliography:
Abbot, S., and B. Love. *Sappho Was a Right-On Woman.* New York: Stein and
Day, 1972.
Abortion. Special issue, *American Journal of Public Health* 61 (March 1971).
Addeigo, F., et al. "Female Ejaculation: A Case Study." *The Journal of Sex
Research* 17 (1981): 13–21.
Appleton, W. "The Battered Woman Syndrome." *Annals of Emergency Medicine*
(Feb. 1980): 84.
Arms, S. "How Hospitals Complicate Childbirth." *Ms.* (May 1975): 108–115.
Banks, J.A., and O. Banks. *Feminism and Family Planning in Victorian England.*
New York: Schocken Books, 1964.
Bardwick, J.M. *Psychology of Women—A Study of Bio-cultural Conflicts.* New
York: Harper and Row, 1971.
Bart, P.B. "Social Structure and Vocabularies of Discomfort: What Happened to
Female Hysteria?" *Journal of Health and Social Behavior* 9 (1968): 188–194.
Belson, A. "What Every Woman Should Know About Calcium Before She Turns
30." *Ms.* (January 1980): 72–76.
Blanchard, M. "Middle-age muddle." *Women* 4: 12–15.
Boston Women's Health Book Collective. *The New Our Bodies, Our Selves.* New
York: Simon and Schuster, 1984.
Broverman, K.B., et al. "Sex-Role Stereotypes and Clinical Judgements of Mental
Health." *Journal of Consulting and Clinical Psychology* 34 (1970): 1–7.
Caress, B. "Sterilization." *Health/PAC Bull.* 62 (1975): 1–6, 10–13.

The Closet Alcoholics. *Harpers Bazaar* (Sept. 1981).

Cooke, C. and S. Dworkin. "Tough Talk about Unnecessary Surgery." *Ms.* (Oct. 1981): 42–44.

Davidson, V., and J. Bemke. "International Review of Women and Drug Abuse (1966–1975)." *Journal of American Women's Medical Association* 33 (1978): 507–512.

Davis, A. "Whoever Said Life Begins at 40 Was a Fink or, Those Golden Years — Phooey." *International Journal of Women's Studies* 3: 583–589.

Dye, N. "History of Childbirth in America." *Signs* (Autumn 1980): 97–108.

Ehrenreich, B., and D. English. *Complaints and Disorders — The Sexual Politics of Sickness*. Old Westbury, N.Y.: Feminist Press, 1973.

Ehrenreich, B., and D. English. *Witches, Midwives and Nurses — A History of Women Healers*. Old Westbury, N.Y.: Feminist Press, 1973.

Elhai, L. "The Quality of Medical Care Delivered by Lay Practitioners in a Feminist Clinic." *American Journal of Public Health* 71 (August 1978).

English, D. "The Politics of Porn: Can Feminists Walk the Line?" *Mother Jones* (April 1980): 20–50.

English, D. "The War Against Choice." *Mother Jones* (Feb./March 1981): 16–32.

Ernst, E., and R. Lubic. "The Childbearing Center: An Alternative to Conventional Care." *Nursing Outlook* (December 1978): 754–760.

Franks, V., and V. Burtle, eds. *Women in Therapy — New Psychotherapies for a Changing Society*. New York: Brunner/Mazel Publishers, 1974.

Friday, N. *My Secret Garden — Women's Sexual Fantasies*. New York: Trident Press, Simon & Schuster, 1973.

Godow, A. "Female Sexual Dysfunction: Contributory Factors and Treatment Considerations." *Journal of Sex Education and Therapy* 3 (1977).

Gomberg, E. "Women, Sex Roles, and Alcohol Problems." *Professional Psychology* 12 (1981).

Gordon, M., and P.J. Shaukweiler. "Different Equals Less: Female Sexuality in Recent Marriage Manuals." *Journal of Marriage and the Family* 33 (1971): 459–466.

Gove, W.R., and J.F. Tudor. "Adult Sex Roles and Mental Illness." *American Journal of Sociology* 78 (1973): 812–835.

Goz, R. "Women Patients and Women Therapists: Some Issues that Come up in Psychotherapy." *International Journal of Psychoanalysis and Psychotherapy* 2 (1973): 298–319.

Greer, G. *The Female Eunuch*. New York: McGraw-Hill Book Company, 1970.

Heppner, M. "Counseling the Battered Wife: Myths, Facts and Decisions." *The Personnel Guidance Journal* 36 (1978): 522–525.

Himes, N.E. *Medical History of Contraception*. New York: Schocken Books, 1970.

Hornstein, F. "An Interview on Women's Health Politics, Part I *Quest* (Summer 1974): 27–37. Part II, *Quest* (Fall 1974): 75–80.

Horrobin, D.F. "The Valium and Breast Cancer Affair: Lessons Relating to the Involvement of Women in Health Care Research and Policy." *International Journal of Women's Studies* 14: 19–26.

Howard, R. "Drugged, Bugged, and Coming Unplugged." *Mother Jones* (1981): 39–59.

Howell, M.C. "What Medical Schools Teach About Women." *New England Journal of Medicine* 219 (1974): 304–307.

Isaacson, W. "The Battle over Abortion." *Time* 20 (April 6, 1981).

"I.U.D. Debate: How Great Are the Risks?" *Time* 115 (1980): 60.

Iyer, P. "The Battered Wife." *Nursing '80* (July 1980): 53–55.

Kaschak, E., and D. Logan. "The Relationship of Sex, Sex Role and Mental Health." *Psychology of Women Quarterly* 4 (Summer 1980).

Kennedy, D.M. *Birth Control in America: The Career of Margaret Sanger*. New Haven, Conn.: Yale University Press, 1970.

Kistner, R.W. "The Menopause." *Clinical Obstetrics and Gynecology* 16 (1973): 106–129.

Krause, C. "The Feminist Complex and Women Therapists." *Journal of Marriage and the Family* 33 (1981): 476–482.

Lennane, K.J., and R.J. Lennane. "Alleged Psychogenic Disorders in Women—A Possible Manifestation of Sexual Prejudice." *New England Journal of Medicine* (1973): 288–292.

Linn, L.S., and M.S. Davis. "The Use of Psychotherapeutic Drugs by Middle-Aged Women." *Journal of Health and Social Behavior* 12 (1971): 331–340.

Lupton, M. "From Leeches to Estrogen: The Menopause." *Women* 4: 22–25.

MacPherson, K. "Menopause as Disease: The Social Construction of a Metaphor." *Annals of Nursing Science* (Feb. 1981): 95.

Maracek, J., and D. Kravetz. "Women and Mental Health. A Review of Feminist Change Efforts." *Psychiatry* (Nov. 1977): 322.

Marieskind, H. "The Women's Health Movement." *International Journal of Health Services* 5 (1975).

McClain, C. "Women's Choice of Home or Hospital Birth." *The Journal of Family Practice* 12 (1981): 1033–1038.

Medea, A., and K. Thompson. *Against Rape*. New York: Farrar, Straus and Giroux, 1974.

Nathanson, B.N. "Ambulatory Abortion: Experience with 26,000 Cases." *New England Journal of Medicine* 286 (1972): 403–407.

Nathanson, B.N. "Deeper into Abortion." *New England Journal of Medicine* 291 (1974): 1189–1190.

Navarro, V. "Women in Health Care." *New England Journal of Medicine* 292 (1975): 398–402.

Paige, K.E. "Women Learn to Sing the Menstrual Blues." *Psychology Today* 7 (1973): 41–46.

Paige, K.E., and J.M. Paige. "The Politics of Birth Practices: A Strategic Analysis." *American Sociologic Review* 38 (1973): 663–676.

Rodewald, R. "Women Healers vs. the AMA." *Quest* 1: 21–27.

Ross, C.H. "Geriatrics and the Elderly Woman." *Journal of the American Geriatric Society* 22 (1974): 230–239.

Scully, D., and P. Bart. "A Funny Thing Happened on the Way to the Orifice: Women in Gynecology Textbooks." *American Journal of Sociology* 78 (1973): 1045–1050.

Seaman, B. *Do Gynecologists Exploit Their Patients?* New York, Aug. 14, 1972, pp. 46–54.

Sexist Society: Studies in Power and Powerlessness, V. Gornick, and B.K. Moran, eds., pp. 99–117. New York: Basic Books, 1971.

Sharpe, J. "The Birth Controllers." *Health/PAC Bulletin* (April 1972): 3–12. An analysis of the politics of population planning.

Sherfey, M.J. *The Nature and Evolution of Female Sexuality*. New York: Random House, 1966.

Solomon, J. "Menopause: A Rite of Passage." *Ms.* 1 (1972): 16–18.

Sontag, S. "The Double Standard of Aging." *Saturday Review* (Sept. 1980): 30–38.

Stone, M. "Tubal Ligation: Why and Why Not." *New York Magazine* (Sept. 25, 1972): 88.

Verbrugge, L. "Recent Trends in Sex Mortality Differentials in the United States." *Women and Health* (Fall 1980): 17.

Walker, L. "Battered Women: Sex Roles and Social Issues." *Professional Psychology* 12 (1981).

Weissman, M.M. "The Depressed Woman: Recent Research." *Social Work* (Sept. 1972): 19–25.

"What Does Exercise Mean for the Menstrual Cycle?" *Journal of the American Medical Association* (May 2, 1980): 1699.

Willis, J. "Cervical Caps—The Perfect, Untested Contraceptive." *F.D.A. Consumer* (April 1981): 20–21.

Wysor, B. *The Lesbian Myth.* New York: Random House, 1974.

Methods of evaluation: Papers, notebooks/journals, presentations.

Brief course description: Course begins with general health statistics overview on morbidity and mortality. It incorporates a feminist theoretical approach from the outset, then focuses on special topics/issues in women's health and health care. Students determine the particular topics to be included during course.

Other features of the course: Each student has the opportunity to select a particular topic for in-depth examination and research. Her endeavors culminate in a major presentation to her student peers.

Syllabus

I.   Theoretical Foundations
     A. Health issues and concerns unique to women
     B. Historical influences on the health care of women
     C. Patterns of mortality and morbidity
     D. The women's health movement
II. Mental Health Issues
     A. Key determinants of mental health in women
     B. Substance addiction
     C. Traditional and alternative therapies
III. Women and the Health Care System
     A. Selecting a health care provider and health care coverage
     B. Principles of self-care
IV. Diet, Nutrition and Fitness
     A. Historical and cultural fashion trends
     B. Madison Avenue and the cosmetic industry
     C. Body image
     D. Weight control and dietary practices
V.   Reproductive Health
     A. The childbearing experience
     B. Pre- and postnatal care
     C. Labor and delivery options
     D. Contraceptive choices
     E. Unwanted pregnancy
     F. Infertility
VI. Women and Illness
     A. Cancer
     B. Menstrual and reproductive disorders
     C. Sexually transmitted diseases
VII. Female Sexuality
     A. Anatomy and physiology
     B. Sexual response cycle
     C. Sexual difficulties
VIII. Women and Intimacy
     A. Heterosexual friendships and relationships
     B. Homosexual friendships and relationships

Author Index

Subject Index

Able-bodiedness, feminist pedagogical methods, 107–114 *passim*

Academia/real world dualism, 90, 94, 97

Age, in Biology and Psychology of Women, 97

American Chemical Society, 69

American Indian Women, 54

American Women in Science, 69

Amniocentesis, benefits and risks, 40–41; definition, of, 41; definition of "abnormal" or "defective," 41; perspectives of class, religion, and race, 41–42; use of to abort female fetuses, 42

Androcentrism, recognition of influence of, 5; of male anthropologists, 8; relationship to "objectivity," 24; scientific method, 26; and reproductive technologies, 38, 47; excluding women from science, 65; in traditional science and health curriculum, 77, 81, 107, 137; dualism, 90; viewed as synonymous with gender-free and "objective" science, 106; to be overcome by numbers of women in science, 135; overcome in women's studies, 137

Animal behavior, and sociobiology, 13; circularity of logic, 13; search for "universal" behavior patterns, 13, 29; in Introductory Biology, 28–29; androcentric and ethnocentric descriptions, 29; feminist critique of, 80; language, 80; types of sexual bias, 80–81

Aristotle, 5

Artificial insemination, positive and oppressive aspects, 40

Asian students, faculty interaction, 111

Aspasia, 62

Attracting women to science, 23, 118, 135

Audience, topics for particular, 130–131

Audio-visual aids, use for self-instruction, 121, 124–130 *passim*

Biological determinism, definition of, 12, 31; Antoinette Blackwell's rebuttal of, 12; Darwin's framework for, 12; relationship to sociobiology, 12; scientific flaws in, 12; relationship to animal behavior, 12–13; relationship to hormone research, 12–13

Biological sciences, history and careers, 66–67

Biology, and substantial work on feminism and science, 10; numbers of women, 10; phases of feminist curricular transformation, 10–17; sexuality, 52; Biology of Women as course for non-majors, 56; Biology of Women as course for majors, 57; androcentric, gynocentric, and women's studies perspectives, 77, 80; exclusion of women

236

About the Author

Sue Rosser is an Associate Professor of Biology, Coordinator of the Division of Theoretical and Natural Sciences, and Coordinator of Women's Studies at Mary Baldwin College, a small liberal arts college for women. Her undergraduate experiences as a female student desiring to become a scientist caused her to seek out other women in science and led her to feminism. Professor Rosser received her Ph.D. in Zoology in 1973 from the University of Wisconsin–Madison. In 1976, while a post-doctoral fellow, she began teaching in the women's studies program at the University of Wisconsin. Since then she has taught courses in both biology and women's studies programs at the University of Wisconsin–Madison and Mary Baldwin College. She has authored numerous publications dealing with the theoretical and applied problems of women and science. As a consultant for the Wellesley Center for Research on Women, she has worked with faculty at several institutions that are attempting to include new scholarship on women in the science curriculum. During 1984–85, Professor Rosser was Visiting Lecturer in Biology and Women's Studies at Towson State University under a grant from the Fund for Improvement of Post-Secondary Education (FIPSE).